Principles of Economics

Principles of Economics

Peter Lewis

MURPHY & MOORE
www.murphy-moorepublishing.com

Murphy & Moore Publishing,
1 Rockefeller Plaza,
New York City, NY 10020, USA

ISBN: 978-1-63987-457-6

Cataloging-in-Publication Data

Principles of economics / Peter Lewis.
p. cm.
Includes bibliographical references and index.
ISBN 978-1-63987-457-6
1. Economics. 2. Economics--Methodology. 3. Microeconomics.
4. Macroeconomics. I. Lewis, Peter.

HB131 .P75 2022
330--dc23

For information on all Murphy & Moore Publications
visit our website at www.murphy-moorepublishing.com

MURPHY & MOORE

Contents

Preface VII

Chapter 1 **Economics: An Introduction** 1
- a. Macroeconomics 5
- b. Microeconomics 7
- c. Financial Economics 13
- d. Business Economics 14
- e. Development Economics 17

Chapter 2 **Economic Growth and Development** 19
- a. Types of Growth Models 24
- b. Growth Accounting 65
- c. Economic Development and Institutions 72

Chapter 3 **Money and Banking** 78
- a. Money 78
- b. Theories of Money Supply 86
- c. Money Multiplier and Reserve Ratio 92
- d. Determinants of Money Supply 96
- e. Interest Rate Determination 102

Chapter 4 **Understanding Supply and Demand** 109
- a. Law of Supply 117
- b. Law of Demand 118
- c. Demand Curve 120
- d. Supply 123
- e. Economic Equilibrium 128
- f. Elasticity 135

Chapter 5 **Diverse Economic Models** 147
- a. Econometric Model 147
- b. Macroeconomic Model 160
- c. Brander-Spencer Model 164

d. Big Push Model 169
e. Mundell-Fleming Model 175

Chapter 6 **Significant Theories in Macroeconomics** **184**
a. Diluted Property Rights Theory 184
b. Induced Innovation 186
c. Supply-side Economics 189
d. Demand-side Economics 196
e. Modern Monetary Theory 198
f. Recursive Competitive Equilibrium 204
g. Twin Deficits Hypothesis 206

Chapter 7 **Microeconomic Theories** **209**
a. Economic Decision Making 209
b. General Equilibrium Theory 214
c. Search Theory 219
d. Theory of the Second Best 220
e. Information Economics 224

Permissions

Index

Preface

Economics is a branch of social science which focuses on production, distribution and consumption of goods and services. It studies the choices which are made by individual, businesses, governments and nations regarding allocation of resources. Economics is divided into two major branches, namely, macroeconomics and microeconomics. Microeconomics deals with the interactions between individuals and firms regarding the allocation of scarce resources with the help of statistics and derivatives. Macroeconomics analyzes the structure, behavior, performance and decision making of an economy as a whole using tools such as GDP, CPI and unemployment rates. Some key areas of focus under this discipline are normative economics, positive economics, Keynesian economics, rational economics, applied economics and behavioral economics. This book is a compilation of chapters that discuss the most vital concepts in the field of economics. This book presents the complex subject of economics in the most comprehensible and easy to understand language. It will provide comprehensive knowledge to the readers.

Given below is the chapter wise description of the book:

Chapter 1- The branch of social science which deals with the production, distribution and consumption of wealth, goods and services is known as economics. It can be classified into microeconomics and macroeconomics. It can be further divided into financial economics, business economics and developmental economics. This is an introductory chapter which will introduce briefly all the significant aspects of economics.

Chapter 2- An increase in the market value of goods and services produced by an economy is known as economic growth. An improvement in the living standards and quality of life is known as economic development. In order to completely understand economic growth and development, it is necessary to understand the processes related to it. The following chapter elucidates the varied processes and mechanisms associated with this area of study.

Chapter 3- Money is any verifiable record that is a generally recognized medium of payment for goods and services. The industry that handles financial transactions is banking. Money and banking play a significant role in the financial stability of the economy of a country. This chapter has been carefully written to provide an easy understanding of the varied facets of money and banking.

Chapter 4- The quantity of a product produced or producers wish to sell is known as supply. The quantity that consumers want to buy is known as demand. This chapter includes some aspects of supply and demand such as law of supply, law of demand, demand curve and economic equilibrium, etc. The topics elaborated in this chapter will help in gaining a better perspective about supply and demand.

Chapter 5- Economic models are a simplified representation of economic processes which helps in observing and making predictions about economic behavior. Some of the models explained in this chapter are econometric and macroeconomic model, Brander-Spencer model, big push model and Mundell-Fleming model. This chapter discusses in detail these models related to economics.

Chapter 6- The branch of economics which is concerned with the structure, decision making, behavior and performance of an economy is known as macroeconomics. This chapter elucidates topics such as induced innovation, supply-side and demand-side economics, modern monetary theory, recursive competitive equilibrium, etc. All the theories related to macroeconomics have been carefully analyzed in this chapter.

Chapter 7- The branch of economics which is concerned with the decision making behavior of individuals to allocate scarce resources is known as microeconomics. This chapter covers economic decision making, general equilibrium theory, search theory, theory of the second best, information economics, etc. The aim of this chapter is to explore these concepts and theories related to microeconomics.

Indeed, my job was extremely crucial and challenging as I had to ensure that every chapter is informative and structured in a student-friendly manner. I am thankful for the support provided by my family and colleagues during the completion of this book.

Peter Lewis

1

Economics: An Introduction

The branch of social science which deals with the production, distribution and consumption of wealth, goods and services is known as economics. It can be classified into microeconomics and macroeconomics. It can be further divided into financial economics, business economics and developmental economics. This is an introductory chapter which will introduce briefly all the significant aspects of economics.

Economics is a social science concerned with the production, distribution, and consumption of goods and services. It studies how individuals, businesses, governments, and nations make choices about how to allocate resources. Economics focuses on the actions of human beings, based on assumptions that humans act with rational behavior, seeking the most optimal level of benefit or utility. The building blocks of economics are the studies of labor and trade. Since there are many possible applications of human labor and many different ways to acquire resources, it is the task of economics to determine which methods yield the best results.

Economics can generally be broken down into macroeconomics, which concentrates on the behavior of the economy as a whole, and microeconomics, which focuses on individual people and businesses.

One of the earliest recorded economic thinkers was the 8th-century B.C. Greek farmer/poet Hesiod, who wrote that labor, materials, and time needed to be allocated efficiently to overcome scarcity. But the founding of modern Western economics occurred much later.

The principle (and problem) of economics is that human beings have unlimited wants and occupy a world of limited means. For this reason, the concepts of efficiency and productivity are held paramount by economists. Increased productivity and a more efficient use of resources, they argue, could lead to a higher standard of living.

Despite this view, economics has been pejoratively known as the "dismal science," a term coined by Scottish historian Thomas Carlyle in 1849. He used it to criticize the liberal views on race and social equality of contemporary economists like John Stuart Mill, though some commentators suggest Carlyle was actually describing the gloomy predictions by Thomas Robert Malthus that population growth would always outstrip the food supply.

Types of Economics

The study of economics is generally broken down into two disciplines:

1. Microeconomics focuses on how individual consumers and firms make decisions; these individual decision making units can be a single person, a household, a

business/organization, or a government agency. Analyzing certain aspects of human behavior, microeconomics tries to explain how they respond to changes in price and why they demand what they do at particular price levels. Microeconomics tries to explain how and why different goods are valued differently, how individuals make financial decisions, and how individuals best trade, coordinate, and cooperate with one another. Microeconomics' topics range from the dynamics of supply and demand to the efficiency and costs associated with producing goods and services; they also include how labor is divided and allocated; how business firms are organized and function; and how people approach uncertainty, risk, and strategic game theory.

2. Macroeconomics studies an overall economy on both a national and international level, using highly aggregated economic data and variables to model the economy. Its focus can include a distinct geographical region, a country, a continent, or even the whole world. Its primary areas of study are recurrent economic cycles and broad economic growth and development. Topics studied include foreign trade, government fiscal and monetary policy, unemployment rates, the level of inflation and interest rates, the growth of total production output as reflected by changes in the Gross Domestic Product (GDP), and business cycles that result in expansions, booms, recessions, and depressions.

Micro and macroeconomics are intertwined. Aggregate macroeconomic phenomena are obviously and literally just the sum total of microeconomic phenomena. However these two branches of economics use very different theories, models, and research methods, which sometimes appear to conflict with each other. Integrating the microeconomics foundations into macroeconomic theory and research is a major area of study in itself for many economists.

Schools of Economic Theory

There are many competing, conflicting, or sometimes complementary theories and schools of thought within economics. Economists employ many different methods of research from logical deduction to pure data mining. Economic theory often progresses through deductive processes, including mathematical logic, where the implications of specific human activities are considered in a "means-ends" framework.

This type of economics deduces, for example, that it is more efficient for individuals or companies to specialize in specific types of labor and then trade for their other needs or wants, rather than trying to produce everything they need or want on their own. It also demonstrates trade is most efficient when coordinated through a medium of exchange, or money. Economic laws deduced in this way tend to be very general and not give specific results: they can say profits incentivize new competitors to enter a market, but not necessarily how many will do so. Still, they do provide key insights for understanding the behavior of financial markets, governments, economies—and human decisions behind these entities.

Other branches of economic thought emphasize empiricism, rather than formal logic—specifically, logical positivist methods, which attempt to use the procedural observations and falsifiable tests associated with the natural sciences. Some economists even use direct experimental methods in their research, with subjects asked to make simulated economic decisions in a controlled environment. Since true experiments may be difficult, impossible, or unethical to use in economics, empirical economists mostly rely on simplifying assumptions and retroactive data analysis. However, some economists argue economics is not well suited to empirical testing, and that such methods often generate incorrect or inconsistent answers.

Two of the most common in macroeconomics are monetarist and Keynesian. Monetarists are a branch of Keynesian economics that argue that stable monetary policy is the best course for managing the economy, and otherwise often have generally favorable views on free markets as the best way to allocate resources. In contrast, other Keynesian approaches favor fiscal policy by an activist government in order to manage irrational market swings and recessions and believe that markets often don't work well at allocating resources on their own.

Types of Economic Systems

Societies have organized their resources in many different ways through history, deciding how to use available means to achieve individual and common ends.

Primitivism

In primitive agrarian societies, people tend to self-produce all of their needs and wants at the level of the household or tribe. Families and tribes would build their own dwellings, grow their own crops, hunt their own game, fashion their own clothes, bake their own bread, etc. This economic system is defined by very little division of labor and resulting low productivity, a high degree of vertical integration of production processes within the household or village for what goods are produced, and relationship based reciprocal exchange within and between families or tribes rather than market transactions. In such a primitive society, the concepts of private property and decision-making over resources often apply at a more collective level of familial or tribal ownership of productive resources and wealth in common.

Feudalism

Later, as civilizations developed, economies based on production by social class emerged, such as feudalism and slavery. Slavery involved production by enslaved individuals who lacked personal freedom or rights and were treated as the property of their owner. Feudalism was a system where a class of nobility, known as lords, owned all of the lands and leased out small parcels to peasants to farm, with peasants handing over much of their production to the lord. In return, the lord offered the peasants relative safety and security, including a place to live and food to eat.

Capitalism

Capitalism emerged with the advent of industrialization. Capitalism is defined as a system of production whereby business owners (entrepreneurs or capitalists) organize productive resources including tools, workers, and raw materials to produce goods for sale in order to make a profit and not for personal consumption. In capitalism, workers are hired in return for wages, owners of land and natural resources are paid rents or royalties for the use of the resources, and the owners of previously created wealth are paid interest to forgo the use of some of their wealth so that the entrepreneurs can borrow it to pay wages and rents and purchase tools for hired workers to use. Entrepreneurs apply their best judgement of future economic conditions to decide what goods to produce, and are earn a profit if they decide well or suffer losses if they judge poorly. This system of market prices, profit, and loss as the selection mechanism as to who will decide how resources are allocated for production is what defines a capitalist economy.

These roles (workers, resource owners, capitalists, and entrepreneurs) represent functions in the capitalist economy and not separate or mutually exclusive classes of people. Individuals typically fulfill different roles with respect to different economic transactions, relationships, organizations, and contracts which they are a party to. This may even occur within a single context, such as a employee-owned co-op where the workers are also the entrepreneurs or a small business owner-operator who self-finances his firm out of personal savings and operates out of a home office, and thus acts as simultaneously as entrepreneur, capitalist, land owner, and worker. The United States and much of the developed world today can be described as broadly capitalist market economies.

Socialism

Socialism is a form of cooperative production economy. Economic socialism is a system of production where there is limited or hybrid private ownership of the means of production (or other types of productive property) and a system of prices, profits, and losses is not the sole determinant used to establish who engages in production, what to produce and how to produce it. Segments of society band together to share these functions.

Production decisions are made through a collective decision making process, and within the economy some but not all economic functions are shared by all. These might include any strategic economic functions that effect all citizens. These would include Public Safety (police, fire, EMS), National Defence, resource allocation (utilities. like water, and electric), education, and more. These are often paid for through income or use taxes levied on the remaining tactically independent economic functions (individual citizens, independent businesses, foreign trade partners, etc).

Modern socialism contains certain elements of capitalism, such as a market mechanism, and also some centralized control over some resources. If more of the economic control is centralized in ever increasing ways, it may eventually become more akin to communism. Note that socialism as an economic system can and does occur under various forms of government, from the Democratic Socialism of the Nordic countries to more authoritarian strands found elsewhere.

Communism

Communism is a form of command economy, whereby nearly all economic activity is centralized, and through the coordination of state-sponsored central planners. A society's theoretical economic strength can be marshalled to the benefit of the society at large. Executing this in reality is far more difficult than in theory, in that it requires no conflicting or competing entities within the society to challenge the allocation of resources. Note that instances of economic communism in the modern era have also been coupled with an authoritarian form of government, although this need not be the case in theory.

Macroeconomics

If we observe the economy of a country as a whole it will appear that the output levels of all the goods and services in the economy have a tendency to move together. For example, if output of food grain is experiencing a growth, it is generally accompanied by a rise in the output level of industrial goods. Within the category of industrial goods also outputs of different kinds of goods tend to rise or fall simultaneously. Similarly, prices of different goods and services generally have a tendency to rise or fall simultaneously. We can also observe that the employment level in different production units also goes up or down together.

If aggregate output level, price level, or employment level, in the different production units of an economy, bear close relationship to each other then the task of analysing the entire economy becomes relatively easy. Instead of dealing with the above mentioned variables at individual (disaggregated) levels, we can think of a single good as the representative of all the goods and services produced within the economy. This representative good will have a level of production which will correspond to the average production level of all the goods and services. Similarly, the price or employment level of this representative good will reflect the general price and employment level of the economy.

In macroeconomics we usually simplify the analysis of how the country's total production and the level of employment are related to attributes (called 'variables') like prices, rate of interest, wage rates, profits and so on, by focusing on a single imaginary commodity and what happens to it. We are able to afford this simplification and thus usefully abstain from studying what happens to the many real commodities that actually are bought and sold in the market because we generally see that what happens to the prices, interests, wages and profits etc. for one commodity more or less also happens for the others. Particularly, when these attributes start changing fast, like when prices are going up (in what is called an inflation), or employment and production levels are going down (heading for a depression), the general directions of the movements of these variables for all the individual commodities are usually of the same kind as are seen for the aggregates for the economy as a whole.

Let us study why, sometimes, we also depart from this useful simplification when we realise that the country's economy as a whole may best be seen as composed of distinct sectors. For certain purposes the interdependence of (or even rivalry between) two sectors of the economy (agriculture and industry, for example) or the relationships between sectors (like the household sector, the business sector and government in a democratic set-up) help us understand some things happening to the country's economy much better, than by only looking at the economy as a whole.

While moving away from different goods and focusing on a representative good may be convenient, in the process, we may be overlooking some vital distinctive characteristics of individual goods. For example, production conditions of agricultural and industrial commodities are of a different nature. Or, if we treat a single category of labour as a representative of all kinds of labours, we may be unable to distinguish the labour of the manager of a firm from the labour of the accountant of the firm. So, in many cases, instead of a single representative category of good (or labour, or production technology), we may take a handful of different kinds of goods. For example, three general kinds of commodities may be taken as a representative of all commodities being produced within the economy: agricultural goods, industrial goods and services. These goods may have different production technology and different prices. Macroeconomics also tries to analyse how the individual output levels, prices, and employment levels of these different goods gets determined.

Macroeconomics tries to address situations facing the economy as a whole. Adam Smith, the founding father of modern economics, had suggested that if the buyers and sellers in each market take their decisions following only their own self-interest, economists will not need to think of the wealth and welfare of the country as a whole separately. But economists gradually discovered that they had to look further.

Economists found that first, in some cases, the markets did not or could not exist. Secondly, in some other cases, the markets existed but failed to produce equilibrium of demand and supply. Thirdly, and most importantly, in a large number of situations society (or the State, or the people as a whole) had decided to pursue certain important social goals unselfishly (in areas like employment, administration, defence, education and health) for which some of the aggregate effects of the microeconomic decisions made by the individual economic agents needed to be modified. For these purposes macroeconomists had to study the effects in the markets of taxation and other budgetary policies, and policies for bringing about changes in money supply, the rate of interest, wages, employment, and output. Macroeconomics has, therefore, deep roots in microeconomics because it has to study the aggregate effects of the forces of demand and supply in the markets. However, in addition, it has to deal with policies aimed at also modifying these forces, if necessary, to follow choices made by society outside the markets. In a developing country like India such choices have to be made to remove or reduce unemployment, to improve access to education and primary health care for all, to provide for good administration, to provide sufficiently for the defence of the country and so on. Macroeconomics shows two simple characteristics that are evident in dealing with the situations we have just listed. These are briefly mentioned below.

Emergence of Macroeconomics

Macroeconomics, as a separate branch of economics, emerged after the British economist John Maynard Keynes published his celebrated book The General Theory of Employment, Interest and Money in 1936. The dominant thinking in economics before Keynes was that all the labourers who are ready to work will find employment and all the factories will be working at their full capacity. This school of thought is known as the classical tradition.

However, the Great Depression of 1929 and the subsequent years saw the output and employment levels in the countries of Europe and North America fall by huge amounts. It affected other countries of the world as well. Demand for goods in the market was low, many factories were lying idle, and workers were thrown out of jobs. In USA, from 1929 to 1933, unemployment rate rose from 3 per cent to 25 per cent (unemployment rate may be defined as the number of people who are not working and are looking for jobs divided by the total number of people who are working or looking for jobs). Over the same period aggregate output in USA fell by about 33 per cent. These events made economists think about the functioning of the economy in a new way. The fact that the economy may have long lasting unemployment had to be theorised about and explained. Keynes' book was an attempt in this direction. Unlike his predecessors, his approach was to examine the working of the economy in its entirety and examine the interdependence of the different sectors. The subject of macroeconomics was born.

Microeconomics

Microeconomics is the branch of economics that considers the behaviour of decision takers within the economy, such as individuals, households and firms. The word 'firm' is used generically to refer to all types of business. Microeconomics contrasts with the study of macroeconomics, which considers the economy as a whole.

Scarcity, Choice and Opportunity Cost

The platform on which microeconomic thought is built lies at the very heart of economic thinking – namely, how decision takers choose between scarce resources that have alternative uses. Consumers demand goods and services and producers offer these for sale, but nobody can take everything they want from the economic system. Choices have to be made, and for every choice made something is forgone. An individual may choose to buy a car, but in doing so may have to give up a holiday which they might have used the money for, if they had not chosen to buy the car. In this example, the holiday is the opportunity cost of the car. Just as individuals and households make opportunity cost decisions about what they consume, so too do firms take decisions about what to produce, and in doing so preclude themselves from producing alternative goods and services.

Producers also have to decide how much to produce and for whom. A simple answer to the first question might be: 'As much as possible of course, using all the resources we can'. However, classical economists teach us that if we combine all of the factors of production land, labour, capital and the entrepreneur in different ways, we can get some surprising results. One of the most famous of these is confirmed by the law of diminishing returns. This law states that if we keep on adding variable factors of production (such as labour) to fixed factors (such as land), we will get proportionally less output from each additional unit of factor added until, eventually, overall output will start to decrease with each additional unit of factor added.

The Price Mechanism

Much of the study of microeconomics is devoted to analysis of how prices are determined in markets. A market is any system through which producers and consumers come together. In early subsistence economies, markets were usually physical locations where people would come together to trade. In more complex economic systems, markets do not depend on humans actually meeting one another, so many markets today arise when producers and consumers come together less directly, such as by post and on the internet.

Producers and consumers generate forces that we call supply and demand respectively, and it is their interaction within the market that creates the price mechanism. This mechanism was once famously described as the 'invisible hand' that guides the actions of producers and consumers.

Markets are essential to produce the goods and services required for everyday life. Even if an individual can produce all the food needed to survive, that person will still need clothes, shelter and other necessities. Therefore, from very early times, communities learned that they would benefit from exchange. The crudest form of exchange was barter, but the evolution of money as a medium of exchange and unit of account accelerated the development of the process.

But how would people know what they could charge, or what they should pay, for goods and services? Before any formal thought was given to this, traders soon discovered that if they fixed their prices too low they would soon run out of inventory, while if they set their prices too high they would not sell what they had produced. In physical markets there would often be perfect knowledge, as traders would be able to check the prices of those who had similar goods and services to trade, simply by walking around the stalls. Once markets became more remote, less perfect knowledge of prices was inevitable and the process became less certain.

Alfred Marshall, whose *Principles of Economics* was published in 1890, drew heavily on the writings of Jevons and Mill. However, much of what you read today about supply and demand, elasticity, revenues and costs and marginal utility are based on Marshall's thoughts. Marshall provided a base upon which formal analysis of supply and demand, and consequently the determination of prices in markets, could be built.

Demand

Demand is created by the needs of consumers, and the nature of demand owes much to the underpinning worth that consumers perceive the good or service to have. We all need necessities, such as basic foodstuffs, but other products may be highly sought after by some and regarded as worthless by others. The level of demand for a good or service is determined by several factors, including:

- The price of the good or service.
- Prices of other goods and services, especially substitutes and complements.
- Income.
- Tastes and preferences.
- Expectations.

In orthodox economic analysis, these determinants are analysed by testing the quantity demanded against one of these variables, holding all others to be constant (or ceteris paribus).

The most common way of analysing demand is to consider the relationship between quantity demanded and price. Assuming that people behave rationally, and that other determinants of demand are constant, the quantity demanded has an inverse relationship with price. Therefore, if price increases, the quantity demanded falls, and vice versa. Figure below portrays the conventional demand curve.

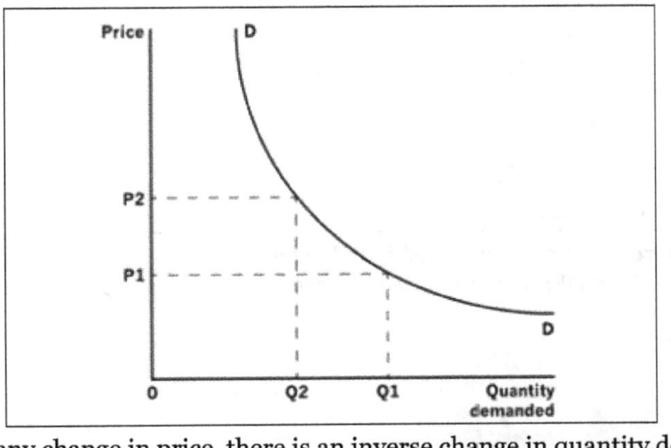

Demand curve: For any change in price, there is an inverse change in quantity demanded. The price increase from OP1 to OP1 results in a reduction in quantity demanded from OQ1 to OQ2.

A change in price will cause a movement along the curve. When the price increases, the quantity demanded will reduce. This happens with most types of goods, with some bizarre exceptions. Demand for what are known as 'Giffen goods' actually rises with an increase in the price for such goods. For example, when the price of rice increases in some regions of China, more rice will be purchased, as there is not enough income left over to some consumers to purchase higher value food items.

If we then relax the assumption that other variables (such as income and tax rates, etc) are constant, what happens then? An increase in income will often cause the demand for a good or service to increase, and this will shift the whole curve away from the origin. Likewise, a reduction in the price of a substitute good will move the demand curve towards the origin as the good in question will then be less attractive to the consumer.

While these generalisations are useful, it is important to remember that economic behaviour is based on human decisions, and so we can never predict fully how people will act. For example, some very basic foodstuffs will become less popular as incomes increase and when consumers find that they no longer have to subsist on basic diets.

Supply

Supply refers to the quantity of goods and services offered to the market by producers. Just as we can map the relationship between quantity demanded and price, we can also consider the relationship between quantity supplied and price. Generally, suppliers will be prepared to produce more goods and services the higher the price they can obtain. Therefore, the supply curve – when holding other influences constant – will slope upwards from left to right, as illustrated in figure below:

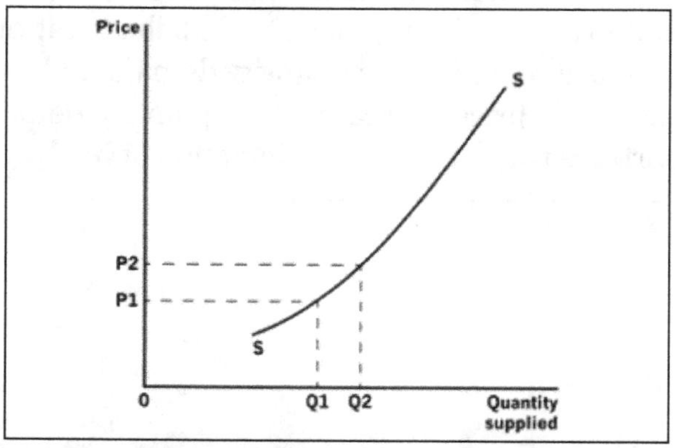

Supply curve: There is a direct relationship between price and quantity supplied. An increase in price from OP1 to OP2 results in an increase in quantity supplied from OQ1 to OQ2.

The determinants of supply are:

- Price.
- Prices of other goods and services.

- Relative revenues and costs of making the good or service.
- The objectives of producers and their future expectations.
- Technology.

Generally, a firm will maximise profit when its marginal revenue (the revenue arising from selling one extra unit of production) equals its marginal cost (the cost of producing that one extra unit of production). However, a firm may continue to produce as long as the marginal revenue exceeds its average variable costs, as in doing so it will be making a contribution towards covering its fixed costs.

Following the same rationale as applied earlier, a movement along the supply curve will be brought about by a change in price, but a movement of the whole curve will be caused by a determinant other than price.

Elasticity

The concept of elasticity is concerned with the responsiveness of quantity demanded or quantity supplied to a change in price. If a small change in price brings about a massive change in quantity demanded, the price elasticity of demand is said to be highly elastic. Conversely, if a change in price has little or no effect on the quantity demanded, the demand is said to be highly inelastic. This concept is obviously very important to producers, who have to estimate the potential effects of their pricing strategies over time. It is also important to government finance departments, which have to model the implications of imposing sales taxes on goods and services in order to predict tax revenues.

Price elasticity of demand is measured by dividing the change in quantity demanded by the change in price and, conversely, price elasticity of supply is measured by dividing the change in quantity supplied by the change in price. Price elasticity of demand occurs when an increase in price leads to a reduction in total revenue ($p \times q$) between those two points on the demand curve, and price inelasticity occurs when an increase in price leads to an increase in total revenue. Unitary elasticity occurs when the change in price causes no change in total revenue. In addition to price elasticity, there are similar concepts of relevance to your study:

- Income elasticity is the responsiveness of quantity demanded or supplied to a change in income.
- Cross elasticity is the responsiveness of quantity demanded or supplied of good X to a change in price of good Y.

Equilibrium

Assuming all determinants of supply and demand are to be constant except price, a firm will produce where the supply curve intersects the demand curve. By definition, this is the point at which the quantity supplied equals the quantity demanded.

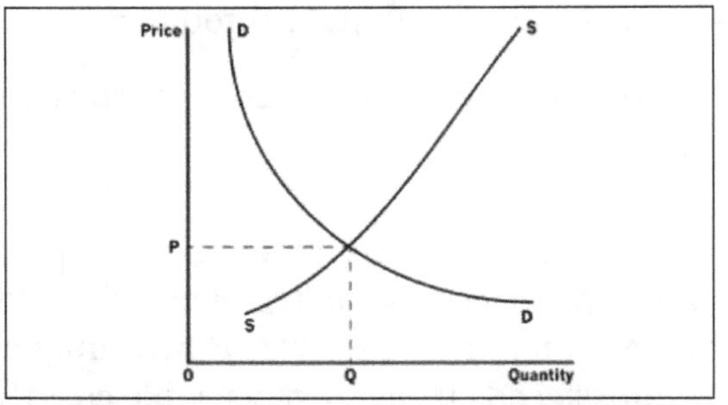

Price is determined at the intersection of the supply and demand curves.

If the price is set above the equilibrium price, this will result in the quantity supplied exceeding the quantity demanded. Therefore, in order to clear its inventory, the company will need to reduce its price. Conversely, if the price is set below the equilibrium price, this will result in an excess demand situation, and the only way to eliminate this is to increase the price.

Market Intervention

In capitalist systems, allowing markets to operate freely is considered to be desirable, but it is generally accepted that market forces cannot be permitted to operate for all the goods and services required by society. Some goods and services are 'public goods and services', which means that they can only be provided adequately by intervention. These include law and order and the military. For this reason, the government or supra-national organisations may choose to introduce and maintain systems that will ensure that such goods and services are produced, and may fix prices either above or below the equilibrium price.

A maximum price is sometimes imposed in order to protect consumers. This will result in a situation in which the quantity demanded will exceed the quantity supplied, provided the maximum price is struck below the equilibrium price. There are numerous examples of this in real life. During World War 2, the UK government intervened in this way in order to ensure that families could obtain adequate supplies of goods such as bread, butter and petrol. One consequence of this is that there was excess demand in the system, and this led to an illegal market developing.

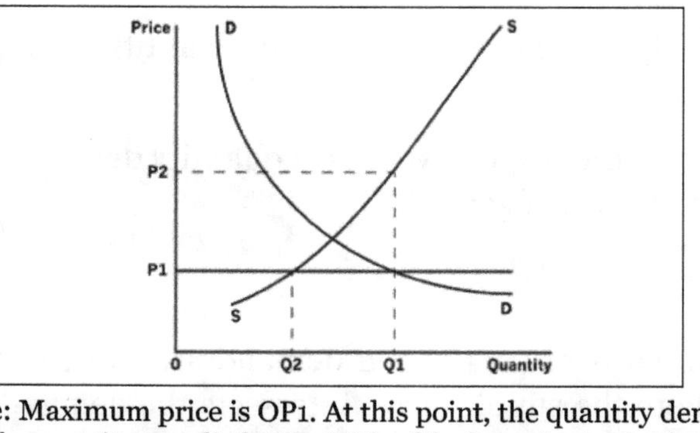

Maximum price: Maximum price is OP1. At this point, the quantity demanded (OQ1) exceeds quantity supplied (OQ2). The 'black market' price is OP2.

A minimum price is sometimes imposed in order to protect producers. Here, the quantity supplied will exceed the quantity demanded, provided the minimum price is struck at a level above the equilibrium price. One of the goals of the European Union (EU) has been to protect the agricultural sector, and the common agricultural policy is a minimum price system. As a consequence of this, the agricultural sector of the EU has periodically generated surpluses.

The impact of intervention in the price system should not be seen as undesirable in all cases. However, one of the contributions that microeconomic analysis makes is that it teaches us that there will be consequences of such interventions, and society has to manage those consequences.

Financial Economics

Financial economics is a branch of economics that analyzes the use and distribution of resources in markets in which decisions are made under uncertainty. Financial decisions must often take into account future events, whether those be related to individual stocks, portfolios or the market as a whole.

Making financial decisions is not always a straight-forward process. Time, risk (uncertainty), opportunity costs, and information can create incentives or disincentives. Financial economics employs economic theory to evaluate how certain things impact decision making, providing investors with the instruments to make the right calls.

Financial economics often involves the creation of sophisticated models to test the variables affecting a particular decision. Often, these models assume that individuals or institutions making decisions act rationally, though this is not necessarily the case. Irrational behavior of parties has to be taken into account in financial economics as a potential risk factor.

This branch of economics builds heavily on microeconomics and basic accounting concepts. It is a quantitative discipline that uses econometrics and other mathematical tools. It necessitates familiarity with basic probability and statistics since these are the standard tools used to measure and evaluate risk. Financial economics studies fair value, risk and returns, and the financing of securities and assets. Numerous monetary factors are taken into account, including interest rates and inflation.

Financial Economics Vs. Traditional Economics

Traditional economics focuses on exchanges in which money is one—but only one—of the items traded. In contrast, financial economics concentrates on exchanges in which money of one type or another is likely to appear on both sides of a trade.

The financial economist can be distinguished from traditional economists by their focus on monetary activities in which time, uncertainty, options and information play roles.

Financial Economics Methods

There are many angles to the concept of financial economics. Two of the most prominent are:

- Discounting: Decision making over time recognizes the fact that the value of $1 in 10 years' time is less than the value of $1 now. Therefore, the $1 at 10 years must be discounted to allow for risk, inflation, and the simple fact that it is in the future. Failure to discount appropriately can lead to problems, such as underfunded pension schemes.

- Risk Management and Diversification: Many advertisements for stock market-based financial products must remind potential buyers that the value of investments may fall as well as rise, so although stocks yield a high return on average, this is largely to compensate for risk.

Financial institutions are always looking for ways of insuring, or hedging, this risk. It is sometimes possible to hold two highly risky assets but for the overall risk to be low: if share A only performs badly when share B performs well (and vice versa) then the two shares perform a perfect hedge. An important part of finance is working out the total risk of a portfolio of risky assets, since the total risk may be less than the risk of the individual components.

Business Economics

Business Economics, also called Managerial Economics, is the application of economic theory and methodology to business. Business involves decision-making. Decision making means the process of selecting one out of two or more alternative courses of action. The question of choice arises because the basic resources such as capital, land, labour and management are limited and can be employed in alternative uses. The decision-making function thus becomes one of making choice and taking decisions that will provide the most efficient means of attaining a desired end, say, profit maximation.

Different aspects of business need attention of the chief executive. He may be called upon to choose a single option among the many that may be available to him. It would he in the interest of the business to reach an optimal decision- the one that promotes the goal of the business firm. A scientific formulation of the business problem and finding its optimals solution requires that the business firm is he equipped with a rational methodology and appropriate tools.

Nature of Business Economics

Traditional economic theory has developed along two lines; viz., normative and positive. Normative focuses on prescriptive statements, and help establish rules aimed at attaining the specified goals of business. Positive, on the other hand, focuses on description it aims at describing the manner in which the economic system operates without staffing how they should operate.

The emphasis in business economics is on normative theory. Business economic seeks to establish rules which help business firms attain their goals, which indeed is also the essence of the word normative. However, if the firms are to establish valid decision rules, they must thoroughly understand their environment. This requires the study of positive or descriptive theory. Thus, Business economics combines the essentials of the normative and positive economic theory, the emphasis being more on the former than the latter.

Scope of Business Economics

As regards the scope of business economics, no uniformity of views exists among various authors. However, the following aspects are said to generally fall under business economics:

- Demand Analysis and Forecasting.
- Cost and production Analysis.
- Pricing Decisions, policies and practices.
- Profit Management.
- Capital Management.

These various aspects are also considered to comprise the subject matter of business economic.

Demand Analysis and Forecasting

A business firm is an economic organisation which transform productive resources into goods to be sold in the market. A major part of business decision making depends on accurate estimates of demand. A demand forecast can serve as a guide to management for maintaining and strengthening market position and enlarging profits. Demands analysis helps identify the various factors influencing the product demand and thus provides guidelines for manipulating demand.

Demand analysis and forecasting provided the essential basis for business planning and occupies a strategic place in managerial economic. The main topics covered are: Demand Determinants, Demand Distinctions and Demand Forecast.

Cost and Production Analysis

A study of economic costs, combined with the data drawn from the firm's accounting records, can yield significant cost estimates which are useful for management decisions. An element of cost uncertainty exists because all the factors determining costs are not known and controllable. Discovering economic costs and the ability to measure them are the necessary steps for more effective profit planning, cost control and sound pricing practices.

Production analysis is narrower, in scope than cost analysis. Production analysis frequently proceeds in physical terms while cost analysis proceeds in monetary terms. The main topics covered under cost and production analysis are: Cost concepts and classification, Cost-output Relationships, Economics and Diseconomics of scale, Production function and Cost control.

Pricing Decisions, Policies and Practices

Pricing is an important area of business economic. In fact, price is the genesis of a firms revenue and as such its success largely depends on how correctly the pricing decisions are taken. The important aspects dealt with under-pricing include. Price Determination in Various Market Forms, Pricing Method, Differential Pricing, Product-line Pricing and Price Forecasting.

Profit Management

Business firms are generally organised for purpose of making profits and in the long run profits earned are taken as an important measure of the firm's success. If knowledge about the future were perfect, profit analysis would have been a very easy task. However, in a world of uncertainty, expectations are not always realised so that profit planning and measurement constitute a difficult area of business economic. The important aspects covered under this area are: Nature and Measurement of profit, Profit policies and Technique of Profit Planning like Break-Even Analysis.

Capital Management

Among the various types business problems, the most complex and troublesome for the business manager are those relating to a firm's capital investments. Relatively large sums are involved and the problems are so complex that their solution requires considerable time and labour. Often the decision involving capital management are taken by the top management. Briefly Capital management implies planning and control of capital expenditure. The main topics dealt with are: Cost of capital Rate of Return and Selection of Projects.

Development Economics

Development economics is a branch of economics that focuses on improving fiscal, economic, and social conditions in developing countries. Development economics considers factors such as health, education, working conditions, domestic and international policies, and market conditions with a focus on improving conditions in the world's poorest countries. The field also examines both macroeconomic and microeconomic factors relating to the structure of developing economies and domestic and international economic growth.

Development economics studies the transformation of emerging nations into more prosperous nations. Strategies for transforming a developing economy tend to be unique because the social and political backgrounds of countries can vary dramatically. Not only is that, but the cultural and economic frameworks of every nation different also, such as women's rights and child labor laws.

Students of economics, and professional economists, create theories and methods that guide practitioners in determining practices and policies that can be used and implemented at the domestic and international policy level.

Some aspects of development economics include determining to what extent rapid population growth helps or hinders development, the structural transformation of economies, and the role of education and healthcare in development.

They also include international trade, globalization, sustainable development, the effects of epidemics, such as HIV, and the impact of catastrophes on economic and human development. Prominent development economists include Jeffrey Sachs, Hernando de Soto Polar, and Nobel Laureates Simon Kuznets, Amartya Sen, and Joseph Stiglitz.

Types of Development Economics

Mercantilism

Mercantilism is thought to be one of the earliest forms of development economics that created practices to promote the success of a nation. It was a dominant economic theory practiced in Europe from the 16th to the 18th centuries. The theory promoted augmenting state power by lowering exposure to rival national powers.

Like political absolutism and absolute monarchies, mercantilism promoted government regulation by prohibiting colonies from transacting with other nations. Mercantilism monopolized markets with staple ports and banned gold and silver exports. It believed the higher the supply of gold and silver, the more wealthy it would be. In general, it sought a trade surplus (exports greater than imports), did not allow the use of foreign ships for trade, and it optimized the use of domestic resources.

Economic Nationalism

Economic nationalism reflects policies that focus on domestic control of capital formation, the economy, and labor, using tariffs or other barriers. It restricts the movement of capital, goods, and labor.

Economic nationalists do not generally agree with the benefits of globalization and unlimited free trade. They focus on a policy that is isolationist so that the industries within a nation are able to grow without the threat of competition from established companies in other countries.

The economy of the early United States is a prime example of economic nationalism. As a new nation, it sought to develop itself without relying so much on outside influences. It enacted measures, such as high tariffs, so its own industries would grow unimpeded.

Linear Stages of Growth Model

The linear stages of growth model was used to revitalize the European economy after World War II. This model states that economic growth can only stem from industrialization. The model also agrees that local institutions and social attitudes can restrict growth if these factors influence people's savings rates and investments.

The linear stages of growth model portrays an appropriately designed addition of capital partnered with public intervention. This injection of capital and restrictions from the public sector leads to economic development and industrialization.

Structural-Change Theory

The structural-change theory focuses on changing the overall economic structure of a nation, which aims to shift society from being a primarily agrarian one to a primarily industrial one. For example, Russia before the communist revolution was an agrarian society. When the communists overthrew the royal family and took power, they rapidly industrialized the nation, allowing it to eventually become a superpower.

References

- Economics: investopedia.com, Retrieved 11, July 2020
- Introduction-to-microeconomics, fundamentals-exams-study-resources: accaglobal.com, Retrieved 27, April 2020
- Financial-economics: investopedia.com, Retrieved 03, August 2020
- Development-economics: investopedia.com, Retrieved 16, March 2020

2

Economic Growth and Development

An increase in the market value of goods and services produced by an economy is known as economic growth. An improvement in the living standards and quality of life is known as economic development. In order to completely understand economic growth and development, it is necessary to understand the processes related to it. The following chapter elucidates the varied processes and mechanisms associated with this area of study.

Economic growth is quite modern phenomenon. For instance, consider the growth rate of world leading industrial countries over the past four centuries. During the period 1580-1820, the Netherlands was the leading industrial nation it experienced an average annual growth in real GDP per worker hour of roughly 0.2 percent. The United Kingdom (UK), the other leading country experienced an annual growth of 1.2 percent during the period approximately 1820-1890. Since 1890, the United States of America (USA) is considered to have usurped the leaders' seat, and its average growth rate during the period 1890-1989 was a relatively dramatic 2.2 percent a year. Clearly, by today's standard even the fastest growing economy two centuries ago would be considered practically stagnant. According to one estimate, even the modest 2 percent growth, a nation's per capita Gross domestic product (GDP) doubles in 35 years. It shows the enormous potential that economic growth carries if sustained.

Economic growth is the increase in the market value of goods and services produced by an economy over time. It is conventionally calculated as the percent rate of increase in real GDP. In economics, economic growth theory typically refers to growth of potential output i.e. production at full employment. As an area of study, economic growth generally distinguished from economic development, the former generally refers to the increase in per capita income while letters tries to focus on quantitative as well as qualitative changes in nation's Alife during the economic advancement. "Economic growth means more output, while economic development implies both more output and changes in the technical and institutional arrangement by which it is produced and distributed. Growth not only involves more output derived from higher amounts of input but also refers greater efficiency i.e. an increase in output per unit of input. Development goes beyond this to imply changes in the composition of output and in the allocation of inputs by sectors".

Difference between Economic Growth and Economic Development

Economic development can be referred as the quantitative and qualitative changes in the economy. Arthur Lewis defined economic development as the enlargement of the range of people choices. Economic development focuses on the spectrum of spheres ranging from health, education, employment, safety, environmental sustainability, social exclusion, gender empowerment, infrastructure, and other activities whereas economic growth measured in terms of rise in GDP or market productivity.

The study of economic development was borne out of an extension to traditional economics that focused entirely on national product, or the aggregate output of goods and services, the latter known as economic growth. Economic development mainly concerned in expansion of people's entitlements and their corresponding capabilities, morbidity, nourishment, literacy, education, and other socio-economic indicators.

Economic growth, that is, more income is only one of the things desired by poor people. Adequate nutrition, safe water, better medical services, more and better schooling for their children, cheap transport, adequate shelter, continuing employment and secure livelihood, and productive remunerative satisfying job do not show up in higher income per head. There are even other non-material benefits that are often more highly valued by poor people than material benefits but they do not reflect in higher income figure. For instances, freedom to choose, movement, speech, safe working condition, expressing cultural, regional, linguistic and religious identity, empowerment are some factors often more important than income.

It is quite often observed in the many parts of world that economic growth can be rapid without the improvement in the quality of life. In other words, per capita increase in GDP only benefits a small section of minority population and rest of the vast majority of population deprived from the fruits of increased GDP. It led to concentration of wealth in few hands, stark inequality, existence of dual economy where one sect enjoyed the increased production of goods and services and remaining large section of population starving and yet to receive any benefits of higher GDP.

Economic growth set the prerequisite condition for economic development. The economic growth accompanied by proper distribution of resources across the population, building institutional mechanisms which ensure qualitative change in the lives of people, and environmental sustainability guaranteed the economic development. It has been observed that there is positive correlation between incomes per head and indicators of human development. It does not refer that higher income led higher development since many countries have achieved high human development at low level of income. This correlation depend on how additional income from growth being used for public education, health, and employment opportunities. Economic is indeed important, not for itself, but for what it allows a country to do with the resources that generated, expanding both individual incomes and the public revenue that can be used to meet the social commitments. Initial endowments like distribution of assets are also important factor in determining economic development. If land are fairly distributed among the population and education is accessible for masses, then the benefits of economic growth can easily percolate down to the end of the population.

Economic growth is quite often considered to be an essential part of development. But growth (known as continuing increase of the quantity of goods and services produced and consumed over time) is simply the inter-temporal dimension of any policy objective, although it has been wrongly monopolized by production and consumption: it should apply to poverty to poverty reduction, employment, investment, a more equitable income distribution, environment protection, leisure and, of course, also to income. But once you specify for income, consumption and production, the 'What?' 'To whom?' 'By whom?' 'For what?' and 'When?' growth becomes the incidental result, not the objective, of a sensible economic policy. Growth is too unspecified, abstract, aggregate and unbounded to be a sensible objective of policy. It also implies an infinite horizon, without the limits to increases in income. What matters is the composition of national income, to what uses it is put, its distribution among beneficiaries, now and for future generations; and with how much efforts and in what conditions it is produced. If and only if the extra resources resulting from growth go largely to the poor, and if they are spent on public health and education, will a contribution to human development result.

In measuring economic growth, the national income is a quite inadequate measure of human development for several reasons. It counts only goods and services that are exchanged for money, leaving out of account the large amount of work done inside family, mainly by women, and work done voluntarily for children or older people or in communities. Public services are counted at their cost, so that doubling the wages of all public services appears to double their contribution to welfare or development. National income accounting does not distinguish between goods and regrettable necessities, like military expenditure or anti-crime expenditure, products needed to combat 'bads'. Addictive eating and drinking is counted twice: when the food and the alcohol are consumed, and when large sums are spent on diet industry and on cures for alcoholism. Much of what is now counted as economic growth is really either combating evils, and fixing the blunders and social decay from the past, or borrowing resources from the future, or shifting functions from community and household to the market.

One more dimension that untouched in discussion of economic growth is related to gender issues. In events where women are provided opportunity to choose the size of their family it has been found that without adverse economic and social consequences, smaller families are indeed chosen. With human development through expanding education, especially for women and girls, the reduction in infant mortality, improved medical facilities led to significant fall in fertility rate among women. There are strong evidences which show that more surviving children also led to reduction in population growth by evading uncertainties in family. Human development is a powerful tool to curb the population growth, and reduced population growth open up the news ways of economic advancement.

Factors Affecting Economic Growth

Natural Resources

The principal factor determining economic growth of a country is the natural resources. A country suffering from non-availability of natural resources would not be able develop rapidly. Having said this, it is also a recognized fact that presence of abundant resources does not guarantee the economic growth; it must be accompanied by proper exploitation of these resources. If the existing resources are not properly utilized or exploited, the country would not be able to develop. One of the main factors which ensure the utilization of resources is technological advancement. Therefore, natural resources can be put in right place to augment economic growth through introducing improved technology. As pointed out by economist that the value of resource depend upon its usefulness, and the usefulness of resource mainly depend on accommodating and updating the technology which can be used a means to define its usefulness.

It is often said that economic growth could be achieved even when an economy is inadequate in natural resources. On such country is Japan which even deficient in natural resource but one of the developed countries of the world because it has been succeeded in forming human capital and discover new used of its limited resources. A country which considered poor in resources in one point of time may considered rich in resources after passage of time, not because of new avenues of resources are discovered but equally because creating new resources and using limited resources most efficient way. Moreover, by importing those resources from other countries, it has been able to overcome the inadequacy of natural resources through using the superior technology, efficient management skills.

Thus for economic growth mere presence of abundant resources are not enough. What is essential is their proper exploitation through improved technology and efficient management skills so there would be little wastage of scarce resources.

Capital Accumulation

The second most important factor in economic growth is capital accumulation. Capital means stock of physical reproducible factor of production. When the capital stock grows over period of time, this is defined as capital accumulation. The process of capital accumulation is cumulative and self-sustaining provided three inter-related stages proceeded: (a) the existence of continuous rise in saving; (b) to us these saving for investment in capital goods; (c) intermediaries to mobilize saving and divert them for investment.

One of the prominent reason of lower growth in underdeveloped countries is lower saving, equally opposite in developed countries higher saving ensure the capital formation and sustain continuous growth. Due to low propensity to save in least developed countries, voluntary saving are not sufficient to ensure desired growth. Due to low level of income poor countries are close to subsistence level of consumption which led to low level of saving. In such circumstances possibility to raise saving are dismal, and economic growth would rely on other sources of capital accumulation, like external loans, grants or aid.

Capital formation is the key component of economic growth. On the one hand it ensure effective demand, and other hand, it creates productive efficiency for future production. Higher investment in capital goods and consumer goods industries creates employment opportunities which led to higher consumption reflects in effective demand. On the other hand new avenues for capital goods open up the ways for productive efficiency in production. The processes of capital accumulation reflect in higher national output, essential to meet the demand of increasing population.

Technological Progress

Technological changes are count as the most important factor in the process of economic growth. They are mostly referring as the change in mode of production through new technique emerges out from research or innovation. Changes in technology lead to increase in productivity of labour, capital and other factors used in production. Schumpeter regards innovation as most important technological factor in economic growth.

Modern economic growth theories even assume that without technical progress, a country cannot sustain the growth in per capita income indefinitely. Due to low technological progress in least developed countries they are not able to break the vicious circle of underdevelopment. Developed countries are succeeded in continuous adaptation of new technology due to higher spending in research and development activities.

Population

Population growth is also another important factor which affects the economic growth. There are evidences which shows that population growth systematically change with the overall development of a society. The changes in population growth along with development process normally are known as demographic transition. The idea is very simple, when the population growth is high, economy has to put more effort for achieving higher growth since higher population pull down the per capita income growth and vice versa. A strong family planning targets or the provision of incentive to have less children, spread of education can pull down the population growth and permit long-run growth.

Other Factors

One of the important factors determining modern economic growth is infrastructural development such as means of transport and communication, facilitating services. Structural changes also important factor determining shape of economic growth. It implies the transition from a traditional primary sector to modern manufacturing sector and service sector. Such structural changes should accompanied by increasing employment opportunities, higher labour productivity and ever increasing stock of capital, and institution promotes new ideas, innovation or research. Sign of structural changes begin with the transfer of population from primary sector to secondary and then tertiary sector.

Creation of human capital another important factor determines the path of economic growth. The skilled labour force of various kinds such as scientist, engineers, managers, administrator, expert on various fields of social science, etc. are crucial to form such institutions which create enough ground for economic growth. The shortage of such skilled labour force poses a serious problem in least developed countries. To overcome such deficiency in human capital, it requires setting up scientific, technological, and various institutions which fill such gaps in human assets.

Human endowments, social attitudes, political conditions, and historical factors greatly influence the process of growth. Therefore, social, cultural, political, and administrative factor have its own importance in economic development. For instance, social attitudes, culture and values determine the spirit of adventure, discoveries, invention which consequently led to new opportunity conducive for economic growth.

Types of Growth Models

Joan Robinson's Model

Mrs. Joan Robinson has given her model of growth in her classic book 'The Accumulation of Capital' in 1956. Joan Robinson's model clearly takes the problem of population growth in a developing economy and analyses the influence of population on the role of capital accumulation and growth of output.

Assumptions

- Labour and capital are the only productive factors. It implies that the national output is the result of combined efforts of these two factors of production.
- The economy is assumed to be closed i.e., there is no foreign trade.
- Total wage bill is the product of real wage rate and number of workers.
- Total income is divided between capital and labour as these are the two factors of production.
- The production is not affected by the technological changes i.e. there is no progress in technology.
- Total profit is the product of profit rate and amount of capital invested.
- There is constancy in price level.

- Wage earners spend all of their wage income on consumption, while profit takers save and invest all of their profit income.
- Capital and labor are combined in a fixed proportion for a given output.
- The national income is the sum of wage bill and total profits.
- There is no scarcity of labor and entrepreneurs can employ as much labor as they wish.
- Entrepreneurs consume nothing but save and invest their entire income for capital formation. If they have no profits, there is no accumulation and if they do not accumulate, they have no profits.

Open Model

In an open economy, the conditions for the steady growth and conditions for rising rate of capital accumulation will be discussed. According to Mrs. Joan Robinson, national income is the sum of the total wage bill and total profit. Total wage bill is the real wage multiplied by the number of workers and total profits are equal to profit rate multiplied by the amount of capital. This relationship can be expressed as under:

$$PY = WN + \pi PK$$

Where,

- P = Average Price level,
- Y = Net national income,
- W= Net money wage rate,
- N=Amount of labor employed,
- K= Amount of capital invested,
- π = Rate of profit.

To convert the expression into real terms, divide both sides of equation by p (average price level), we get,

$$PY = WN + \pi PK$$

$$Y = \frac{WN}{P} + \pi K$$

$$\pi K = Y - \frac{W}{P}N$$

$$\pi = \frac{Y - \frac{W}{P}N}{K}$$

Dividing both sides b N, we get,

$$\pi = \frac{\frac{Y}{N} - \frac{W}{P}}{K/N}$$

$$\pi = \frac{\rho - \frac{W}{P}}{\theta}$$

Where,

- ρ Y/N i.e Labor/Productivity.
- W/P real wage rate.
- θ = K/N i.e. Capital Labour Ratio.

The above equation indicates that the profit rate is a function of labour productivity (ρ) and real wage rate (W/P) and capital labour ratio. In other words, the profit rate is shown as capable of varying directly with the rate of net return to capital and inversely with the coefficient of capital intensity. The necessary condition for maximization is that the first derivative must be zero.

Keynesian income expenditure analysis shows that the net national real income (Y) is the sum of real consumption expenditure (C) and real net investment which can be expressed as:

$$Y = C + I$$

Now we know that labour spends its entire income and saves nothing. The profit earning class makes saving in the form of profit. According to Mrs. Robinson, savings must be equal to total profits. Thus, savings in a given period are equal to capital investment multiplied by rate of profit.

$$S = \pi K$$

I is simply increase in real capital i.e.

$$I = \Delta K$$

Substituting the value S and I in saving investment function,

$$S = 1$$

$$\pi K = \Delta K$$

$$\pi = \frac{\Delta K}{K}$$

The above relation implies that profit rate is equal to growth rate of real capital. Now,

For the economy to be in equilibrium, the growth rate of capital must be equal to rate of profit. A higher rate of profit is archive when,

$$\pi = \frac{\Delta K}{K}$$

$$\pi = \frac{\rho - \frac{W}{P}}{\theta}$$

For the economy to be in equilibrium, the growth rate of capital must be equal to rate of profit. A higher rate of profit is archived when,

$$\left(\rho - \frac{W}{P}\right) > \theta,$$

The above equation illustrates that the rate of growth of capital is capable of increasing if the net returns to capital rise in greater proportion than the capital-labour ratio and vice-versa. In other words, lower rate of profit always affects the supply of capital adversely which in turn widens the gap between supply of capital and labour. The main feature of the model is that the rate of growth of capital is dependent on profit rate.

Closed Model

In a closed economy, the concepts of Golden age and Platinum age are to be discussed. In simple words, Golden age is a situation of smooth steady growth with full employment arising out of the equality of the 'Desired' and 'Possible' rates of accumulation and has been designated by Mrs. Joan Robinson as the Golden age equilibrium.

However, if an increase in labour supply is not accompanied by proportionate increase in the capital supply, then it will cause unemployment in the economy. To achieve full employment of labour the growth rate of population must be equal to growth rate of capital i.e.

$$\Delta N/N = \Delta K/K$$

When the rate of growth of labour and capital are equal to each other, then there is full utilisation of capital in the economy. Such a switch on is called Golden age. The existence of Golden age is the indicator of full employment level.

The concept of Golden age implies that there must be equality in actual, warranted and natural growth rates. In short, in Mrs. Robinson Joan's words, when technical progress is neutral and proceeding steady, without any change in the time pattern of production, the competitive mechanism works freely, population grows (if at all) at a steady rate and accumulation goes on fast enough to supply productive capacity for all available labour, the rate of profit tends to be constant and the level of real wages rises with output per head.

Then there are no internal contradictions in the system, we may describe these conditions as a Golden age (thus indicating that it represents a mythical state of affairs not likely to obtain in any actual economy). This is explained with the help of a figure.

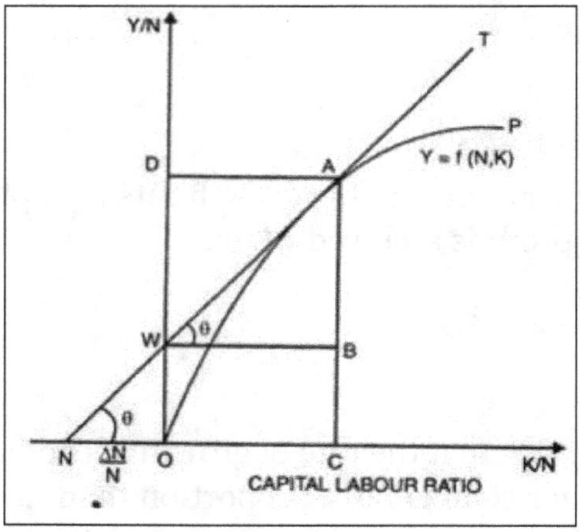

In the figure, capital labour ratio is illustrated along positive direction of X-axis and wage rate of labour on Y-axis and the growth rate of labour on negative side of X-axis. The production function is represented by OP. Each point on this curve shows the proportion in which capital and labour are combined to produce a particular level of output.

Tangent NT touches the curve OP at A and intersects Y-axis at W. At point A capital labour ratio is OC, the productivity of labour is OD and out of which OW is the wage rate. The surplus DW is rate of return to capital.

The point A shows the position of equilibrium because the slope of tangent NT and the slope of production curve OP is the same. It can also be said that at A, the growth rate of capital ΔK/K is equal to growth rate of labour ΔN/N.

$$\text{Growth rate of capital} = \frac{\Delta K}{K}$$

$$= \frac{\text{output} - \text{Input}}{\text{Input}} = \frac{\text{surplus}}{\text{Input}}$$

$$= \frac{DW}{OC \times OW}$$

But, DW = AB

and OC = WB

$$\frac{\Delta K}{K} = \frac{AB}{WB \times OW}$$

In Δ AWB and Δ ONW,

$$\angle AWB = \angle WNO$$
$$\angle AWB = \angle WON$$

$\therefore \Delta AWB$ is similar to ΔONW.

Since the triangles are similar so the sides are in same proportion.

$$\frac{AB}{OW} = \frac{WB}{ON}$$

$$\frac{AB}{WB} = \frac{OW}{ON}$$

Putting the value of AB/BW in $\frac{\Delta K}{K} = \frac{AB}{WB \times OW}$,we get,

$$\frac{\Delta K}{K} = \frac{AB}{WB \times OW}$$
$$= \frac{OW}{ON} \times \frac{1}{OW} = \frac{1}{ON}$$

= Growth rate of labour

$$= \frac{\Delta N}{N}$$

- $\Delta N/N > \Delta K/K$
- $\Delta K/K > \Delta K/A$

The first possibility (i.e., $\Delta N/N > \Delta K/K$) shows that the growth rate of population is greater than growth rate of capital. This type of situation occurs in underdeveloped countries. Mrs. Robinson is of the view that it is the 'profit wage relation' which pushes the economy back on the path of Golden age. The excess of labour supply would depress the money wage rate and if the prices remain constant, the real wages would fall.

This fall in real wages would increase the level of profit, which in turn would stimulate the growth of capital. The increase in the growth rate is unable to fulfil the labour supply of population. When the parity between the two growth rates are restored, then the economy would be on Golden age.

On the other hand, if real wages do not fall because of subsistence wage floor or if the general price level does not fall in same proportion as money wage rate, it would be difficult to restore the position of Golden age and it will lead to under employment.

The second possibility comes out as the economy is in the disequilibrium and can be expressed as $\Delta N/N < \Delta K/K$ Under the situation, the growth rate of population is less as compared to growth rate of capital. This type of situation occurs in developed countries. The possibility of advanced countries returning to the path of Golden age equilibrium is greater than that of underdeveloped economies.

Harrod-Domar Model-I

Roy Harrod and Evsey Domar worked separately to develop their highly similar models of economic growth and business cycles. The two economists expanded the short-run Keynesian framework to analyze the growth process in the developed economies. Both of them criticized the basic Keynesian framework of income determination in the short run for ignoring the role of investment to create more capacity for the production of output.

The investment in physical capital, according to these economists, has a dual role. Dual role of investment here means that investment spending generates income on one hand and also increases the productive capacity of the economy on the other hand. Increase in the income as a result of increase in investment is called the demand side effect while the increase in the productive capacity of economy due to investment is called the supply side effect. Both the economists were interested in finding out an equilibrium growth path which would guarantee a full employment in some sense. Although the two models of Harrod and Domar are similar in many respects but they have some crucial differences as well.

Harrod's Model

His first concern was to find that does there exist an equilibrium growth rate of output which if the economy grows at then it will continue to grow at the same rate moving over time? His second concern was to investigate that whether such an equilibrium growth path is stable in the sense that if ever the economy grew at some different rate then would it automatically move towards equilibrium growth rate in due time?

Basic Assumptions of the Harrod's Model

- Savings and investment refer to income of the same period. Both Saving and Investment are net, i.e. over and above the depreciation.
- The economy saves a constant proportion of its income, which implies that the marginal propensity to save (MPS) i.e. $\frac{ds}{dy}$ is equal to average propensity to save (APS) i.e. $\frac{s}{y}$ Since if $MPS \neq APS$, then the latter could not stay constant.
- Income is determined by investment through the multiplier process while investment is determined through the process of accelerator.

- If plans of investment are realized then the firms don't change the rate of desired investment whereas if plans are under realized i.e. actual investment is less than planned investment or over realized i.e. actual investment is more than planned then firms increase or decrease respectively the rate of desired investment.
- The economy is assumed to begin with full employment of capital.
- There are no lags in the adjustment between demand and supply, especially between investment and creation of productive capacity.
- Aggregate output in the economy can be written as a function of aggregate physical capital and aggregate labor measured in suitable units respectively i.e. $Y = F(K, L)$. It is further assumed that there are constant returns to scale in the aggregate production function which means that if both the factors are changed by some equal proportion then output also gets by same proportion.
- General Price level and the rate of interest remains fixed. It means that the relative prices of capital and labor remain constant as the economy grows. This assumption has a very crucial implication for the Harrod model. A constant relative factor price implies a constant capital-labor ratio i.e. $\frac{K}{L}$ in the economy over time. Some authors like Branson formulate the requirement of fixed $\frac{K}{L}$ in the Harrod model using an Lshaped fixed proportion production function of the form $Y = \text{Min}\,(aK, bL)$.

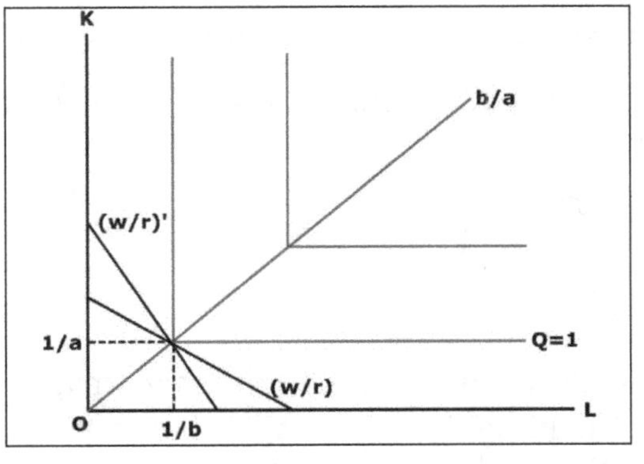

If the production function is conceived to be of a perfectly complementary form as above then a change in relative factor prices from say (w/r) to (w/r)'will not change the ratio $\frac{b}{a}$ in which the factors are used. Although there is no need to assume such a functional form of aggregate production provided we assume constant relative price of factors.

- The implication of constant returns to scale along with fixed proportion of factors implies constant capital-output ratio as well as constant labor-output ratio overtime. The constancy of capital-output ratio is a very important assumption of the Harrod's model.

- There is no role of government in influencing aggregate demand and supply.

Structure and Working of the Harrod's Model

Harrod wanted to find out that rate of growth of investment or output which will sustain itself overtime. In order to find that out Harrod does the marriage of multiplier and accelerator to arrive at his most fundamental growth equation. Keynesian multiplier can be written says that:

$$\Delta y = \frac{\Delta I}{s}$$

Here Y stands for the aggregate output, I for net investment and s for the savings ratio in the economy.

The accelerator theory of investment tells us that the net investment planned or desired in any period in an economy is a fixed multiple of the expected change in output during that period i.e.

$$I = C_r \Delta Y$$

Here $C_r = \frac{\Delta K_r}{\Delta Y}$ stands for the desired change in capital stock per unit increment in output. C_r is also known as desired incremental capital-output ratio. If we combine equations $\Delta y = \frac{\Delta I}{s}$ and $I = C_r \Delta Y$ above by eliminating ΔY then we get that rate of growth of planned investment.

$$\frac{\Delta I}{I} = \frac{s}{C_r}$$

We know that in any short run equilibrium of the economy, planned net savings must equal planned net investment i.e. I = S which implies that in a short run equilibrium I = S = sY or I/Y = s. In other words, to keep their ratio fixed, planned investment and output must grow at the same rate i.e $\frac{\Delta I}{I} = \frac{\Delta Y}{Y}$ if the economy has to always remain in short run equilibrium at all points in time while growing. Substituting $\frac{\Delta Y}{Y}$ in place of $\frac{\Delta I}{I}$ in equation $\frac{\Delta I}{I} = \frac{s}{C_r}$, we get,

$$\frac{\Delta Y}{Y} = \frac{s}{C_r}$$

Equation above is the most fundamental equation in Harrod's model since it says that if economy is growing at the rate given in the right hand side of equation above, then planned investment is always equal to planned savings along the moving growth path. To see why this happens we can rewrite the equation above as $C_r \Delta Y = sY$ where the right hand side is nothing but the planned savings and the left hand side is nothing but the planned investment. Since we generally assume in Keynesian framework that savings are always realized and by truism we know that actual savings must always equal actual investment therefore equation above can be understood to give us that growth path where planned investment must equal actual investment. The assumption number of above tells us that if the plans of firms are met, then there is no reason for them to change their rate of investment which through multiplier would ensure an unchanged rate of growth. Therefore if the economy grows at the rate $\frac{s}{C_r}$ then there is no force to deviate it from this constant growth path. Such an equilibrium growth rate is defined as Warranted (Required) rate of growth by Harrod and denoted as g_w. In his own words, it is "that rate of growth which, if occurs, will leave all the parties satisfied that they have produced neither more nor less than the right amount. ... It will put them into a frame of mind which will cause them to give such orders as will maintain the same rate of growth". Therefore we may write,

$$g_w = \frac{s}{C_r}$$

In fact he defines the following three different types of rate of growth for an economy:

- Warranted (Required) rate of growth denoted as g_w.
- Actual rate of growth denoted as g_a.
- Natural rate of growth denoted as g_n.

Using a similar terminology as in case of warranted rate of growth we may write that,

$$g_a = \frac{\Delta Y}{Y} = \left(\frac{\Delta Y}{I} \times \frac{I}{Y}\right) = \left(\frac{\Delta Y}{\Delta K} \times \frac{I}{Y}\right) = \frac{s}{C}$$

Here S is the saving ratio and C is the actual (not desired) ratio of actual change in capital i.e. actual net investment to the change in output i.e. $C = \frac{\Delta K}{\Delta Y} = \frac{I}{\Delta Y}$ Thus C is the actual incremental capital-output ratio.

Natural rate of growth is defined by Domar as that rate of growth of output which is required to fully employ the entire growing labor force. Since labor-output ratio is assumed to be constant, therefore the natural rate of growth of output must be equal to the rate of growth of labor. Suppose if the rate of growth of population is given by n then the natural rate of growth must be equal to n.

$$g_n = n$$

You may think of growth of labor force as not just an increase in number of labor but an increase in number of effective labor to incorporate the increases in labor productivity.

We know that in the short run disequilibrium occurs whenever actual investment is not equal to planned investment i.e. there is either an unplanned positive or an unplanned negative addition to stock of inventories. This equilibrium is restored by the firms in subsequent periods through increase or decrease in output in case of unplanned removal or unplanned addition to inventories respectively. Does a similar response mechanism also bring the economy back to required equilibrium growth path in case of any deviation from it? After deriving the warranted or equilibrium rate of growth, Harrod's next concern was to check if the equilibrium is stable i.e. is any deviation from the equilibrium path self-correcting over time? Let us look at the following formulation of the adaptive expectation response model of the firms wherein,

$$I_t = C_r\left(Y_t^e - Y_{t-1}\right)$$
$$g_t^e - g_{t-1}^e = \lambda\left(g_{t-1} - g_{t-1}^e\right)$$

The first equation says the investment in any period is a function of the increase in output expected in this period over the previous period's output. The second equation says that the expected rate of growth of output increases by a constant positive multiple of the difference between actual and expected rate of growth of output in the previous observed period. For example, if actual output in previous period was more than expected output i.e. actual growth was more than expected growth in previous period then the firms will revise their expectations of growth of output upwards in the current period implying a larger expected output in the current period and therefore a larger investment given by the first equation. The reverse will hold true whenever actual will be less than expected. Let us consider the following two scenarios:

- $g_a > g_w$
- $g_a < g_w$

Using equations $g_w = \frac{s}{C_r}$ and $g_a = \frac{\Delta Y}{Y} = \left(\frac{\Delta Y}{I} \times \frac{I}{Y}\right) = \left(\frac{\Delta Y}{\Delta K} \times \frac{I}{Y}\right) = \frac{s}{C}$ above, we may write that if,

$g_a > g_w \Rightarrow C < C_r \Rightarrow \Delta K < \Delta K_r \Rightarrow$ rate of planned I is increased $\Rightarrow g_a$ increases.

$g_a < g_w \Rightarrow C > C_r \Rightarrow \Delta K > \Delta K_r \Rightarrow$ rate of planned I is decreased$\Rightarrow g_a$ decreased.

The first implication above considers the situation when for some reason the actual rate of growth in the economy happens to be more than the warranted rate of growth. Under such a situation, the actual incremental capital per unit of incremental output will be less than the desired incremental capital per unit of incremental output. A shortfall in actual capital vis-à-vis planned capital will take either the form of unplanned shortfall in the stock of inventories or an excess demand for the equipment. Both the situations will be inflationary and responded by the firms through increase in the rate of planned investment. Such an increase will cause a further increase in the actual rate of growth of output through the multiplier mechanism. It means that whenever the actual growth rate of output is more than the warranted rate of growth, the response by the firms will make the actual growth rate even larger than the warranted growth rate. Therefore the response mechanism which worked to create equilibrium in the short run will create further disequilibrium in the long run and take the economy further away from the equilibrium growth path towards a boom.

The second implication above considers the situation when the actual rate of growth in the economy happens to be less than the warranted rate of growth. Under such a situation, the actual incremental capital per unit of incremental output will be more than the desired incremental capital per unit of incremental output. A shortfall in actual capital vis-à-vis planned capital will again take either the form of unplanned addition to the stock of inventories or an excess capacity of the equipment. Both the situations will be deflationary and responded by the firms through decrease in the rate of planned investment. Such a decrease will cause a further decrease in the actual rate of growth of output through the multiplier. It means that whenever the actual growth rate of output is less than the warranted rate of growth, the response by the firms will make the actual growth rate even smaller than the warranted growth rate. Therefore the response mechanism will create further disequilibrium in the long run and take the economy further away from the equilibrium growth path towards a depression. The above analysis concludes that the equilibrium growth path of Harrod is completely unstable and any deviation is further aggravating rather than self-correcting. For this reason, the equilibrium growth is said to have a Knife-Edge Stability. If you make a slip on either side, you keep falling.

The instability of equilibrium in the Harrod model can be used to explain the business cycles above and below the trend path of warranted growth. But we know that business cycles always have peaks and troughs. Harrod explained these through the use of natural rate of growth of output. Remember from equation $g_n = n$ that $g_n = n$. Harrod argues that in an economy with constant capital-labor ratio, the actual growth rate of output can never be more than the natural rate of growth of output i.e. $g_a \leq g_n = n$. In other words, growth is constrained by labor. Here again we consider two possible scenarios:

- $g_a \leq g_n < g_w$
- $g_n > g_w$

In the first situation, natural rate is less than the warranted rate which implies that the actual rate which has to be less than or equal to the former will also be less than the warranted rate. Such a situation as we have seen above will push the actual rate further below and bring a deflationary gap in the economy. During this gap, neither the labor nor the capital will be fully employed. The less than full employment of capital is obvious since at all rates of growth below the warranted, actual capital stock must be more than planned capital stock. Correction will only be possible if the warranted rate of growth falls below to become equal to the actual.

A fall in warranted rate requires a fall in savings or an increase in C_r. But an increase in latter is not profitable and thus possible under conditions of deflation. In fact, C_r is bound to fall. But Harrod argues that the savings rate in the economy will fall during the deflation due to redistribution in income against the capitalists and will fall more in proportion to fall in C_r thereby decreasing the warranted rate. When it has fallen enough, then actual will once again become greater than warranted and begin to recover thereafter.

In the second situation, natural rate is more than the warranted rate. In this situation, if actual is equal to warranted then there the economy will move along a constant growth path where there will full employment but persistent growing unemployment of labor. However, if actual is more than warranted, then actual rate will keep growing till it reaches its bounds of natural rate of growth. Although the unemployment will keep o reducing but the capital will be in excess demand putting inflationary pressures. But this rate high rate of growth will not be sustained forever since due to inflation there will be a redistribution of income in favor of capitalists implying an increase in savings rate faster than the increase in desired incremental capital output ratio.

On the other hand, if actual is less than warranted, then the economy will move further in depression with high labor unemployment levels and also unused capacity. This will keep happening unless the warranted rate falls below through the mechanism discussed in the above paragraph. Note that although warranted growth rate changes, but the warranted growth path does not which requires that actual rate of growth must be equal to warranted rate of growth.

Harrod-Domar Model-II

Evsey Domar published his work on "Capital Expansion and Growth" in 1946, seven years later than a very similar work by Roy Harrod. Although there are many similarities in conclusions of the two models by Domar and Harrod but there are some very important differences in the two models.

Domar's Model of Economic Growth

Domar's starting point was to criticize Keynesian framework for its incompleteness in addressing two important issues related to the long-run:

- Keynesian analysis considers investment only to be an income generating (i.e.

demand side) instrument through the multiplier while ignoring the essential productive capacity changing (i.e. supply side) role of investment. It is precisely because of this reason that Keynes assumed that employment of labor is a function of national income. But Domar points out that this is true only in the short run. He assumes that overtime employment of labor is a function of 'ratio of national income to productive capacity'.

- Keynesian analysis, while giving over importance to the need of full employment of labor, almost ignores the issue of unemployment of capital, which in turn becomes the source of labor unemployment. According to Domar, it is the premature obsolescence of capital equipment that discourages investment and growth, thereby causing the labor unemployment.

Main Assumptions of Domar's Model

- Savings and investment refer to income of the same period.
- Both Saving and Investment are net, i.e. over and above the depreciation.
- Depreciation is measured not in respect to historical costs of the depreciated equipment but in respect to the cost of replacement of the depreciated asset by another one of same productive capacity. The latter cost may be different from the former owing to technological progress.
- There is a constant general level of prices.
- No adjustment lags are present in any market.
- Productive capacity of an asset or of the entire economy can be measured. This assumption is very strong since the productive capacity of a given physical stock of capital does not depend just upon the technical factors but economic and institutional factors as well, for example distribution of income, preferences of consumers', wage rates, relative prices, and structure of industry, etc.
- Average and marginal propensities to save are equal for the economy.
- The ratio of productive capacity of capital to the size of capital for the entire economy is equal to that of the new investment projects. It means nothing but that average potential output to capital ratio is equal to marginal potential output capital ratio.
- Employment rate depends upon the ratio of actual output and productive capacity, also known as the utilization ratio.

Structure of Domar's Model

1. National Income (output) is determined by investment through the multiplier as per the following relation,

$$Y_t = \frac{I_t}{S}$$

Where *s* (assumed to be constant) is the marginal propensity to save.

2. Productive capacity of an economy (or capital stock) is defined by Domar as its output when the entire labor force is fully employed in some conventional sense.

3. For the new investment projects, the ratio of potential productive capacity created by these new investment projects to the size of capital invested in them (i.e.*I*), is denoted by η. Domar in his original work had used a different symbol though,

$$\eta = \frac{dP}{dK}$$

we can write $\eta = \frac{P}{K} = \frac{dP}{dK}$.

4. The addition in potential productive capacity of the entire economy's capital stock may be less than the potential productive capacity of just the new investment projects. This is because operation of new projects may involve transfer of scarce labor from older projects making the latter less productive and thereby increasing the overall productive capacity of the economy due to new investment less than the potential. The ratio of change in productive capacity of the economy (due to new investment) to the amount of investment is termed by Domar as the "potential social average investment productivity" and is denoted by σ. Therefore,

$$\sigma = \frac{dP / dt}{I}$$

where *P* stands for the productive capacity of the economy.

5. Domar assigns the following characteristics to σ:

- Its magnitude depends on the technological progress (as embodied in new investment projects). Thus we can say that σ refers to increase in capacity which accompanies rather than caused by investment.

- σ refers to increase in potential capacity to supply. Its realization depends upon the presence of adequate demand for it.

- The maximum value which σ can attain is equal to η. The shortfall would depend upon the magnitude of the rate of investment, growth of labor force and natural resources, technological progress, misdirection of investment etc. Therefore,

  $\sigma \leq \eta$

- It is assumed by Domar that σ and η remain constant.

6. When $\sigma < \eta$ then following an investment I new projects with productive capacity of $I\eta$ are built. The productive capacity of entire economy however increases only by ($I\sigma < I\eta$). This implies that somewhere in the economy (not excluding new projects because of misdirection of investment), productive capacity must be reduced by $I\eta - I\sigma$. But since Domar has assumed in assumption number 8 above that the ratio of productive capacity of capital to the size of capital for the entire economy is constant at η, therefore every year an amount of capital (or capital value) equal to $\frac{I(\eta-\sigma)}{\eta}$ becomes useless. Such an untimely (unintended) demise of capital equipment (over and above depreciation) is termed by Domar as "Junking". Junking of capital is a result of unprofitability of old type of capital assets which in turn may be caused by either shortages in supply of labor or loss of demand of produce because of lower costs and better quality of newer products.

7. The incentives for investment are provided by the rate of growth of output and hurt by the amount of junking. We may write that,

$$\frac{\Delta I}{I} = f\left(\overbrace{\frac{\Delta Y}{Y}}^{+}, \overbrace{\frac{\eta-\sigma}{\eta}}^{-}\right)$$

The increase in proportion of capital junked negatively affects the business confidence thereby reducing the rate of investment.

Working of Domar's Model

The Question Harrod asks is that what must be the rate of growth of investment if the increase in productive capacity (due to change in capital stock) is to be exactly matched by the increase in output (due to change in demand for investment), so that the economy always remains in full employment (of labor) equilibrium over time.

Rewriting equation ($\eta = \frac{dP}{dK}$) above as follows gives us the rate of change of productive capacity.

$$\frac{dP}{dt} = I\sigma$$

Note that productive capacity increases so long as net investment and potential social average investment productivity are positive.

The rate of growth of output is obtained by differentiating equation ($Y_t = \frac{I_t}{S}$) with respect to time as given below,

$$\frac{dY}{dt} = \frac{dI}{dt} \times \frac{1}{s}$$

For simplification, Domar assumes that the economy is in equilibrium to begin with,

$$P_0 = Y_0$$

The equilibrium condition then is that change in productive capacity equals change in output,

$$\frac{dP}{dt} = \frac{dY}{dt}$$

Substituting from ($\sigma = \frac{dP/dt}{I}$) and ($\frac{dP}{dt} = I\sigma$), we obtain the equilibrium condition as follows,

$$\frac{1}{I} \times \frac{dI}{dt} = s\sigma$$

The above condition implies that equilibrium over time requires investment to grow at a constant continuous rate equal to $s\sigma$. Equation ($Y_t = \frac{I_t}{S}$), ($\frac{dY}{dt} = \frac{dI}{dt} \times \frac{1}{s}$) and ($P_0 = Y_0$) together imply that,

$$\frac{1}{Y} \times \frac{dY}{dT} = \frac{1}{I} \times \frac{dI}{dT}$$

This implies that output grows as the same rate as investment, i.e. $s\sigma$. If the economy fails to grow at this warranted rate then the capacity will be under-utilized implying less than full employment of labor as well as capital.

Notice the similarity between the expression of the warranted (required) rate of growth of Domar and that of Harrod. The warranted rate of Harrod is $\frac{s}{C_r}$ where *Cr* is reciprocal of the marginal output-capital ratio.

The consequences of an economy to grow at a rate different from the warranted rate i.e. $s\sigma$ are demonstrated by Domar under the following two conditions:

$\sigma = \eta$ (No Junking)

This is a situation in which no junking of capital equipment occurs. Under such situation, suppose the investment and output grow at a constant rate of *r*,

$$I = I_0 e^{rt}$$

Now since $\frac{dK}{dt} = I$, therefore capital stock at any point of time is nothing but the continuous sum of all net investments, we can therefore write,

$$K = K_0 + \int_0^t I_0 e^{rt} dt = K_0 + \frac{I_0}{r}\left(e^{rt} - 1\right)$$

As $t \to \infty, K_0 + \frac{I_0}{r}\left(e^{rt} - 1\right) \to \frac{I_0}{r} e^{rt}$, as the other terms become relatively insignificant. This implies that the capital will also grow at the rate approaching r.

Since, $Y = \frac{I}{s}$ and $\eta = \sigma = \frac{P}{K}$,

$$\lim_{t\to\infty} \frac{Y}{P} = \lim_{t\to\infty} \frac{I_0 e^{rt}}{S\sigma K}$$

$$= \lim_{t\to\infty} \frac{I_0 e^{rt}}{S\sigma\left[K_0 + \frac{I_0}{r}\left(e^{rt} - 1\right)\right]} = \lim_{t\to\infty} \frac{1}{s\sigma\left[\left(\frac{K_0}{I_0} - 1\right)e^{-rt} + \frac{1}{r}\right]}$$

$$= \frac{r}{S\sigma}$$

The expression $\frac{r}{S\sigma}$ is termed by Domar as the coefficient of utilization and denoted by θ. When,

- $\theta < 1 \Leftrightarrow r < s\sigma$: The economy fails to utilize its capacity i.e. $Y < P$. The proportion of capital stock unutilized is given by (1−K). This not only creates unused capital but unused labour force as well.
- $\theta = 1 \Leftrightarrow r = s\sigma$: Only under this situation wherein actual growth rate is equal to the warranted growth rate, full capacity is utilized and the economy is in equilibrium.

$\sigma < \eta$ (Junking)

As seen above, whenever $\sigma < \eta$, the amount $\frac{I(\eta - \sigma)}{\eta}$ of capital is junked every year. This implies that $\frac{dK}{dt} \neq I$ but rather $= I - \frac{I(\eta - \sigma)}{\eta} = \frac{I\sigma}{\eta}$.

Therefore,

$$K = K_0 + \frac{I_0 \sigma}{r\eta}\left(e^{rt} - 1\right)$$

$$\lim_{t\to\infty} \frac{Y}{P} = \lim_{t\to\infty} \frac{I_0 e^{rt}}{S\eta K}$$

$$= \lim_{t\to\infty} \frac{I_0 e^{rt}}{S\eta\left[K_0 + \frac{I_0\sigma}{r\eta}\left(e^{rt}-1\right)\right]} = \lim_{t\to\infty} \frac{1}{s\eta\left[\left(\frac{K_0}{I_0}-1\right)e^{-rt} + \frac{\sigma}{r\eta}\right]}$$

$$= \frac{r}{S\sigma}$$

Thus Domar demonstrates that even under the case of junking, the capacity will be fully utilized so long as the rate of growth is equal to the warranted rate of growth. Under this case, although there is full employment of labour but less than full employment of capital owing to premature death of capital. Entrepreneurs are discouraged for further investments in such case.

Stability of Equilibrium in Domar's Model

Domar only considers the question of downward stability of his equilibrium, although not explicitly. According to Domar, even in the situation of no junking, if the investment ever fails to grow at the warranted rate then the economy would progress towards depression because investors would further reduce the rate of investment following developed unused capacity due to fall of output below productive capacity.

The situation becomes even grimmer in the case of junking. Under this situation, the business confidence would be negatively affected despite the fact the economy is on the equilibrium path i.e. $P = Y$. This owes to the junking of capital following new investments. Junking (i.e. unused capital stock due to shortfall in labour force or demand or both) leads to lack of desire to invest further and thereby a reduction in rate of invest below the warranted rate of growth even when the economy started with the latter rate of growth. One way Domar points out that in which entrepreneurs will react to a high unused capacity would be by decreasing the real wage rates and thereby increasing their share of profits. However this move, since capitalists have a higher savings rate than the rest, would leads to increase in the savings rate of the economy as a whole and thus the warranted rate of growth, making it even more difficult to achieve the warranted rate and therefore further building of the excess capacity.

Conclusions of Domar's Model

- Without Junking or unwanted scrapping of capital, the income, investment, productive capacity and capital stock can grow at the warranted rate of growth $s\sigma$ ensuring the full employment of both labour and capital.
- With junking of capital every year, the economy would move towards acute depression.

- It is the unused capital equipment that endangers the attainment of full employment equilibrium in the economy.

Comparison between Harrod's and Domar Model

As noted above, the two models are similar in the following ways:

- For both the economists, the started point to make the Keynesian framework dynamic.
- Both have assumed, to some extent, constancy of capital-output ratio C_r in case of Harrod and its inverse, the related output-capital ratio σ in case of Domar.
- Both obtain constant growth paths.
- Both assume that output follows demand thereby implying that output can fall below potential leading to entrepreneurial reaction of change in rate of investment.
- Both conclude a grimmer future if ever the economy diverges from its unstable equilibrium path.

Although similar on many broad counts, the two differences in models can be summarized as below:

Issue	Domar	Harrod
1. Key concept	Rate of growth which equate output to productive capacity, ensuring full employment of labor but if junking is present, it is possible with less than full employment of capital.	Equilibrium rate of growth for entrepreneurs, which requires full employment of capital but is compatible with less than full employment of labor.
2. Long-run problem	Junking of capital decreasing the rate of investment below the warranted.	Labor shortage not allowing economy to reach warranted rate of growth.
3. Feature of economy	Unused capacity.	Less than full employment of labor.
4. Role of Labor	Shortages lead to junking of capital and thus negatively affects rate of investment.	Determines the natural rate of growth which is a cap on the rate of growth an economy can achieve.
5. Cause of instability	Continuously decreasing investment incentive due to increasing unused capacity.	The process of adjustment which results in expected rate of growth diverge further and further from the warranted rate of growth.
6. Causes of fixed capital-output ratio	Simplification assumption	Fixed relative rate of interest and thus fixed capital-labor ratio combined with CRS.

Solow Growth Model

The Solow Growth Model is an exogenous model of economic growth that analyzes changes in the level of output in an economy over time as a result of changes in the population growth rate, the savings rate, and the rate of technological progress.

The Solow Growth Model, developed by Nobel Prize-winning economist Robert Solow, was the first neoclassical growth model and was built upon the Keynesian Harrod-Domar model. The Solow model is the basis for the modern theory of economic growth.

Simplified Representation of the Solow Growth Model

Assumptions

- The population grows at a constant rate g. Therefore, current population (represented by N) and future population (represented by N') are linked through the population growth equation N' = N(1+g). If the current population is 100 and the growth rate of population is 2%, the future population is 102.
- All consumers in the economy save a constant proportion, 's', of their incomes and consume the rest. Therefore, consumption (represented by C) and output (represented by Y) are linked through the consumption equation C= (1+s)Y. If a consumer earns 100 units of output as income and the savings rate is 40%, then the consumer consumes 60 units and saves 40 units.
- All firms in the economy produce output using the same production technology that takes in capital and labor as inputs. Therefore, the level of output (represented by Y), the level of capital (represented by K), and the level of labor (represented by L) are all linked through the production function equation Y = aF(K,L).
- The Solow Growth Model assumes that the production function exhibits constant-returns-to-scale (CRS). Under such an assumption, if we double the level

of capital stock and double the level of labor, we exactly double the level of output. As a result, much of the mathematical analysis of the Solow model focuses on output per worker and capital per worker instead of aggregate output and aggregate capital stock.

- Present capital stock (represented by K), future capital stock (represented by K'), the rate of capital depreciation (represented by d), and level of capital investment (represented by I) are linked through the capital accumulation equation K'= K(1-d) + I.

Solving the Solow Growth Model

In our analysis, we assume that the production function takes the following form: $Y = aK^bL^{1b}$ where $0 < b < 1$. The production function is known as the Cobb-Douglas Production function, which is the most widely used neoclassical production function. Together with the assumption that firms are competitive, i.e., they are price-taking firms, the coefficient b is the capital share (the share of income that capital receives).

Therefore, output per worker is given through the following equation: $y = ak^b$ where $y = Y/L$ (output per worker and $k = K/L$ (capital stock per worker). Under the assumption of competitive equilibrium, we get the following:

- The income-expenditure identity holds as an equilibrium condition: Y = C + I.
- Consumer's budget constraint: Y = C + S.
- Therefore, in equilibrium: I = S = sY.
- The capital accumulation equation becomes: K' = (1–d)K + sY.

The capital accumulation equation in per worker times is given through the following equation: $(1 + g)k' = (1 - d)k + sy = (1 - d)k + saf(k) = (1 - d)k + sak^b$.

The solution concept used is that of a steady state. The steady state is a state where the level of capital per worker does not change. Consider the graph below:

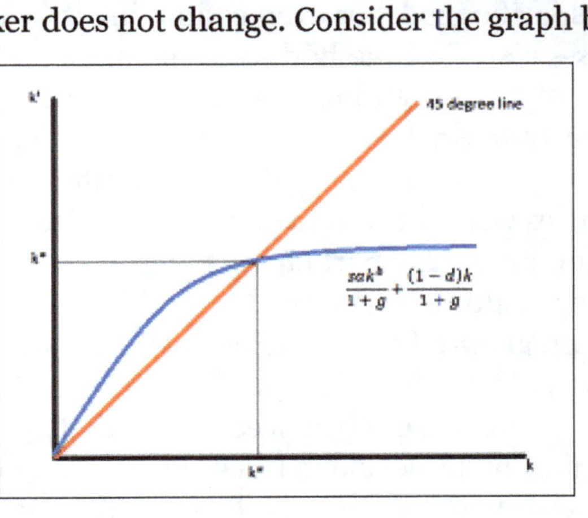

The steady state is found by solving the following equation: k' = k => (1 + g)k = (1 – d)k + sak^b. Therefore, the steady state value of capital per worker and the steady state value of output per worker are the following:

$$k^* = \left(\frac{sa}{g+d}\right)^{\frac{1}{1-b}}$$

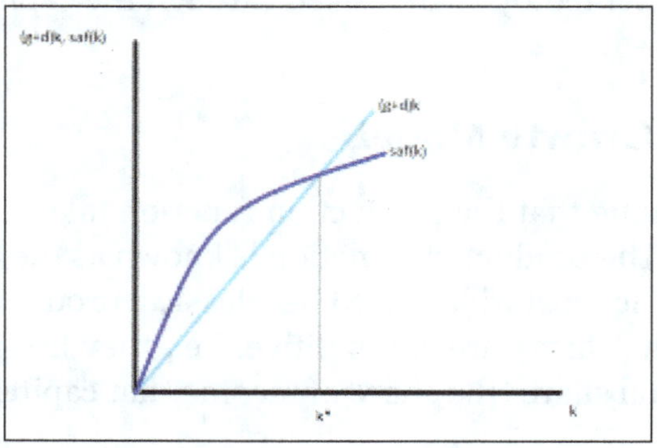

Implications of the Solow Growth Model

There is no growth in the long term. If countries have the same g (population growth rate), s (savings rate), and d (capital depreciation rate), then they have the same steady state, so they will converge, i.e., the Solow Growth Model predicts conditional convergence. Along this convergence path, a poorer country grows faster.

Countries with different saving rates have different steady states, and they will not converge, i.e. the Solow Growth Model does not predict absolute convergence. When saving rates are different, growth is not always higher in a country with lower initial capital stock.

Neo-Classical Model

Before disapproving a specific model or even estimating its' success it is significant to understand the various-- historical methods of economic development. Various paths to economic development have been taken ever since the Industrial Revolution. The first contributors in the Industrial revolution witnessed very productive agricultural sectors which created surpluses. These surpluses permitted for specialization in other industries. These countries were the first to develop organized markets and took an export-led industrialization path. Late participants in the Industrial Revolution suffered from a less productive agricultural sector, had less advanced markets and institutions, and had to rely on inward growth because of lack of trade. Many land scarce countries throughout history have suffered from low productivity growth and experienced massive poverty. Others have gained from balanced productivity growth in agriculture and industry, allowing them to build developed markets and rely on a diverse export led economy. Economists have understood from history. The most prosperous countries gained from more developed markets, high factor endowments, human resources, and political systems accessible to capitalism.

At the end of World War II the ideologies of the United States and the Soviet Union were at odds. The 2 super powers could not reach an agreement on how to rebuild the economies destroyed by the war. The development approaches produced in the US sought to contain communism while spreading capitalism throughout the world. The conflict that ensued came to be known as the Cold War and development strategy was only one of many areas in which this clash played out. Years after the Cold war prevailing development models still compete against the communist theory. One such model is the Neo-Classical development model.

Embedded in early economic thought, Neo-Classical development purposes to spur economic growth through government support. A sequence of market failures in the 1960's led to the indication that the government should provide infrastructure to support the market. Based on the theory of Neo-Classical economics, this model purposes to construct organized markets to rise productivity and development. It hinges on the idea that investment will raise the growth rate of per capita output.

Neo-Classical Development Model

The Neo-Classical development model is focused on Neo-Classical economic theory. Neo-Classical economics emphases on prices, outputs, and income distributions in markets accessed through supply and demand. The prime goal of Neo-Classical Economics is to offer efficient allocation of scarce resources. It assumes an individual's rationality allows them to maximize their utility or profit. An emphasis is placed on equilibrium. The interactions of consumers and firms in a free market should exercise an equilibrium quantity and supply. The architects of the Neo-Classical Development model knew that highly developed markets and institutions were required for the theory to work. It calls for the government to gather capital by eliminating trade barriers and encouraging foreign direct investment.

Once capital is gathered it should flow from areas of low productivity to areas of higher productivity. As per capita productivity grows economic growth will follow. This is only a brief synopsis of the model, but it illustrates the basic assumptions made. The Neo-Classical Development model points us in the right direction. It recognizes the importance of advanced markets and institutions to economic growth. History has demonstrated their importance. It also recognizes the importance of free trade to economic growth. The major contributors to the neo-classical theory of growth have been R.M.Solow, T.W.Swan, j.R.Hicks, and J.E.Meade.

In 1945, around the time of the Australian White Paper on Employment Policy, Swan wrote a memorandum on "The Principle of Effective Demand – A 'Real Life' Model". This paper laid out the first macroeconomic model of the Australian economy. While still Chief Economist in the Prime Minister's Department, Swan made his first venture into trying to reach some understanding of "the theory underlying any policy of economic development" with a sixteen-page memorandum entitled "Size and Composition of Investment, and the Industrial Distribution of Labour in a Closed Progressive Economy." Although no formal mathematical model was written down, the discussion involved Several formal assumptions including:

- Savings a constant proportion of income and unaffected by the rate of interest.
- Complete mobility of labour.
- Constant physical returns from land.
- Full employment.
- No inventions.

Setting savings equal to investment, Swan reasoned using a simple numerical example that if capital and population is increasing at the same rate, then "the population increase will wholly exhaust net investment" and capital and output per head will remain constant. In this case, the "increment of consumpion demanded is an increment in the existing 'average' consumption in proportion to the rate of population increase", but most of the analysis is concerned with a more complicated, but policy relevant case, in which marginal consumption as real income rises is biased towards specific uses, such as housing. According to him Consumption goods were divided into three categories: Houses produced with capital alone, Manufactures produced with current labor and capital (in the form of machinery) and Services produced with current labor alone. The capital used to produce housing and manufactures embodies past labor services (classified as Building and Engineering services respectively). Capital and labor are substitutable in the production of manufactures.

However, given the difficulties of verbal analysis, it is not surprising that the general equilibrium effect of an increase in capital on relative factor prices and hence on the proportions of labor and capital in manufacturing is ignored. He argued that if the population is constant, but at the margin, desires only increased housing, all increments in capital are diverted to housing and "capital per head will remain constant in manufactures". However, if the Population desires only more manufactures, then all next investment is in machines and "capital per head will rise steadily in manufactures, which will have constant current labor". If it is services that people desire marginally, then all net investment is in machinery for manufactures, but the increase in capital per-head and output per head in manufactures "means that manpower must be released from manufactures" to production of services.

Harrod-Domar Model

As stated by Harrod-Domar model "steady states and stability" in which the most powerful and characteristic and powerful conclusion is that even for long run the economic system which assumed fixed-coefficient production technologies that gave their models "knife-edge" equilibrium with the implausible implication that any deviation at all from equilibrium would cause the model to diverge further and further away from Equilibrium. There are so many economists has given solutions to the dis-equilibrium among them one of the pioneer was Swan.

Swan Model

The original contribution of swan was not the elimination of the Harrod-Domar knife edge by making the output/capital and capital/labor ratios endogenous rather Swan created a simple, convenient, and powerful apparatus for finding the steady-state growth path of a one-commodity world. Swan demonstrates the importance of technical progress for long-run growth. In considering technical progress, Swan introduces a third factor, land, which is fixed in supply and hence induces diminishing returns. Swan considers the rate of technical Progress that is necessary to prevent population pressure from moving the economy to a Malthusian outcome.

A higher savings rate (and a faster accumulation of capital) raises the growth rates at every point, but only temporarily interrupts the inevitable progress towards the stationary state determined by technical progress. "Swan notices that the model makes technical progress a powerful way of improving the standard of living and capital accumulation a disconcertingly weak reed. He looks for an answer to 'this anti-accumulation, pro-technology line of argument' and mentions two possibilities. One is very classical: if higher output per head will induce faster growth of the labor force, then something like Arthur Lewis's unlimited supply of labor is present, and additional capital accumulation becomes much more powerful. His second idea is that 'the rate of technical progress may not be independent of the rate of accumulation of capital, or accumulation may give rise to external economies, so that the true social yield of capital is greater than any 'plausible' figure based on common private experience.

This point would have appealed to Adam Smith, but it will not be pursued here. Trevor Swan independently developed the standard neoclassical growth model. Swan was published ten months later than Robert Solow but included a more complete analysis of technical progress. Swan is able to directly illustrate the effects of variations in the rate of technical progress. Swan was also involved in developing the constant elasticity of substitution production function, of which Cobb-Douglas (elasticity of substitution equal to one) and Leontief fixed coefficients technology (zero elasticity of substitution). In deciding on the contribution of economic analysis (whether theory or econometric estimation), Swan placed a huge weight on the importance of the work for economic policy in addition to requirements for originality and rigor. 18 Swan, "Growth models: Of golden ages and production functions", prepared for the Roundtable Conference in Japan, explains some of the inadequacies of growth models for practical development. It is also likely that Swan's interest in further contributions to the growth literature was reduced by the frustrations of dealing with bureaucracy while working on India's five year plan in 1958.

Swan had first to develop a composite growth model in which he had introduced some deeper determinants of growth which varies from country to country. Those factors are basically non-economic factors which can be classified into four broad categories are: geographical, institutional, political and cultural. Geographical differences are perhaps the most obvious. He has emphasized, countries that are landlocked, that suffer from a hazardous disease environment and that have difficult obstacles in the way of internal transportation, will almost certainly produce at a lower level than countries without these problems, even if they use the same technology and the same array of capital.

In addition, the lower productivity of these countries will serve to reduce the rate of return to accumulating capital and to generating new technologies. Institutions matter because of the way they affect private contracts and also because of the way they affect the extent to which the returns to different kinds of investments can be appropriated by the government.

In long run productivity growth requires technical progress, it depends on political, institutional and regulatory factors that affect the way the conflict between the winners and losers of technical progress will be resolved, and hence affect the incentives to create and adopt new technologies. Economic policies matter not only because of the way they affect the return to investing in capital and technology but also because of the inefficiencies that can be created by taxes and subsidies. But how these policies affect economic growth can vary from one country to another. Culture is a difficult factor to measure. In principle, however, it is capable of explaining a great deal of cross-country variation in growth, because a society in which people are socialized to trust each other, to work hard, to value technical expertise and to respect law and order is certainly going to be thriftier and more productive.

Among the neo classical economist "solow" was so impressed by the growth model developed by "swan" that he has given all credit to swan for the neoclassical model of growth. The model developed by swan and solow has such similarities that the model of growth named as swan-solow model. But "Solow model" has over shadowed on swan model of development. Though there is some different approach of the theory but due to similarities the approach is known as "swan –solow" model of growth. The growth model is saying that the economy is self-stable and the equilibrium comes naturally.

Result and Drawback of Swan-Solow Model

This model actually shows how the rate of economic growth, the population growth and the technological progress influence the economic growth during a definite period of time. The properties used in this model are: economy is perfectly competitive; two production factors which are perfectly substitutable (work L and capital K – in the initial analysis does not appear the technical progress); the perfect mobility of the production factors; Complete employment in using the resources. The model takes into concern a closed economy, with a single sector in which the homogeneous production has as target either they consume or the investments, in order to create new capital units and the savings are equal to the investments. The capital will have a constant and positive depreciation rate. According to the neo-classical theory, the saving rate will not affect the long-term rate of economic growth, but will long-term influence the level of the output/capita. According to this theory the saving rate represents one of the main indicators of an economy, but it reflects the level of the financial education of one nation (if the saving rate is high, of course the amount of incomes for consume is more reduced.

The major shortcoming of the theory of swan model is overlook of behavioral economics. The psychological fundamentals of the human behaviour determined the population – who was facing a risk and so was mentally forced – to take precautions measures, in order to evade being unprepared in the following period.

Another big problem of the models aiming to explain the economic growth and to offer recovering scenarios is represented by the implementation of these models. There are big gaps of the transfer of knowledge between those who develop models (academic world, researchers) and those who are supposed to ensure the smooth running of the economy (both governments and the business community).

The key criticisms of the Swan model development model should be in the scope of its' assumptions. There are a wide range of difficulties faced by developing countries and this model addresses very few of them. It leads to creating an economy receptive to capitalism, but fails to benefit the population as a whole. There is historical evidence displaying developed markets and advanced institutions are crucial to economic development. How about the accumulation of human capital or the effects of corruption? The Neo-Classical Development model fails to address these issues. Barriers to economic development are not always measurable. The greatest failure seems to be its reliance on weak sustainability. It is a simple evidence which states overall capital stock should be non-decreasing. It permits for natural resources to be entirely exhausted as long as other forms of capital recompense for this loss. A country could quickly find itself on a track to unsustainable development.

Kaldor and Pasinetti Model

Kaldor's Model of Economic Growth

Kaldor's model of economic growth considers the causation of technical progress as endogenous and provides a framework that relates the genesis of technical progress to capital accumulation. The model is based on Keynesian techniques of analysis and the well-known dynamic approach of Harrod in regarding the rates of changes in income and capital as the dependent variables of the system. Pasinetti's model has made a correction to the Kaldor's theory of distribution and points out that in any type of society, when any individual saves a part of his income, he must also be allowed to own it, otherwise he would not save at all. Kaldor's growth model is based on certain assumptions. The basic assumptions of the model are the following:

Assumptions

- The model assumes that in a growing economy the general level of output at any point of time is limited by the availability of resources and not by effective demand. In other words, the model assumes full employment in the strictly Keynesian sense – a state of affairs in which the short-run supply of aggregate goods and services is inelastic and irresponsive to further increase in monetary demand.
- Technical progress depends on the rate of capital accumulation and technical invention.
- The variables of the model such as income, capital, profits, wages, savings and investment are expressed in real terms i.e. values are expressed at constant prices.
- The model assumes an investment function which makes investment of any period partly a function of the change in output and partly of the change in the rate of profit on capital in the previous period.
- Monetary policy is assumed to play a passive role which means that interest rates follow the standard set by the rate of profit on investment in the long-run. The model is consistent with continued price-inflation (with money wages rising faster than productivity) or with a constant price level. It is also consistent with constant money wages.
- It is assumed that there are no effects of a change in the share of profits and wages, and of a change in rate of profit on capital (or of interest rates) on the choice of techniques adopted.

Framework of the Model

Kaldor postulates the following three relationships:

- Given savings propensities for profit-earners and wage-earners.
- Investment decisions in any period are governed by the desire to maintain the capital stock in a given relationship to turnover, modified by any change in the rate of profit on capital.
- A given technical relationship between the rate of growth in productivity per person and the rate of growth in capital per person.

Let Y_t, K_t, P_t, S_t and I_t denote respectively real income, capital, profits, savings and investment at time t. Income is divided into two categories, wages and profits, where wages comprise salaries as well as the earnings of manual labour, and profits comprise entrepreneurial incomes and also incomes accruing to property owners. The familiar saving-investment identity is represented in the following equation,

$$S_t \equiv I_t \equiv K_{t+1} - K_t$$

The three relationships mentioned above can be represented through linear equations as follows:

Savings Function:

$$S_t = \alpha P_t + \beta (Y_t - P_t)$$

where $1 > \alpha > \beta \geq 0$

Investment Function:

$$K_t = \alpha' Y_{t-1} + \beta' \left(\frac{P_{t-1}}{K_{t-1}} \right) Y_{t-1}$$

$$I_t = K_{t+1} - K_t = (Y_t - Y_{t-1}) \left(\alpha' + \beta' \frac{P_{t-1}}{K_{t-1}} \right) + \beta' \left(\frac{P_t}{K_t} - \frac{P_{t-1}}{K_{t-1}} \right) Y_t$$

where $\alpha' > 0$ and $\beta' > 0$.

Technical Progress Function:

$$\frac{Y_{t+1} - Y_t}{Y_t} = \alpha'' + \beta'' \frac{I_t}{K_t}$$

Where $\alpha'' > 0$ "and $1 > \beta'' > 0$.

Equation ($S_t = \alpha P_t + \beta (Y_t - P_t)$) shows total savings as consisting of a proportion, α of total profits and a proportion β of total wages $(Y_t - P_t)$. Equation ($K_t = \alpha' Y_{t-1} + \beta' \left(\frac{P_{t-1}}{K_{t-1}} \right) Y_{t-1}$) shows the stock of capital at time (which is assumed to be equal to the desired stock of capital at time t-1). Capital stock at time t is equal to a constant fraction, α' of the output of the preceding period plus a constant proportion, α' of the rate of profit of previous period, multiplied by the output of the preceding period. Equation ($I_t = K_{t+1} - K_t = (Y_t - Y_{t-1}) \left(\alpha' + \beta' \frac{P_{t-1}}{K_{t-1}} \right) + \beta' \left(\frac{P_t}{K_t} - \frac{P_{t-1}}{K_{t-1}} \right) Y_t$) gives the investment demand function which is derived from ($K_t = \alpha' Y_{t-1} + \beta'\left(\frac{P_{t-1}}{K_{t-1}}\right)Y_{t-1}$) by difference equation, and shows that investment in period t(I_t) assumed to match to the difference between desired and actual capital at time, and is equal to the increase in output over the previous period $(Y_t - Y_{t-1})$ multiplied by the relationship between desired capital and output in the previous period $(K_t - Y_{t-1})$ plus a proportion, β' of the change in the rate of profit over that period, multiplied by the output of current period, since it is implicit in equation ($K_t = \alpha' Y_{t-1} + \beta'\left(\frac{P_{t-1}}{K_{t-1}}\right)Y_{t-1}$) that $\alpha' + \beta'(P_{t-1}/K_{t-1}) = (K_t / Y_{t-1})$.

Equation ($I_t = K_{t+1} - K_t = (Y_t - Y_{t-1})\left(\alpha' + \beta'\frac{P_{t-1}}{K_{t-1}}\right) + \beta'\left(\frac{P_t}{K_t} - \frac{P_{t-1}}{K_{t-1}}\right)Y_t$) implies that investment of period t (expressed as a proportion of the existing stock of capital) is equal to the expected rate of growth of turnover (which is assumed to be equal to the actual rate of growth in turnover for the previous period) if the rate of profit on capital is constant, and it is greater (or smaller) than this if the rate of profit on capital is rising (or falling). Equation ($\frac{Y_{t+1} - Y_t}{Y_t} = \alpha'' + \beta''\frac{I_t}{K_t}$) shows the rate of growth of income (and labour productivity) as an increasing function of the rate of net investment expressed as a proportion of the stock of capita.

$$S_t = \alpha P_t + \beta(Y_t - P_t),\ K_t = \alpha' Y_{t-1} + \beta'\left(\frac{P_{t-1}}{K_{t-1}}\right)Y_{t-1}$$

and,

$I_t = K_{t+1} - K_t = (Y_t - Y_{t-1})\left(\alpha' + \beta'\frac{P_{t-1}}{K_{t-1}}\right) + \beta'\left(\frac{P_t}{K_t} - \frac{P_{t-1}}{K_{t-1}}\right)Y_t$ taken together provide the mechanism underlying savings and investment. In simple words, the savings function indicates that savings are determined by the propensity to save out of profits and wages respectively. The investment function shows that investment is determined by the rate of profit and the changes associated with it. The technical progress function shows that the rate of growth of income is a function of the rate of investment, capital per person and the technical progress.

Taking into account the assumptions and the implications of the three functions, the operation of the model can be examined under two conditions: (a) constant working population, and (b) Expanding population. In the former case the proportionate rate of growth in total real income, Y_t, will be the same as the proportionate rate of growth in output per head, O_t, and in the latter case the proportionate change in total real income will be the sum of the proportionate change in productivity, O_t, and the proportionate change in the working population, L_t. These two versions of the model are discussed below:

Constant Working Population

Starting from an arbitrary point of time, $t=1$, the existing stock of capital, K_1 can be considered as a datum which is inherited from the past. Y_1 can be taken as given which the fully employed labour force produces with the capital stock . K_1 Similarly, the income and capital in the previous period, Y_0 and K_0 respectively are given. Capital stock satisfies the following condition:

$$\frac{K_1}{Y_0}=\alpha'+\beta'\frac{P_0}{K_0}$$

Since K_1, K_0 and Y_0 are given, equation,

$(I_t=K_{t+1}-K_t=(Y_t-Y_{t-1})\left(\alpha'+\beta'\frac{P_{t-1}}{K_{t-1}}\right)+\beta'\left(\frac{P_t}{K_t}-\frac{P_{t-1}}{K_{t-1}}\right)Y_t)$ can be rewritten as,

$$\frac{I_1}{Y_1}=\frac{Y_1-Y_0}{Y_0}\cdot\frac{K_1}{Y_1}\beta'\left(\frac{P_1}{K_1}-\frac{P_0}{K_0}\right)$$

Equation above shows that the rate of investment in period 1, as proportion of income of that period equals the rate of growth of income over the previous period multiplied by the capital-output ratio of the current period, plus a proportion of the change of the rate of profit over the previous period. Equation above can be written as,

$$\frac{I_1}{Y_1}=\frac{Y_1-Y_0}{Y_0}.\frac{K_1}{Y_1}+\beta'\left(\frac{P_0}{K_0}\right)+\beta'\frac{Y_1}{K_1}.\frac{P_1}{Y_1}$$

and equation $(S_t=\alpha P_t+\beta(Y_t-P_t))$ can be written as,

$$\frac{S_1}{Y_1}=\alpha\frac{P_1}{Y_1}+\beta\left(\frac{Y_1-P_1}{Y_1}\right)=\beta+(\alpha-\beta)\frac{P_1}{Y_1}$$

These two equations shown above jointly determine both the distribution of income between profits and wages, and the proportion of income saved and invested at. Given a particular income distribution, the level of profits acts as the equilibrating mechanism between savings and investment. The level of profits has to be such as to induce a rate of investment that is just equal to the rate of savings at that particular distribution of income.

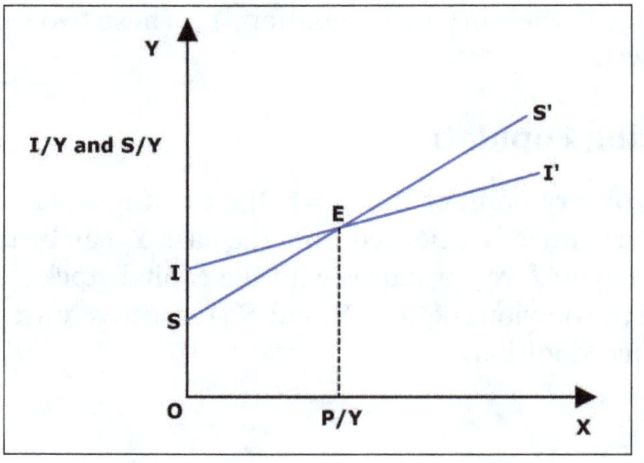

This mechanism is illustrated in figure. Profits as a ratio of income $\left(\frac{P}{Y}\right)$ are measured on X-axis, and savings and investment as a ratio of income $\left(\frac{S}{Y}\right)$ and $\left(\frac{I}{Y}\right)$ respectively are measured on Y-axis. The line represents the saving function given by equation $\left(\frac{I_1}{Y_1} = \frac{Y_1 - Y_0}{Y_0}.\frac{K_1}{Y_1} + \beta\left(\frac{P_0}{K_0}\right) + \beta'\frac{Y_1}{K_1}.\frac{P_1}{Y_1}\right)$ and II′ represents the investment function given by equation $\left(\frac{S_1}{Y_1} = \alpha\frac{P_1}{Y_1} + \beta\left(\frac{Y_1 - P_1}{Y_1}\right) = \beta + (\alpha - \beta)\frac{P_1}{Y_1}\right)$. The point of intersection indicates the short-run equilibrium level of profits and investment as a proportion of income. If the level of profits is lower than the equilibrium value, investment will tend to exceed savings until the difference is eliminated through the consequential rise in profits. Similarly, if the level of profits is higher than the equilibrium value, savings will exceed investment. The equilibrium will be stable if the slope of the curve exceeds the slope of the II′ curve, which implies that the following condition is satisfied,

$$\alpha - \beta > \beta'\frac{Y_t}{K_t}$$

The implication of this condition is that the stability of the equilibrium depends upon the changes in the acceleration coefficient which in turn depends on the changes in the rate of profit and ultimately on the income distribution. According to Kaldor this is only a necessary condition of the equilibrium growth path. The stability of the model depends on two further restrictions (known as the sufficient condition for the stable equilibrium of the system). These two restrictions are:

$$P_t \leq Y_t - W_{min}$$

$$\frac{P_t}{Y_t} \geq m$$

where W_{min} stands for minimum wages and m represents minimum margin of profit.

The first restriction implies that profits should not be greater than the surplus available after the labour force has been paid a subsistence wage. If this condition were not satisfied, investment would be less than that indicated by equation $\left(I_t = K_{t+1} - K_t = (Y_t - Y_{t-1})\left(\alpha' + \beta'\frac{P_{t-1}}{K_{t-1}}\right) + \beta'\left(\frac{P_t}{K_t} - \frac{P_{t-1}}{K_{t-1}}\right)Y_t\right)$. The second constraint implies that profits should be higher than the minimum margin of profits (m) that the entrepreneurs must obtain in order to continue further investment. In other words, the prevailing rate of profit should be adequate so as to induce the entrepreneurs to continue further investment. According to Kaldor, this minimum margin of profit is the degree of monopoly. If this condition were not satisfied, full-employment savings indicated by equation $S_t = \alpha P_t + \beta(Y_t - P_t)$ would exceed investment, so that income and employment would be reduced below the full-employment level to the point where savings generated by that income are no more than sufficient to finance investment. Figure elucidates this point.

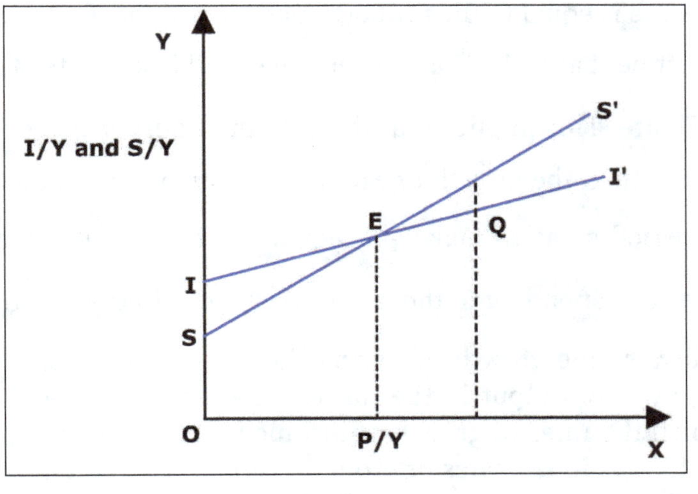

In the above diagram, the dotted line represents the minimum level of profits (m). If this minimum level were to fall to the right of E, the equilibrium would not be at point E, but at point Q as shown in figure and income will fall to the point where the savings income ratio is reduced to the level indicated by Q.

Assuming these conditions are satisfied, the technical progress function ensures the growth of income and capital from t=1 onwards, and the gradual shift of the economy from a short-run equilibrium to a long-run equilibrium of steady growth. This is illustrated in figure.

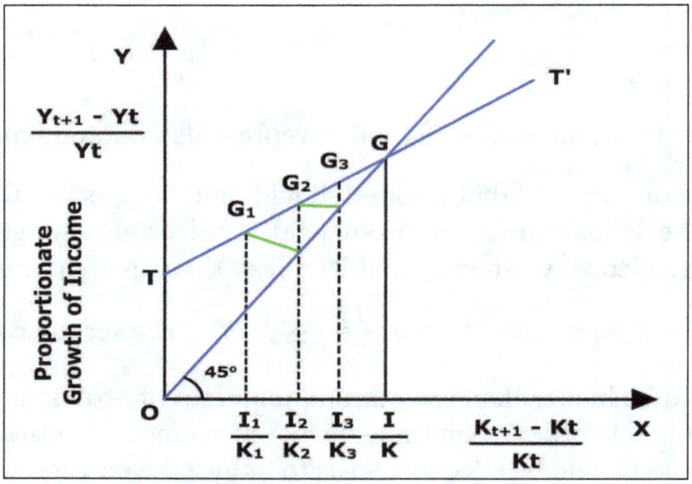

Proportionate growth of capital.

The proportionate growth of capital $\left(\frac{K_{t+1}-K_t}{K_t}\right)$ is measured on X-axis and the proportionate growth of income $\left(\frac{Y_{t+1}-Y_t}{Y_t}\right)$ is measured on Y-axis. TT represents the technical progress function. Point G denotes the long-run equilibrium where the proportionate growth of income is equal to the proportionate growth of capital. Suppose that the initial rate of investment at $t=1, \frac{I_1}{K_1}$ is less than the equilibrium rate of growth of capital $\frac{I}{K}$ as shown in Figure. This implies that the growth of output g in successive units of time will be greater than the growth of capital, the rate of investment will increase in the subsequent period so as to make $\frac{I_2}{K_2}$ equal to g_1 (g_1, g_2, etc. denote the rates of growth of income corresponding to the points G_1, G_2, etc. in the figure).

This in turn will raise the growth of income in the second period to g_2. By similar reasoning, the growth of output in the third period will increase to and so on until is reached at which the rates of growth of income and capital are equal. The indirect effects through changes in the rates of profit on capital will reinforce this process and any associated change in the rate of profit on capital $\frac{P_t}{K_t}$ will make the rate of increase in investment even greater.

The long-run equilibrium rate of growth of income and capital is independent of the savings and investment functions. It depends only on the technical progress function, and is given by,

$$G = \frac{\alpha''}{1-\beta''}.$$

Expanding Population

The model discussed earlier was modified by Kaldor to account for the expansion of the population. This version of the model assumes the Malthusian theory that population growth is a function of the rate of increase of the means of subsistence which is assumed to be equal to the rate of increase in total production. Kaldor takes into account two limitations of the Malthusian theory. These two limitations are as follows:

- For a given fertility rate, the rate of growth of population cannot exceed a certain maximum, regardless of how fast is the growth of real income.
- The rate of population growth will rise only moderately as a function of the rate of growth in income over some interval of the latter before that maximum is reached.

Given these limitations, and denoting $I_t, g_t,$ for the rates of growth of population and income at time t, and λ for the maximum rate of growth of population, Kaldor express the relationship between population growth and income growth algebraically as follows:

$$I_t = g_t \left(g_t \le \lambda\right)$$
$$I_t = \lambda\left(g_t > \lambda\right)$$

Assuming to start with that the rate of population growth is λ(i.e $g_t > \lambda$), $\frac{I_t}{K_t}$ in equation ($I_t = K_{t+1} - K_t = (Y_t - Y_{t-1})\left(\alpha' + \beta'\frac{P_{t-1}}{K_{t-1}}\right) + \beta'\left(\frac{P_t}{K_t} - \frac{P_{t-1}}{K_{t-1}}\right)Y_t$) is replaced by $\frac{I_t}{K_t} - \lambda$ by $\frac{Y_{t+1} - Y_t}{Y_t} - \lambda$.

Hence, the long-run equilibrium rate of growth of both income and capital becomes,

$$G = \gamma'' + \lambda$$

where $\frac{\alpha''}{1-\beta''}'' = \gamma''$

If $g_t < \lambda$ (and hence $I_t < \lambda$), the rates of growth of income and population will continually accelerate until the latter approaches λ. Therefore, in the long-run equilibrium population must grow at its maximum rate which is indicated by the horizontal section of the curve in figure.

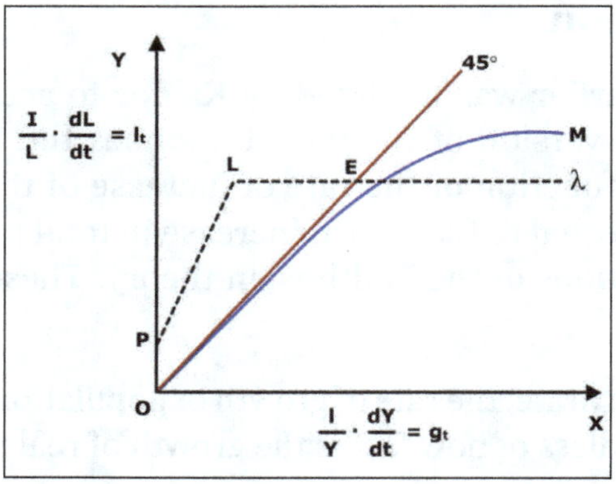

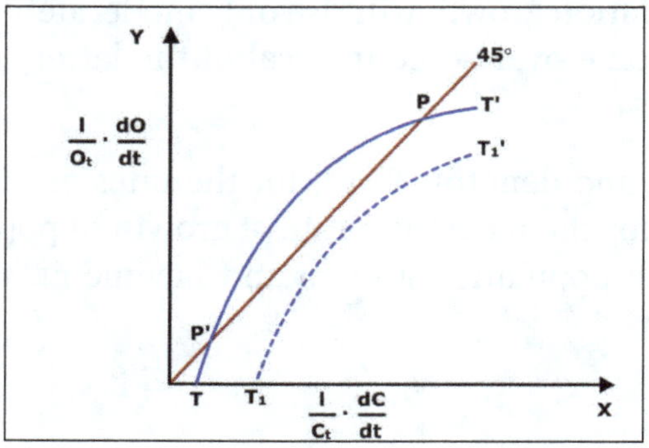

In figure, the rate of growth of income is measured horizontally and the rate of growth of population is measured vertically. OM curve shows the income growth path. The rates of growth of income and population will increase continually till the rate of growth of population approaches λ. This assumes that the shape and position of the technical progress function as given by the coefficients α'' and β'' in equation $\frac{Y_{t+1} - Y_t}{Y_t} = \alpha'' + \beta'' \frac{I_t}{K_t}$ and hence γ'' remain unaffected by changes in population. This implies that there are constant returns to scale. In other words, an increase in numbers, given the amount of capital per head, leaves output per head unaffected. This assumption may be valid enough in the case of a relatively under-populated country, but in the case of over-populated countries, the scarcity of land will cause diminishing returns. With given techniques and capital per head, an increase in population will cause a fall in productivity. Given the rate of the flow of new ideas, the curve denoting technical progress function will be lowered by an extent depending on the rate of increase in population. In this situation, the technical progress function will cut the capital-axis positively as shown in figure above.

This implies that in order to maintain output per head (O_t) at a constant level, a certain percentage growth in capital per head (C_t) will be required. In this case we have two points of intersection of the curve with the diagonal line, P' and P, of which only the latter is stable. If the economy is in a position which is to the left of P', the rates of growth of income and capital will steadily diminish until the growth of income and capital come to a complete standstill. In this situation it is even possible that the position of the technical progress function TT' curve is below the diagonal line as shown by the dotted line T_1T_1' in figure.

In this case no long-run equilibrium is attainable, and this may give rise to a situation of stagnation in the economy. Whether an expanding population will be consistent with an equilibrium of growth or not will primarily depend on the relative magnitude of two factors: (1) the maximum rate of population increase λ, and (2) the rate of technical progress which causes a certain percentage increase in productivity, α'' in equation ($\frac{Y_{t+1} - Y_t}{Y_t} = \alpha'' + \beta'' \frac{I_t}{K_t}$) when both population and capital per head are held constant.

The Pasinetti Model

The Pasinetti model postulates a simple relation between the rate of profit, the income distribution and the rate of economic growth. The model has made a correction to the Kaldor's theory of distribution and points out that in any type of society, when any individual saves a part of his income, he must also be allowed to own it, otherwise he would not save at all. This implies that the stock of capital which exists in the system is owned by those (capitalists and workers) who in the past made the corresponding savings. In other words, even if workers save and own a part of the capital stock (either directly or indirectly through loans to the capitalists) they will also receive a share of the total profits. Thus, total profits must be divided into two categories: profits accrue to capitalists and profits received by workers (Kaldor's theory of distribution did not consider this distinction). Pasinetti reformulated the model to eliminate the confusion regarding the two different concepts of distribution of income: distribution of income between profits and wages, and distribution of income between capitalists and workers. These two concepts of income distribution only coincide in the particular case in which workers do not save (i.e. there is no saving out wages).

Formulation of The Model

Total income (Y) is divided into two broad categories, wages (W) and Profits (P). Aggregate savings (S) is the sum of worker's savings (S_w) and capitalist's savings (S_c), and total profits is the sum of profits (P) accruing to the capitalists (P_c) and profits accruing to the workers (P_W). Therefore,

$$Y \equiv W + P$$

$$S \equiv S_w + S_c$$

$$P \equiv P_c + P_w$$

Substituting identity $P \equiv P_c + P_w$ into identity $Y \equiv W + P$ the latter can be written as ,

$$Y \equiv W + P_w + P_c$$

The savings functions of the workers and the capitalists are defined as given below:

$$S_w = S_w\left(W + P_w\right)$$

$$S_c = S_c P_c$$

The condition under which the system will remain in a dynamic equilibrium is the saving-investment equality (I=S). Substituting the savings functions into the saving investment identity, the equilibrium condition becomes:

$$I = S_w\left(W + P_w\right) + S_c P_c = S_w Y + \left(S_c - S_w\right) P_c$$

From equation above we obtain,

$$\frac{P_c}{Y} = \left(\frac{1}{S_c - S_w}\right)\frac{I}{Y} - \frac{S_w}{S_c - S_w}$$

$$\frac{P_c}{K} = \left(\frac{1}{S_c - S_w}\right)\frac{I}{K} - \left(\frac{S_w}{S_c - S_w}\right)\frac{Y}{K}$$

Equation ($\frac{P_c}{Y} = \left(\frac{1}{S_c - S_w}\right)\frac{I}{Y} - \frac{S_w}{S_c - S_w}$) expresses the distribution of income between capitalists and workers. But, the distribution of income between profits and wages is something different, and to obtain it, we need to add the share of workers' profit to both sides of equation ($\frac{P_c}{Y} = \left(\frac{1}{S_c - S_w}\right)\frac{I}{Y} - \frac{S_w}{S_c - S_w}$). Equation above represents the ratio of a part of profits (Pc) to total capital. In order to obtain the ratio of total profits to total capital (the rate of profit), we must add the ratio $\left(\frac{P_w}{K}\right)$ to both sides of equation above. We need to find suitable expressions for,

$$\frac{P}{Y} = \frac{P_c}{Y} = \frac{P_w}{Y}$$

$$\frac{P}{K} = \frac{P_c}{K} = \frac{P_w}{K}$$

We already know (P_c/K) from equation ($\frac{P_c}{K} = \left(\frac{1}{S_c - S_w}\right)\frac{I}{K} - \left(\frac{S_w}{S_c - S_w}\right)\frac{Y}{K}$). Writing K_w for the amount of capital that workers own indirectly – through loans to the capitalists – and for r the rate of interest on these loans, we obtain,

$$\frac{P}{K}=\frac{1}{S_c-S_w}\frac{1}{K}-\frac{S_w}{S_c-S_w}\frac{Y}{K}+\frac{rk_w}{K}$$

We require an expression for (K_w/K) which is given below. In dynamic equilibrium:

$$\frac{K_w}{K}=\frac{S_w}{S}\frac{S_w(Y-P_c)}{I}=\frac{S_wS_c}{S_c-S_w}\frac{Y}{1}-\frac{S_w}{S_c-S_w}$$

Substitution of equation ($\frac{P}{K}=\frac{P_c}{K}=\frac{P_w}{K}$) into equation ($\frac{P}{Y}=\frac{P_c}{Y}=\frac{P_w}{Y}$) finally gives us:

$$\frac{P}{K}=\frac{1}{S_c-S_w}\frac{1}{K}-\frac{S_w}{S_c-S_w}\frac{Y}{K}+r\left(\frac{S_wS_c}{S_c-S_w}\frac{Y}{I}-\frac{S_w}{S_c-S_w}\right)$$

By exactly following the same procedure, equation ($\frac{P}{Y}=\frac{P_c}{Y}=\frac{P_w}{Y}$) can be written as,

$$\frac{P}{Y}=\frac{1}{S_c-S_w}\frac{1}{Y}-\frac{S_w}{S_c-S_w}+r\left(\frac{S_wS_c}{S_c-S_w}\frac{K}{I}-\frac{S_w}{S_c-S_w}\frac{K}{Y}\right)$$

Equation ($\frac{P_c}{Y}=\left(\frac{1}{S_c-S_w}\right)\frac{I}{Y}-\frac{S_w}{S_c-S_w}$) shows the distribution of income between capitalists and workers, equation ($\frac{P}{K}=\frac{1}{S_c-S_w}\frac{1}{K}-\frac{S_w}{S_c-S_w}\frac{Y}{K}+r\left(\frac{S_wS_c}{S_c-S_w}\frac{Y}{I}-\frac{S_w}{S_c-S_w}\right)$) expresses the rate of profit, and above equation represents the distribution of income between wages and profits.

Rate and Share of Profits in Relation to the Rate of Growth

In a long-run equilibrium model, it is obvious to assume that the rate of interest is equal to the rate of profit. If we formulate such a hypothesis and substitute $\frac{P}{K}$ for in equation ($\frac{P}{K}=\frac{1}{S_c-S_w}\frac{1}{K}-\frac{S_w}{S_c-S_w}\frac{Y}{K}+r\left(\frac{S_wS_c}{S_c-S_w}\frac{Y}{I}-\frac{S_w}{S_c-S_w}\right)$), we get,

$$\frac{P}{K}\left(1-\frac{S_wS_c}{S_c-S_w}\frac{Y}{1}+\frac{S_w}{S_c-S_w}\right)=\frac{1}{S_c-S_w}\frac{1}{K}-\frac{S_w}{S_c-S_w}\frac{Y}{K}$$

$$\frac{P}{K}\frac{S_c(I-S_wY)}{I}=\frac{I-S_wY}{K}$$

Provided that $I - S_w Y \neq 0$ (otherwise the ratio $\frac{P}{K}$ would be indeterminate) the whole expression becomes,

$$\frac{P}{Y} = \frac{1}{S_c}\frac{I}{K}$$

Similarly, equation ($\frac{P}{Y} = \frac{1}{S_c - S_w}\frac{1}{Y} - \frac{S_w}{S_c - S_w} + r\left(\frac{S_w S_c}{S_c - S_w}\frac{K}{I} - \frac{S_w}{S_c - S_w}\frac{K}{Y}\right)$) becomes,

$$\frac{P}{Y} = \frac{1}{S_c}\frac{I}{Y}$$

Equations ($\frac{P}{Y} = \frac{1}{S_c}\frac{I}{K}$) and ($\frac{P}{Y} = \frac{1}{S_c}\frac{I}{Y}$) represent the most striking result of the Pasinetti model. It shows that in the long-run workers' propensity to save influences the distribution of income between capitalists and workers, but, not the distribution of income between profits and wages. Further, it has no impact on the rate of profit.

The model is based on the institutional principle that profits are distributed in proportion to the ownership of capital. This implies that in the long-run, profits are distributed in proportion to the amount of savings contributed. In other words, profits are proportional to savings, and the ratios of profits to savings are same for the workers and capitalists. Thus,

$$\frac{P_w}{S_w} = \frac{P_c}{S_c}$$

In order to determine the actual value of the ratio of profits to savings for the whole system, substitute the savings functions into equation above. So, we obtain,

$$\frac{P_w}{S_w (W + P_w)} = \frac{P_c}{S_c P_c}$$

which can also be written as,

$$S_w (W + P_w) = S_c P_c$$

Equation ($S_w (W + P_w) = S_c P_c$) states that in the long-run, when workers save they receive an amount of profits (P_w) such as to make their total savings exactly equal to the amount that the capitalists would have saved out of worker's profits (P_w) if these profits remained to them. In other words, the workers will always receive, in the long-run, an amount of profits proportional to their savings, whatever the rate of profit may be. Hence, the rate of profit is indeterminate on the part of the workers.

However, there is a direct relation between savings and profits in the case of capitalists since all their savings come out of profits. Therefore, for any given S_c, there is only one proportionality relation between profits and savings which makes the ratio $P_c / S_c P_c$ equal to P_c / S_c. According to Pasinetti, "This proportionality relation can be nothing but S_c, which will therefore determine the ratio of profits to savings for all the saving groups, and consequently also the income distribution between profits and wages and the rate of interest for the whole system".

The Pasinetti model illustrates that there exists a distribution of income between profits and wages which keeps the system in long-run equilibrium. In order to maintain full employment over time, a specific amount of investment has to be undertaken which is uniquely and exogenously (from outside the economic system) determined by technology and population growth. In this case, the equilibrium rate of profit is determined by the natural rate of growth (S_c) divided by the capitalists' propensity to save (S').

Growth Accounting

In economics, growth accounting is a procedure to measure the contribution of various factors to economic growth. Growth accounting refers to the breaking down the rate of growth of total output of an economy into contribution from the growth of such inputs as capital and labour and as well as technological growth. Growth accounting is also related to the sources of growth. In an economy, the rate of technological progress is indirectly compute, measured as a residual.

Basically, growth accounting decomposes the growth rate of an economy's total output into two part, firstly that which is due to increase in the amount of capital and labor and secondly, that which cannot be accounted for by observable changes in factor utilization i.e. unexplained part of growth in total output is then taken to represent increases in productivity or due to technological progress. It is also known Solow residual. The residual is the difference between the growth rate of output and the measured growth rates of inputs.

Solow residual or technical progress is the residual between output growth rate and weighted growth rates of inputs.

There are following three leading economists who have measured the contribution of the residual in terms of sources of growth to the overall growth rate of the United States economy:

- Robert Solow's Sources of Growth.

- Denision's Sources of Growth.
- Jorgenson-Griliches Sources of Growth.

Assumptions of Growth Accounting

- It is based on constant returns to scale (Euler's Theorem) i.e. Capital share + Labour Share = 1.
- It is based on perfect completion.
- Capital Stock is in complete homogeneity.
- The production function is linear and homogenous i. e. neoclassical production function.
- It breaks down the growth of output into the growth of the factors of production and technical change.
- This approach is based on long run period.
- Technical change is based on Hicks-neutral augmentation.

Growth Accounting or Solow Residual

R. Solow published a model in 1956 that representing a simplified but at the same time powerful framework for the analysis of the causes and dynamics of economic growth. After one year, in 1957, he published a paper entitled 'Technological Change and the Aggregate Production Function'. This paper indicates that growth of aggregate production is represented as a combination of the contributions of growth rates of factors of production and technological change or total factor productivity. He separates variation in output per head due to technical change from those due to changes in availability of capital per head.

R. Solow assumes technical change as disembodied, where capital as treats as homogeneous and he also assumes that the technical change are exogenous. Disembodied technical change is capital augmented in which existing capital is made more productive. Thus, the productivity depends upon the amount of capital stock not on it age. The production function for such technical change is written as, $Q = F(K, L, t)$.

- Q = Output,
- L = Labour Input,
- K = Capital,
- T = Technical Change.

Taking Hick Neutral technical change as a basis, R. Solow postulated the following specification of production function:

$$Y_t = A_t.F[K_t, L_t]$$

Where,

- Y_t = Aggregate production/Total income,
- K_t = Stock of Physical Capital used in production,
- L_t = Amount of labour input,
- A_t = Level of technology.

Equation ($Y_t = A_t F[K_t, L_t]$) can be transformed as,

$$\frac{Y'_t}{Y_t} = \frac{A'_t}{A_t} + a_t \frac{K'_t}{K_t} + b_t \frac{L'_t}{L_t}$$

$$a_t + b_t = 1$$

The shares of capital and labour costs in total costs are at and b_t respectively. So the of shares is equal to one. The equation above can be written as,

$$\frac{A'_t}{A_t} = \frac{Y'_t}{Y_t} + a_t \frac{K'_t}{K_t} - b_t \frac{L'_t}{L_t}$$

Solow Residual/ Technological Change

=

Rate of Growth in Aggregate Production

-

Growth Rate of Physical Capital and Labour Input

Empirical Results

Robert Solow proceeded to focus on rate of technical change by using data on the share of capital and labour and the rates of growth of capital per head. He stated that the contribution of the residual is obtained after calculating the contribution of capital. The residual is attributed to technical progress. He concluded that the average growth rate of output per head in United States could be attributed 12.5 per cent to increase in capital per worker and the residual 87.5 per cent to technical change during the period 1940-49.

Graphical Representation

The latter calculation is also known as Solow residual. The diagrammatical representation of technological change is given below. The third part of diagram indicates the output growth due to higher productivity or Solow residual and due to increases in factor of production.

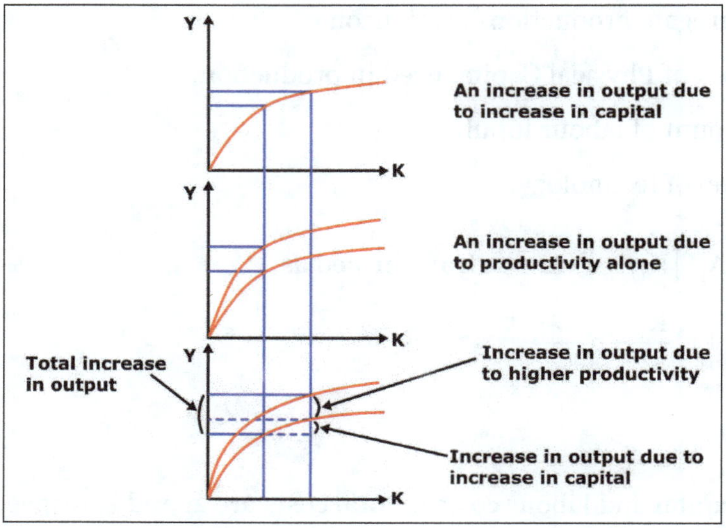

Examples of Solow Residual

For an example, consider Indian economy, whose total output grows at 5 per cent per annum. Assuming that there are two factors of production i.e. capital and labour. During the same period its capital stock grows at 7 per cent per annum and its labor force by 3 per cent per annum. The contribution of the growth rate of capital to output is equal to that growth rate weighted by the share of capital in total output and the contribution of labor is given by the growth rate of labor weighted by labor's share in income. The share of capital's and labour in total output are 1/3 and 2/3 respectively. This means that the portion of growth in output which is due to changes in factors is $0.07 \times (1/3) + 0.03 \times (2/3) = 0.043$ or 4.3 per cent per annum. This means that there is still 0.7 per cent per annum of the growth in output that cannot be accounted for. This remainder/ residual are the increase in the productivity of factors that happened over the period, or the measure of technological progress during this period.

Criticism of Solow Residual

Robert Solow has been criticized for his approach of measuring the residual/ technical change on the following grounds:

- This approach is based on several unrealistic assumptions such as perfect competition, complete homogeneity of capital stock and constant returns to scale.

- Solow estimates undermine the role of investment in context to technical change in process of growth. According to Phelps, 'The results of Solow approach produced a wave of investment pessimism'.
- Solow further admitted that there are index number problems involved in the measurement of every variables in his measurement of the residual.
- This approach ignored the various components of sources of growth such as improvement in skill and quality of labour force, improvement in technological level, change in composition of inputs and output of an industry, investment in research and education and so on.
- Several economists point out that Solow emphasis the role of capital by assuming disembodied technical progress, whereas the most significant advances in technical progress requires capital embodiment. R. Solow himself admitted it in 1959.
- Abramovitz considered residual as 'a measure of our ignorance'. While according to Rosenberg, residual 'provided a wide response on the part of economists wakened, as it were from their dogmatic slumber.'
- Griliches pointed out that the residual approach is not of much use in understanding the growth process because it is based on the concept of unstable production function which is the causes of very large unexplained shifts in it.

Denison's Sources of Growth

Robert Solow, Denison, and Jorgenson-Griliches are the leading economists of growth accounting approach. By using this approach they have discuss sources of growth or technical change by different way. Solow approach has been discussed in previous module. The present module is relating to Denision's and Jorgenson-Griliches sources of growth. Firstly, Denison approach will be discussed.

A number of studies for United States have done by Denison. He have identifies a number of sources of growth and estimates the portion of the growth rate attributable to each. He divides the sources of growth into four important categories:

- The contribution of two factor of production i.e., labour and capital, adjusted for quality changes but not depend on technical change.
- Advancement in knowledge, which is a true measure of total factor productivity (TFP), obtained as a residual.
- Resource allocation improvement.
- Economies of scale.

Measurement of Sources of Growth

In his study entitled 'The Sources of Economic Growth in the United States', he estimated the contribution of different sources with the help of Cobb-Douglas type production function. He kept all inputs i.e., labour and capital together. Denison marked an index of the stock of inputs on the basis of the base year 1929. For constructed this weighted index, he used relative share of income in the base period. In calculating the contribution of education to output, he has treated workers of different educational categories as different inputs. Then the growth rates of the number of workers in different educational categories were aggregated into an index of the growth rate of total labour input according to their shares of total labour hours.

For index of capital, he was taken four types of capital inputs:

- Non-farm residential structures.
- Other structures and equipment.
- Inventories.
- US international assets.

Each types of capital was weighted by its own base year returns in the estimating its contribution to growth. The index of the contribution of increases in output per unit of input comprised advancement in knowledge, resource shift from agriculture to industry and economies of scale.

Table: Sources of growth of real national income of the US during 1929-57.

Sources of Growth	Growth Rate	Per cent of Growth Rate
Real National Income	2.93	100.0
Increase in Total Inputs	2.00	68.3
(a) Labour	1.57	53.6
(b) Capital	0.43	14.7
(c) Land	0.00	0.00
Increase in Output per Unit Input	0.93	31.7
(a) Advance in Knowledge	0.59	20.1
(b) Resource Shift	0.07	2.4
(c) Economies of Scale	0.34	16.6
(d) Irregular Factors	-0.07	-2.4

The above table shows that the growth rate of real national income was 2.93 per cent per annum during the period 1929-57 in the United States economy. The growth rate is calculated from the real net national product at the factor cost. Out of the 2.93 per cent growth rate, 2 per cent are accounted by increase in total inputs and 0.93 per cent increase by productivity (increase in output per unit of input). Out of 2 per cent increase in inputs, 1.57 per cent is accounted by labour and 0.43 per cent by capital.

The contribution of productivity of US real income growth was 0.93 percentages. That is 32 per cent of total sources of growth. According to Denison, this is the residual factor. He divides the increases in output per unit of input into three main components i.e., advance in knowledge, resource shift from agriculture to industry and economies of scale. Thus of the 32 per cent contribution of increase in productivity is comes from advance in knowledge (20 per cent), resource shift (2.4 per cent) and economies of scale (12 per cent).

According to Denison, the contribution of education increases the quality of labour force while the advancement in knowledge is a technical change. Denison regards advancement in knowledge as the 'true residual' and education as 'guesstimated'. So far as other factors like recourse shift and economies of scale are concerned as the lower size of true residual.

Criticisms of Denison's Approach

Denison approach of sources of growth is different from Solow's approach of sources of growth. R. Solow attributes the residual to technical change on the other side Denison breaks the residual into further components. Denison attributes increases in growth to improvement in the quality of labour force as a consequence of better and more education and advancement in knowledge However, he has been criticized for the following weakness in his study of sources of growth:

- Economists have questioned the effect of education on earnings which is the index of quality of labour. They find the adjustment factor of 40 per cent for ability, leaving 60 per cent of differences on income differentials.
- Lundberg has criticized the use of Cobb-Douglas production function by Denison for calculating the contribution of factors of production to growth rate of national income. According to him, the specific C-D function attributes large share of labour income and low share of capital. He also points out that a static equilibrium concept like the production function is a doubtful tool for analysis the dynamics of growth.
- Denison's estimates are based on constant returns to scale, which are available after making payments to all factors according to their marginal productivity. This is unrealistic assumption.
- Denison has also been criticized for assuming 'disembodied technical' progress. In fact, this process should be 'embodied' in plant and equipment. According to J. Sandee, 'the believer of 'embodied' progress usually finds at least twice the yield deduced by the classical Cobb-Douglas disembodied trend analyst, because he consider the whole 'residual' as the result of new investment'.

- Denison does not consider joint effects of capital and technology. Rather, he treats them as separate elements and does not attribute technical progress to the extra capital.

Economic Development and Institutions

Economic development is a complex phenomenon involving not only the changes in output per capita which are related to the physical capita, human capital and technology but also depends upon social attitude, political conditions and various economic organizations. One of the fundamental causes which may explain the differences in the levels of development amongst various countries is differences in these institutions and their role in affecting economic development of a country.

Growth Dynamics of Development

The most important question which social scientists face across the Globe concerns the reasons for the cross country differences in economic growth and development. Why do some countries achieve economic growth while the others are not able to do so? This question also leads to another question as to what can be done to induce economic growth and improve the standard of living of people in a society. Before answering these questions we must differentiate between growth and development. The traditional approach to growth was that it is a process in which the output per capita would increase over a long period of time and that of development implied a sustained increase in Gross Domestic Product (GDP) along with structural changes in an economy. The idea was based on the assumption that the rapid growth of output per capita would trickle down eliminating poverty and economic inequalities by generating more employment.

Since a vast majority of people could not benefit, the concept of development was redefined in terms of 'Redistribution with Growth', thereby implying progressive changes in the socio-economic structure of an economy. The process of development, thus, was combined with social changes. It implied that people are the major participants in the process of change and they only enjoy the benefits of these changes. These changes therefore should include better living standards, equitable distribution of income and wealth productive employment and adequate facilities for health, education and sanitation etc. reflected through various social indicators.

Economists have long recognized that growth can take place without development as has happened in Liberia but development without growth cannot be conceived. Growth in output Per Capita in a society is affected by the amount of Physical capital, human capital and technology that the workers and entrepreneurs have access to as well as to the ability of the society to increase physical and human capital and improvement in technology. Here techniques would also involve the organization of production which would also involve the organization of production which would mean more efficient utilization of resources. The capacity of an economy will be used more effectively not only with the accumulation of more machines and equipment but also with skill formation in the form of managerial and organization skills.

But the study of dynamism of economic development is not limited to the simplistic mind set of general economic theory. The realization that economics is not only limited to the simple quantitative assessment of inputs and output or cost and benefit, there is a greater interest in the influence of institutions on the process and outcome of development. To get more satisfactory answer to the questions of some countries having less physical and human capital and technology and making worst use of their resources and some countries growing much faster than others, we shall have to look to more fundamental causes. It is here that there is a strong support for the overwhelming importance of institutions in determining the levels of development in countries around the world. Once the importance of these institutions is clear one can develop a framework for policy recommendations.

Understanding the Meaning of Institutions

"Institutions are the rules of the game in a society, or more formally are the humanly devised constraints that shape human interactions". Three important features emerge from here:

- That these are "humanly devised constraints" which contrast them with others like geographical factors beyond human control.
- That these are the rules of the game setting constraints on human behaviour.
- That their effect will be through incentives.

These constraints which have been developed by human beings are in the form of formal laws or informal constraints like conventions or self-imposed norms. Although formal laws can be changed very easily, the informal rules change very slowly. But it is the interaction of both that leads to economic development. In fact institutional economics combines economics with other social science disciplines like Political Science, Sociology, Law, Organizational theory and even to anthropology.

The purpose to link development with institutions is to show the relative importance of these institutions in determining the differences in income between the world's most developed and the poorest countries. It is not a new subject that institutions do matter for prospering the economic activities.

Institutions can differ between societies due to their methods of collective decision making e.g. in democracy or dictatorship. These can also differ as a given sets of institutions are expected to and do function differently as the political power lies with different groups or social classes.

Classification of Institutions and their Role in Economic Development

Broadly these institutions can be classified into:

- Economic institutions,
- Political institutions,
- Social institutions.

Economic institutions do affect economic development directly as they influence investment in physical and human capital, technological changes and the organization of production. They not only affect the aggregate growth potential of the economy but the distribution of resources in the society also. Therefore they are not only linked with growth through different degree of efficiency but also through different distributions of the gains this growth. It is because of this influence that all individuals and groups in the society would not prefer the same set of institutions. This leads to a conflict of interest over the choice of institutions among various groups.

Political institutions allocate political power and those who hold political power influence the development of political institutions. They try to maintain those institutions which give them political power. The interaction between the two will create a mechanism of persistence those who are getting more resources will have more political power and will push for such economic and political institutions which are favorable to their own interests. While political institutions work through political power economic institutions of markets, infrastructure, financial organizations, property right and economic organization like planning etc. have their influence through costs, return on investment, distribution of resources cooperation and increased social capital. In Harket Organizations, buyers and sellers meet to determine the prices of commodities. The rational prices thus determined are good indicators of decision making and help in allocation of resources. To take advantages of opportunities for trade with different groups and increase the size of economic transactions only cultural ties are not enough.

There is a need for institutions like organized markets which ensure agreements on the details of exchange and compliance to agreed conditions which will include contracts, codes of conduct, standardized weights and measures and enforcement through law etc. Institutions which provide all these facilities reduce the transaction cost the bargaining costs and the enforcement costs and are thus conducive to economic development. In most of the less developed countries particularly in their agricultural sector the markets are unorganized where the producers are not able to take risks through long term contracts therefore, they restrict output and investment to take advantages of trade opportunities and increase the size of the market.

There is a need for greater information about trading partners and those institutions which ensure agreements on exchange and implementation of the agreed conditions.

The institutions of private property rights increase the security so that the risk in any economic transaction is matched by the appropriation of its benefits. If this right is protected individuals are more willing to invest and even to incur sunk costs. The study of land ownership system in Ghana shows that where individual perception of security of land tenure is low, investment in land is reduced and output thereby drops. The protection of property rights requires a greater role of state for which individuals and groups are ready to sacrifice some degree of freedom. They are ready to pay taxes and accept state monopoly for common security. But here also the risk is that the states which have the power to enforce property rights may use that power to expropriate property too. Thus only the property rights are not sufficient to improve the pace of economic growth. This institution can be effective only when it is balanced by institutions which limit the extractive capacity of state.

It will need independent parliament and judiciary and democratic institutions strongly contribute to this process. Countries which have faced colonial domination suffer from such extractive institutions which have outlived even after gaining of independence. Their control has been taken over by the local elites and the effects of these lie deep in the socio-economic fabric of these societies.

The institutions matter a great deal in determining the level of development as inclusive and participatory institutions increases not only the flow of information but also help increasing the resources. The financial system which helps in economic development includes many institutions and the mechanism which generates more savings and help in its mobilization and effective distributions among those who can use it for investment. The banking and financial institutions if working effectively can bridge the gap between those who save and those who invest for capital formation. The insurance sector by bearing a part of the business risk can also help in inducing development activities.

The pace of development is also affected by the strategy of organizing the process of decision making. Economic planning is one such institution which helps this process not only in communist countries but even in those economics where the concept of democratic planning has been adopted. Although the scope of democratic planning is limited yet its impact on growth and development cannot be ignored. The purpose of economic planning here is to reconcile the conflicting interest so that they sub serve the national interests. Its success would depend upon:

- The extent to which public sector is able to pursue the socially desirable goals.
- The extent to which the state is able to guide the private sector to follow these goals.
- The extent to which the state is able to check the distortions in investment decisions.

The welfare state is another example of an institution which pools resources to limit the negative effects of trade cycles on incomes and employment in an economy. The political environment and the decisions of the government help in providing more funds for investment in infrastructure which is an essential Pre-condition for economic growth. It is not only economic infrastructure in the form of transport communication and power etc. but investment in education, health and information sector is also necessary which will be complementary to private investment. Informal institutions like public agencies, trade unions, community structures and professional associations also help in promoting the growth process. Besides in less developed countries the provision for safe drinking water and sanitation has to be made under expanded social infrastructure.

The declining state expenditure on social infrastructure in these economies is creating a social relationship which is not conducive to economic development. Moreover there is a need for political stability which can generate faith of the people in the programs and policies of the government. It is this faith which drives the people to make investment in various fields of economic activities. The impact of economic institutions is sometimes limited by negative social institutions. The caste system, the joint family system and the laws of inheritance etc. have their powerful negative effect on economic development in a country like India. The required changes in these institutions bring social dynamism which is a critical parameter of change in the context of development.

It is clear, therefore, that institutions do play an important role in the process of economic development. Since these are humanly devised constraints and are both formal and informal in nature, these can support or can put obstacles in the path of development. The question which emerges is that if institutions are so important for economic growth why do some societies choose and maintain these dysfunctional institutions. The answer to this question lies in the relationship between economic institutions, political power and political institutions.

Economic and Political Institutions

Economic institutions not only matter because they influence investment in physical and human capital, technology and organization of production, but they also determine the distribution of resources in the society. The problem arises when the economic institutions may lead to a conflict of interest among various groups and the political power of different groups decides about the choice of economic institutions. When a particular group is rich relative to others it will increase its political power and will be able to push for those economic and political institutions which are favorable to its own interests. It is due to this persistence that reforms become so difficult. But despite this persistence, there is a potential for change in terms of shocks to the political power in terms of new technologies and the international environment.

This may generate major changes in political institutions leading changes in economic institutions and thus to economic growth. It is therefore very important to focus on the political institutions and the distribution of political power along with economic institutions while deciding about the potential institutional reforms. Moreover a direct reform in a specific economic institution may be ineffective and may even backfire as there are different ways and instrument to achieve any goal. Taking away one instrument without changing the balance of power can lead to just a replacement of one instrument with the other. Historically, various countries while attempting institutional reforms have faced various problems and have remained unsuccessful in such reforms. Nevertheless countries do change their institutions and move into different development paths. The obvious examples in the post-world war II are Taiwan, China in late 1950's, Singapore. The Republic of Korea and Botswana in 1960 and Chile and Mauritius in 1970's. Britain also underwent an important process of institutional changes successfully, firstly in the 17th Century and then in the 19th Century.

These changes in various countries took place both under the authoritarian regime as well as under democracy. The obvious result of the discussion above is that one of the main determinant of cross country differences in income per capita is the differences in institutions. These differences in institutions are the outcome of different collective choices which further reflect the different in political institutions and distribution of political power. Although it is a difficult task to change these institutions and thereby to solve the problem of poverty and inequality yet there are examples that countries do reform their negative institutions and solve the problem of stagnation and move to rapid rates of economic growth. The example of economic development of China after 1978 shows that this takes off was the result of the institutional and policy reforms. Growth did not occur in China because some geographical constraints were removed or their culture changed but growth occurred because more power came in the hands of those who wanted to push through reforms.

References

- Joan-Robinson-Model-of-Economic-Growth: ac.in, Retrieved 23, June 2020
- Solow-growth-model, knowledge, economics, resources: corporatefinanceinstitute.com, Retrieved 02, January 2020

3

Money and Banking

Money is any verifiable record that is a generally recognized medium of payment for goods and services. The industry that handles financial transactions is banking. Money and banking play a significant role in the financial stability of the economy of a country. This chapter has been carefully written to provide an easy understanding of the varied facets of money and banking.

Money

Economists have considered various aspects of money, such as the reason for its existence, changes in its form, and its role in economic growth and development. Income and wealth are often considered synonymous to money but while they may be expressed in terms of money they are not the same thing. We therefore need to define money by its use in an exchange economy, in terms of its specific functions within the financial system. By specifying precisely what it does, we can distinguish money from all other assets in the financial system. We also need to know how money comes into existence and what causes it to change over time. This requires an analysis of its nature, role and origin.

Barter Exchange

Disadvantages of Barter Exchange

The first disadvantage would be a lack of double coincidence of wants. It would be extremely difficult to find someone who wishes to purchase right now, exactly what you would like to sell. Thus, exchange under a barter system is costly in terms of the search time and effort. Barter presents even more serious difficulties when the articles to be exchanged are not of the same value and cannot be divided without loss of value. This makes it an inefficient and cumbersome way to conduct transactions. It raises the transactions costs and holds down the volume of exchange in the economy.

The second disadvantage of pure barter is the lack of any common unit in terms of which to measure and state the values of goods and services. The value of each good would be expressed in terms of each of the other goods. If there are n goods in the barter economy, there would be $n(n - 1)/2$ prices. No meaningful accounting system would be possible in such an economy.

The third disadvantage of pure barter is the lack of any satisfactory unit in terms of which to write contracts requiring future payments. These future payments would have to be stated in terms of specific goods and services. Though this would be possible, it would lead to three difficulties (1) regarding the quality of the good or service to be repaid (2) the parties would often be unable to agree on the specific commodity to be used for repayment (3) both parties would run the risk that the commodity to be repaid would increase or decrease in value over the duration of the contract.

The fourth disadvantage of pure barter, which results from its other shortcomings, is the lack of any method of storing generalized purchasing power. People could store purchasing power for future use only by holding specific commodities or claims against specific commodities. The stored commodity may deteriorate or appreciate in value, its storage may be costly, and it may be difficult to dispose off quickly without loss, if its holder wishes to buy something else.

All the disadvantages mentioned above make pure barter a highly inefficient means of trade and to overcome these difficulties every society invented some kind of money, early in its development. The development of money has passed through various stages in accordance with time, place and circumstances with the progress of civilization.

This can be summarized as: Transaction costs associated with barter → encourages → Development of Money → facilitates → Exchange Trading → facilitates → Specialization and division of labour → facilitates → Economic Development.

Functions of Money

Money performs four specific functions, each of which obviates one of the difficulties of pure barter. These functions are to serve as 1) a medium of exchange 2) a unit of value 3) a standard of deferred payments and 4) a store of value. The first two are called the primary functions of money. The last two are called the derivative or secondary functions because they are derived from the primary functions.

Money as a Medium of Exchange

One of the unique function and in fact an essential and primary distinguishing characteristic of money is that it is anything generally acceptable as a means of payment in the settlement of all transactions, including debt. It is a commonly used medium of exchange or means of transferring generalized purchasing power.

It is a device to permit people to exchange goods and services without need for conversion into anything before being spent. Hence, ATM cards, property, gold, FDR's are not money. However, faith or belief or confidence in its general acceptability is very important. The assets which are generally acceptable in exchange may vary from one country to another or from one period to another within the same country.

Money saves time and energy and allows people to buy what they want, how much, at the best bargain or terms, at the time they think best. By economizing on the use of scarce real resources, money promotes transactional or operational efficiency.

In addition, it promotes allocation efficiency by making it possible to exploit potential gains from specialization in trade and production. It also leads to emergence of specialized markets in all types of goods and services. By giving freedom of choice to individuals as a bearer of options, it thereby promotes economic welfare.

By separating the act of sale and purchase, it replaces bilateral trading with multilateral trading leading to specialization and division of labor. As one moves from a barter exchange economy to one of monetary exchange, the length of transaction period and the total trading cost decrease. The use of money for similar transactions also enhances competition. A monetary economy eliminates the problem of double coincidence of wants.

Money as a Unit of Account, Value, Standard and Measure of Value

This is the second primary function of money where the monetary unit is the unit in terms of which the value of all goods and services are measured and expressed. It therefore helps in determining the price or the number of monetary units each good or service would exchange for, making it possible to compare prices and have relative prices.

It simplifies the problem of measuring the exchange value of commodities and makes accounting of national income, costs, profits assets and liabilities possible. It permits rational economic calculations and transmits economic information about market preferences of consumers to producers and makes possible specialization and division of labor. Unlike physical units which are inter temporally and inter regionally constant, the value of money is inversely related to the price level and hence does not remain constant in terms of the goods and services you can buy with it, making money a poor unit of account.

Money as a Standard of Deferred Payment or Unit of Contract

Money serves as the standard or unit in terms of which deferred or future payments like interest, rent, salaries, pensions etc. are stated. This is concomitant with the first two functions because the person who pays cash later quotes money price as a unit of account. These contracts are for the payment of principal and interest on debt where future payments are stated in terms of monetary units. Money is a satisfactory standard of deferred payment if and only if its purchasing power, that is, the value of money remains constant.

Money as a Store of Value

This function is also concomitant with the other functions and since money as a medium of exchange, separates the act of sales and purchase, the two are made at different points of time, i.e. you can sell now, get money, store that money and purchase later.

What you store is generalized power that can be used any time. This is particularly relevant in a money using economy where income and expenditure are discontinuous i.e. wages, interest, salary etc. are got at one point of time and spent over the month till the next receipt. Therefore, money is stored in the form of generalizing purchasing power.

As a store of value, money scores over physical assets which may involve storage costs, deteriorate or become obsolescent or have transaction or brokerage costs since they are not acceptable in exchange for goods and services. Money is also a good store of value because it is perfectly liquid.

Money and Liquidity

Liquidity is a term used by economists to describe how cheaply and easily an asset may be converted into a medium of exchange. This has the following aspects:

- Marketability: Money is readily acceptable in exchange for goods and services.
- Predictability: Money value can be anticipated for making payments in the future. Unlike money, values of shares on stock exchanges are not predictable and hence considered illiquid.
- Reversibility: Money value in payments and receipts are the same. Real assets as well as financial assets lack reversibility as their purchases / sales are subject to tax. A car loses its value once out of the showroom. Travelers' cheques and mutual funds also lack reversibility as commission charges and administrative charges are levied but not refunded.
- Divisibility: Money can be denominated in the smallest unit in which exchange dealings can take place in an asset. This is an important determinant of the flexibility and divisibility of the asset in exchange.

Marketability, reversibility, divisibility and predictability are all relevant attributes in the definition of a liquid asset since liquidity is a collection of characteristics which may be present in varying degrees in various assets, it is a multi-dimensional and subjective concept. Different individuals may have different evaluations about marketability and predictability of assets. However, since the characteristics of liquidity, marketability, predictability and divisibility of assets are designated in terms of cash, money is liquidity par excellence, making the relationship between money and liquidity, bi directional.

Physical Properties of Money

Here, we need to conceptualize what are the desirable physical properties that any commodity should have to be a good choice to serve as money. It needs to have the following characteristics:

- Portability: It should have high enough value relative to its weight to make transportation easier, and. it should be valuable in small quantities. This was the reason why gold and silver coins as currencies were better compared to rice, horses, cows etc. in the evolution of money.

- Durability: It should not deteriorate with time or wear down when handled.
- Divisibility: Into fairly small units to facilitate transactions of various sizes. Here we may find that diamonds may be durable and portable, but they are not divisible as compared to gold and silver.
- Intrinsic or recognizable value: To be accepted in transactions. This was possible with gold coins stamped by authority with respect to value or even paper currency.

Having considered the various functions performed by money, the question arises as to what things are included and what things are excluded in money. Money needs to be defined precisely.

Legal Definition

We could have a legal definition where money is defined in purely legal terms that is, money is what the law states it to be. Laws can help a thing to achieve general acceptability by proclaiming it to be money. It may grant legal tender powers by ensuring that refusal to accept it would be punishable by law. However, things that are not legally defined as money may still come to be generally acceptable in payment for example chequable deposits at banks are a part of money but they are not legal tender.

Legal tender or fiat money serves as money on the fiat or order of the government. It has to be accepted or it cannot be refused in settlement of payments of all kinds. However, small coins are usually limited legal tender for a certain maximum amount beyond which they cease to be legal tender. Pounds two and above currency notes are unlimited legal tender. Demand deposits of banks are fiduciary money and are accepted as money on trust only and are non-legal tender. A payee can legally refuse to accept payment from demand deposits made through a cheque because it may be dishonoured at the issuer's bank. Here there may be insistence on payment in cash.

Functional Definition

The functional definition of money includes in it all those things that perform the functions of money and excludes all others. Since the derivative or secondary functions of money can be performed by a variety of assets, all economists agree that money supply should include all those things that are in fact generally acceptable in payment of debt and as payment for goods and services. A thing that is generally acceptable in payment and generally used as a medium of payments is money whatever its legal status may be.

Narrow and Broad Definition of Money

The narrow definition of money is based on the function of money as a medium of exchange and includes in it only currency and chequable deposits.There may be other assets which have a high degree of moneyness or liquidity, but are not generally acceptable in payment or there is a delay or cost involved in exchanging them for money. These assets which are widely used as a store of value like saving and fixed deposits at banks are called NEAR MONEY and are frequently included only in a broader definition of money. Since all assets possess the quality of moneyness to some degree, any broad definition is likely to have troublesome borderline cases.

Theoretical and Empirical Approach to Definition of Money

There are two approaches for defining money:

- A priori or theoretical approach.
- The empirical approach.

In the theoretical approach, money is first conceptualized in the form of specific functional or institutional attributes and then the corresponding measure of money is obtained by aggregating relevant financial assets possessing those specific attributes like medium of exchange, unit of value, standard of deferred payments and store of value i.e. distinction should be made between the concept of money and the measure of money where conceptualization should be distinguished from and precede its measurement.

Second is the empirical approach which however does not rely on any pre conceived notion of money and instead it directly arrives at a measure of money as an aggregate of financial assets which when introduced in certain functions gives the best results in terms of specific criteria like the highest correlation with national income or having a stable and sturdy demand function.

Among the two approaches, the theoretical approach has a greater analytical appeal and as a sequence, you should empirically only test the adequacy of concepts and verify theoretical hypothesis. This implies that the empirical stage comes only after the relevant concepts have been defined and hypothesis derived from a suitable economic model.

The empirical approach confuses empirical verification with hypothesisation and therefore forecloses the possibility of generating a testable hypothesis capable of empirical verification as a theory, the Theoretical approach is more scientific because it first develops an appropriate concept of money as an analytical entity followed by suitable measurement of money.

We should start with a behavioral hypothesis and subject it to empirical testing. Given the analytical superiority of the theoretical approach the next logical step is to identify the specific attributes with which to conceptualize money. As a statistical construct, money should reflect assets with monetary characteristics and should be specific liquid liabilities of a particular set of financial intermediaries.

Evolution of Money

Having discussed the various functions and roles of money, one could discuss the evolution of, and changes in the monetary system. Such is the importance of money that the breakdown of one monetary system was immediately followed by the development of another system. Primitive economies overcame the inconvenience of barter by the use of uncounted metals like copper, gold and silver as means of exchange because they were generally acceptable in payment.

This could be, because they possessed the above mentioned properties of having high value relative to its weight, durability and portability etc. However these metals continued to be used for non-monetary purposes also and hence metal flowed freely into and out of monetary uses. The use of bullion as money had serious disadvantages of short weighing and adulteration. Coinage solved the problem with an official certification as to the weight and purity of the metal by the issuer who could be the king. Though an important innovation, coinage still had the disadvantage of danger of theft and storage problems, costs of long distance transportation along with the absence of any interest or return.

To remove this problem, people started keeping these coins with a custodian who could be a goldsmith who kept them in a safe box and issued an I.O.U. Initially one would have to go to the goldsmith to get the coins to make payments. Later with faith in the goldsmith the, I.O.U was given as payments to others and passed several hands. The I.O.U as a written order authorized that the goldsmith would pay the specified amount of metal to whosoever presented it. This was the birth of the bank and bank notes. A debt or a promise to pay, evidenced by a piece of paper.

These paper claims were acceptable because they were believed to be fully backed by the metal. These papers could be transferred and used as payments for goods and services. Initially the goldsmith/bank held gold to cover all possible redemptions of bank notes and deposits. This was 100% reserve banking because the reserves/gold was equal to the total value of outstanding bank notes and deposits. The only profit that the goldsmith/bank got was charging fee for deposits or trade gold for bank notes.

At another step in this evolution of money, the person leaving gold or silver with the banker would not receive a paper representing the debt of the banker but simply a deposit credit evidenced by an entry on the banks books. For making payments an order could be written on the banker to pay someone else. Thus these deposit claims came to be used as a means of payment.

The emerging bankers soon realized that to meet their promises to pay in specie on demand they did not need to hold gold and silver equal to 100% of their outstanding debts in the form of deposits and bank notes. Instead they could hold specie equal to only a fraction of their liabilities. This was the birth of fractional reserve banking. This principle gave banks the power to increase or decrease the total money supply which was not there when they issued bank notes and deposits only in exchange for an equal value of gold and silver. That was mere substitution of one type of money for another in the hands of the public. With fractional reserve banking, banks held some deposits as reserves in the vault but loaned out the remainder to people in need of funds. The bank could charge interest on this loan and hence had a second source of revenue in addition to the storage charges assessed on deposits. Here Banks are financial intermediaries because they are accepting deposits and lending those funds to borrowers in the evolution of banking. Bank deposits emerged as the primary medium of payments. However the advances in computer technology and the rapid growth in credit and debit card usage, we may be moving to a chequeless or cashless society and electronic money or bitcoins a virtual or electronic alternative currency that uses technology to facilitate instant payments. The main development is the movement from commodity money such as gold coins to credit money.

Basis of Classification of Money

1. Physical characteristics of the material of which money is made of i.e. whether money is in the form of gold, paper or any commodity.

2. Nature of the issuer i.e. whether money has been issued by the government, central bank or commercial bank.

3. Relationship between value of money as money and the value of money as a commodity, according to which we could have:

- Full bodied money i.e. money whose value as a commodity for non-monetary purposes is as great as its value as money e.g. rice, wool, cattle, gold coins.
- Representative full bodied money, which by itself may have no significant commodity value but it represents in circulation an amount of metal with a commodity value equal to the value of money.
- Credit money/debt money: This is any money except representative full bodied money that circulates at a face value which is greater than the commodity value of the material from which it is made. It is also called fiduciary money or money that circulates as money on the basis of trust commanded by its issuers. This could take the form of:
    - Token coins like 50 paise or one rupee coins which are a small proportion of money supply.

- Representative token coins which represent the receipt of token coins or an equal weight of metal deposited with the government and is usually made of paper.
- Circulating promissory notes issued by the government. This is also called fiat money and is usually made of paper and at present is inconvertible into anything of value except small change.
- Circulating promissory notes issued by private banks. This was present initially in the evolution of money but this right was later taken away.
- Circulating promissory notes issued by centralized banks. These are presently in the form of notes of pounds two and above issued by the Bank of England.
- Checking deposits with banks which form a major part of money supply and are bank deposits payable on demand and transferable by cheques and are acceptable in exchange for goods and service. They are mere entries in the ledgers of the bank to the credit of their holders.

Theories of Money Supply

The supply of money is determined jointly by the public authority, banks and the public. In this determination the monetary authority plays an active and dominant role, but that of the public and banks cannot be ignored or taken for granted. Understanding this role is essential for a successful policy of monetary control.

In the context of developing countries and emerging market economies, there are essentially two main approaches to money supply determination: the money multiplier approach with its foundation in the works of Friedman and Schwartz and Cagan and the balance sheet or structural approach. The money multiplier approach focuses on the relationship between money stock M and reserve money H and through the money multiplier m to the public's preference between currency, demand deposits and time deposits and to the banks holding of reserves as a proportion of aggregate deposits/liabilities, while the structural approach favours analysis of individual items in the balance sheet of the consolidated monetary sector in explaining variations in money stock. The difference between them reflects the division between monetarists and non-monetarists.

Money Mulitiplier Approach

Ordinary Money and High Powered Money

As a preliminary to the study of the Theory of Money Supply, it is essential to understand the distinction between two kinds of money. (a) Ordinary Money (M) and (b) High Powered Money (H).

The alternative empirical measures of money discussed in the previous modules were all measures of ordinary money M. Here we will define money narrowly as M = C + DD + OD that is, sum of currency and demand deposits of banks including the Nation Banks held by the public and since other deposits of the Nation Banks are less than 1% of the total money supply, we ignore OD in the future discussion, This M is the money produced by the Nation Banks, government, and the banking system and held by the public.

$$M = C + DD$$

High powered money (H) is the money produced by the Nation Banks, Government and held by the public and banks. It is also called Reserve or Base Money. H = C + R + OD that is, H is the sum of (a) Currency held by the public C (b) Cash Reserves of banks R and (c) other Deposits of the Nation Banks OD. Since OD are 1% of total H, we ignore it and hence,

$$H = C + R$$

This definition of H is by its use or holders, not by its producers the Nation Banks and the Government.

Comparing equation M = C + DD and H = C + R we find that C is common to both M and H, but while M has DD, H has this difference is of crucial importance in the theory of Money Supply. This is because of the presence of banks who are the producers of DD, which is counted as money at par with C. But to be able to produce DD, banks have to maintain R which is a part of H produced only by the monetary authority and not by banks themselves. In a fractional reserve banking system, DD are certain multiple of which is a component of H. This makes H High powered compared to M. It serves as the base for multiple creation of which is a part of M. This is the reason why H is called base Money. At any point of time only R lends the high poweredness of H, but C has the potential to become high powered the moment it is converted into DD by the public and the banks reserves would increase equivalently.

The H Theory of Money Supply

The H theory of money supply is so called because H is the dominant factor determining money supply. Since money multiplier is the outcome of this approach, it is also called the Money Multiplier Approach. We discuss this in the demand supply framework. We initially assume supply of H to be policy determined given exogenously to the public and banks.

$$H^s = H$$

The demand for H comes from the public demand for currency C and banks demand for Reserves R. The demand for C and DD, the two components of ordinary money are affected by the same set of factors like level of income and the rate of interest, and is therefore correlated. That is, demand for C is a proportional function of DD.

$$C^d = c\ DD$$

Where c is the desired currency deposit ratio of the public. It is assumed to be a behavioral constant. Moving to the banks demand for reserves R, We first look at the components of R,

$$R = RR + ER$$

RR are the reserves which the scheduled banks are required to hold statutorily as balances with the Nation Banks. The Nation Banks stipulates the cash reserve which can vary between 3 to 15% of the total demand and time liabilities of a bank. The banks have no choice about the holding of these reserves.

ER is all reserves in excess of RR. Banks are free to hold them as cash on hand or vault cash or even as balances with the Nation Banks. These reserves are held voluntarily by the banks as a certain proportion of Total Liabilities of the bank. They are held by the banks for transactions, precautionary and speculative purposes. Dividing throughout equation R = RR + ER by total Deposits D we have,

$R^d/D = RR/D + ER^d/D$ which can be represented as,

$$r = RR + e$$

that is, reserve ratio (r) is equal to the statutory cash reserve ratio (rr) plus the excess reserve ratio (e),

$$R^d = r.\ D$$

The total reserves R are a certain proportion r of the total deposits of banks, Here r is called the reserve deposit ratio.

$$D = DD + TD$$

Now Bank Deposits are of two kinds DD or demand deposits which are treated as a part of money in the narrow definition.TD are near money, and a part of the broader definition of money. The choice of division of D between DD and TD is done by the Public. We hypothesis that TD is an increasing proportional function of DD. where it is the ratio of TD to DD.

$$TD^d = t.\ DD$$

Now, from equation $R^d = r.\ D$ and $D = DD + TD$ we have,

$$D = (1 + t)\ DD$$

From equation $R^d = r. D$ and $TD^d = t. DD$ and substituting for (r) from equation r =RR + e,

$$R^d = (rr + e)(1 + t) DD$$

From equation H = C + R and $R^d = (rr + e)(1 + t) DD$,

$H^d = [c + (rr + e)(1 + t)] DD$ which gives us in equilibrium, $H^d = H^s$.

$$DD = 1H$$

$$C + (rr + e)(1 + t)$$

where 1 is the value of the deposit multiplier,

$$c + (rr + e)(1 + t)$$

Now from equation M = C + DD and DD =1H we have the key equation in the H Theory of Money supply,

$$\frac{M = 1 + c}{c + (rr + e)(1 + t)} H$$

This makes the supply of money a function of H and the behavioral ratios c, rr, e, t where the expression $\frac{1 + c}{c + (rr + e)(1 + t)}$ is the value of the narrow money multiplier. This can be represented as m1 and hence we can represent the money supply equation as,

$$M = m(\ )H$$

Here the money multiplier is treated as a behavioural constant as a function of the variables c, t, rr and e and the money multiplier systematically responds to a set of impulses.

In this general formulation, the money multiplier approach suggests that determinants of the money stock can be classified into two broad groups: (1) those that affect the reserve money, and (2) those that affect the money multiplier.

Criticism of the Money Multiplier Approach

The critics of the money multiplier theory have the following arguments:

- The money multiplier approach is based on an identity, an analytically convenient tautology, offering just a description of movements in money stock, rather than a behavioral theory of its determination.
- In its general form M =m ( ) H It is an equilibrium condition rather than a money supply function and process involved is rather mechanical. The only facets

of portfolio choice considered are those of the public in the determination of desired C/DD and desired TD/DD ratio and banks in the determination of R/D ratio. This is inadequate as the analysis does not involve or require any interest changes.

- The theory of Money stock determination should be treated as a branch of a general theory of portfolio adjustment in response to relative price or yield changes. By taking the reserve money as given. The money multiplier identity short circuits this approach.

- The reserve money is taken as exogenously given (whose values are considered to be determined outside the system under consideration), fixed by monetary authorities, and no steps are taken to examine the factors determining its level As a matter of fact level of reserve money is a target (control variables whose values the authorities attempt to set) rather than an exogenous variable. To treat the policy targets as exogenous variables implies that the authorities do not alter their control variables in response to the system. The money multiplier identity obscures rather than illuminates the fundamental nature of the process of money stock determination.

There is essentially, a divergence of views regarding the usefulness of the money multiplier which could be traced to division between the monetarists and the no monetarists. The former argue that monetary authorities can exercise effective control over the stock of money while the latter question the feasibility of this exercise. The controversy between them boils down to 3 issues:

- Which of the variables in equation ($\frac{M=1+c}{c+(rr+e)(1+t)}H$) can be controlled by the monetary authorities?

- If some of the variables are not controllable, can monetary authorities offset influences of such variables by using instruments at their disposal?

- Are the behavioral functions explaining these variables stable and predictable?

According to the non-monetarists, not only are most of the variables entering the equation endogenous, the behavioral functions explaining the determinants are also unstable and Since the monetary authorities in the developing economies do not have potent policy instruments to offset the impact of changes in these variables on money stock and hence are not in a position to effectively control the process of money stock determination.

The monetarists agree that both real and financial sectors of the economy exert influence on the money stock, but the behavioral patterns of the public and the banks are sufficiently stable and predictable so as to permit the monetary authorities to control the money stock. The issue is therefore empirical and country specific, depending on the stage of financial development of the economy.

Structural Approach

Balance Sheet Approach

Balance sheet of the consolidated Banking Sector	
Liabilities	Assets
(A)Monetary Liabilities	(A) Financial Assets
1. Currency with the public	1. Net Bank Credit to Government
2. Deposit liabilities of Banks	2. Bank Credit to Commercial sector
3. Other deposits with the Nation Banks	3. Net foreign exchange assets of Banking Sector
	4. Government's Currency Liabilities to the Public
(B)Non-monetary Liabilities	(B) Other Assets

This approach is based on the balance sheet of the consolidated banking sector rather than of the central bank as in the money multiplier approach. Since broad money M3 comprises the monetary liabilities of the consolidated banking sector, it follows from the asset side that:

M3 = Net Bank credit to govt.

- + Bank credit to commercial sector.
- + Net foreign exchange assets of the banking sector.
- + Govts currency liabilities to the public.
- - Net non-monetary liabilities of the Banking Sector.

The essence of the balance sheet approach lies in the examinations of variations in money stock through analysis of credit creation by the consolidated banking system through credit given to government and the commercial sector and movements in the foreign exchange asset holding etc. By focusing on a dis aggregated analysis of the consolidated banking sector, the balance sheet approach obviates the need for a mechanistic appraisal of the money multiplier.

Goodhart's General Equilibrium Model

This provides a behavioural Theory of money supply determination the model identifies four critical issues influencing the determination of money stock:

- The size of the public sector Deficit.
- Market reactions to the authorities open market operations.

- The elasticity of substitution between foreign and domestic assets.
- Interest elasticity of the demand for bank credit.

It works with a flow of funds identity:

$$PSD = OMO + NMD + ECF - MAT + \Delta H$$

Where,

- PSD = Public Sector deficit.
- OMO = Outcome of operations in marketable debt.
- NMD =Outcome of transactions in non-marketable debt.
- MAT = Use of funds to pay off maturing debt.
- ECF = Finance obtained from, or required for accommodating external currency Flows.
- Δ H = Change in reserve money.

The flow of funds identity is combined with a set of behavioural equations in the model covering the factors above in a general equilibrium framework. The determination of money stock is seen as a process of general portfolio adjustment in response to relative interest rate changes. The time path of the process depends on the relevant speeds of adjustment of various sectors to relative price changes, rather than the mechanistic process embedded in the money multiplier approach.

Money Multiplier and Reserve Ratio

The Money Multiplier refers to how an initial deposit can lead to a bigger final increase in the total money supply. For example, if the commercial banks gain deposits of £1 million and this leads to a final money supply of £10 million. The money multiplier is 10. The money multiplier is a key element of the fractional banking system.

- There is an initial increase in bank deposits (monetary base).
- The bank holds a fraction of this deposit in reserves and then lends out the rest.
- This bank loan will, in turn, be re-deposited in banks allowing a further increase in bank lending and a further increase in the money supply.

The Reserve Ratio

The reserve ratio is the % of deposits that banks keep in liquid reserves. For example 10% or 20%.

Formula for Money Multiplier

$$\text{Money Multiplier} = \frac{1}{\text{Reserve Ratio}}$$

In theory, we can predict the size of the money multiplier by knowing the reserve ratio:

- If you had a reserve ratio of 5%. You would expect a money multiplier of 1/0.05 = 20.
- This is because if you have deposits of £1 million and a reserve ratio of 5%. You can effectively lend out £20 million.

Example of Money Multiplier

- Suppose banks keep a reserve ratio of 10%. (0.1).
- Therefore, if someone deposits $100, the bank will keep $10 as reserves and lend out $90.
- However, because $90 has been lent out – other banks will see future deposits of $90.
- Therefore, the process of lending out deposits can start again.

Banks	Deposit	Money lent out	Reserves	Total deposits
Stage 1	100	90	10	100
Stage 2	90	81	9	190
Stage 3	81	72.9	8.1	270
Stage 4	72.9	65.6	7.3	343.9
Stage 5	65.6	59.0	6.6	409.5
Stage 6	59.0	53.1	5.9	468.6
Stage 7	53.1	47.8	5.3	521.7
Stage 8	47.8	43.0	4.8	569.5
Stage 9	43.0	38.7	4.3	612.6
Stage 10	38.7	34.9	3.9	651.3
....				
Ending at 10	651.3	586.2	65.1	651.3

This example stops at stage 10. In theory, the process can continue for a long time until deposits are fractionally very small.

- If allowed to repeat for an infinite number of times, the final total deposits would be $1,000.

- Money multiplier = 1/0.1 = 10.
- Final increase in money supply = 10 × $100 = $1,000.

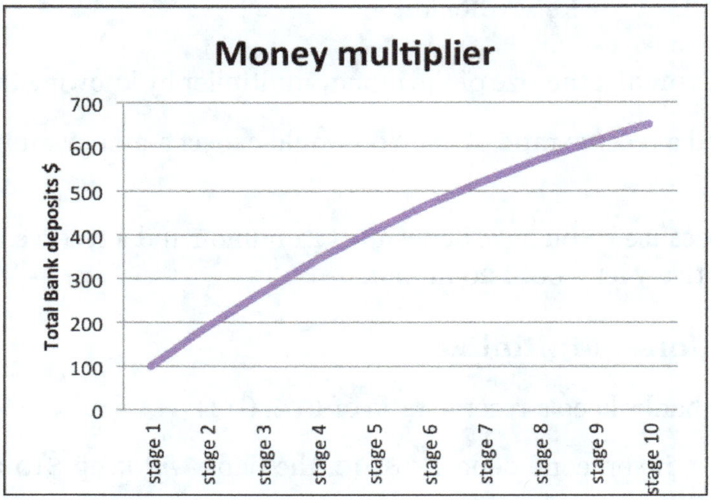

Using the Reserve Ratio to Influence Monetary Policy

In theory, if a Central Bank demands a higher reserve ratio – it should have the effect of acting like deflationary monetary policy. A higher reserve ratio should reduce bank lending and therefore reduce the money supply.

Money Multiplier in the Real World

In a simple theory of the money multiplier, it is assumed that if the bank lends $90 – all of this will return. However, in the real world, there are many reasons why the actual money multiplier is significantly smaller than the theoretically possible money multiplier.

- Import spending: If consumers buy imports the money leaves the economy.
- Taxes: A percentage of income will be taken in taxes.
- Savings: Not all money is spent and circulated, a significant percentage will be saved.
- Currency Drain Ratio: This is the % of banknotes that individual consumers keep in cash, rather than depositing in banks. If consumers deposited all their cash in banks, there would be a bigger money multiplier. But, if people keep funds in cash then the banks cannot lend more.
- Bad loans: A bank may lend out $90 but the company goes bankrupt and so this is never deposited bank into the banking system.

- Safety reserve ratio: This is the % of deposits a bank may like to keep above the statutory reserve ratio. i.e. the required reserve ratio may be 5%, but banks may like to keep 5.2%.
- It might not be possible to lend more money out. Just because banks could lend 95% of their deposits doesn't mean they can, even if they wanted to. In a recession, people may not want to borrow, but they prefer to save.
- Banks may not want to lend Also, at various times, the banks may not want to lend, e.g. during a recession they feel firms and individuals more likely to default. Therefore, the banks end up with a higher reserve ratio.

Therefore, due to these factors, the reserve ratio and money multiplier are theoretical.

Loan First Multiplier

The money multiplier model suggests banks wait for deposit and then lend out a fraction. However, in the real world, banks may take it upon themselves to issue a loan, and then seek out reserves from other financial institutions/Central Bank or private individuals.

For example, in the credit bubble of 2000-2007, many banks were lending mortgages by borrowing on short-term money markets. They were lending money that wasn't related to saving deposit accounts.

Money Multiplier and Quantitative Easing

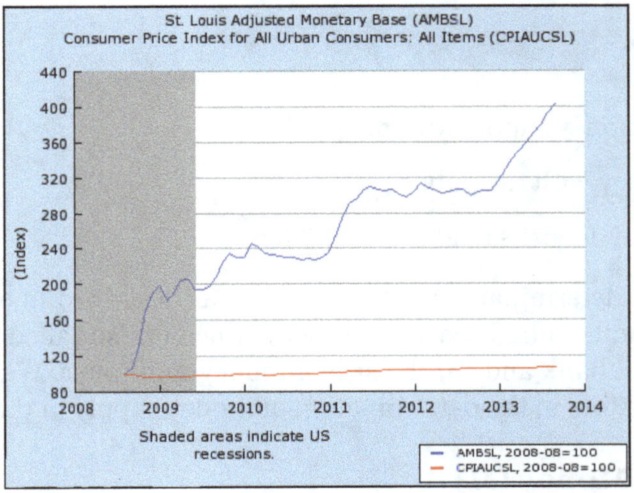

In 2009-12 Central Banks pursued quantitative easing. This involves increasing the monetary base. – Buying bonds off banks gave them greater cash reserves. In theory, this increase in the money multiplier should increase the overall money supply by a large amount due to the money multiplier.

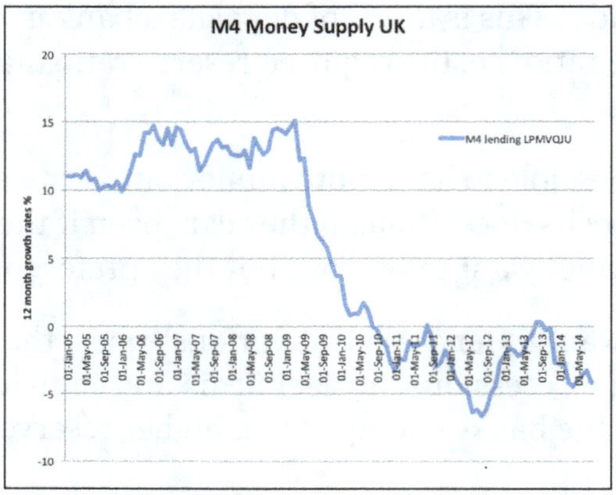

However, in practice, this didn't occur. The money supply didn't increase because banks were not keen to lend any extra money. Also, banks were trying to improve their reserves following the credit crunch and their previous over-extension of loans.

Determinants of Money Supply

In order to explain the determinants of money supply in an economy we shall use M, concept of money supply which is the most fundamental concept of money supply. We shall denote it simply by M rather than M_1. This concept of money supply is composed of currency held by the public (C_p) and demand deposits with the banks (D). Thus,

$$M = C_p + D$$

Where,

- M = Total money supply with the public.
- C_p = Currency with the public.
- D = Demand deposits held by the public.

The two important determinants of money supply as described in equation ($M = C_p + D$) are (a) the amounts of high-powered money which is also called Reserve Money by the banks to central bank and (b) the size of money multiplier. We explain below the role of these two factors in the determination of money supply in the economy.

High-Powered Money (H)

The high-powered money which we denote by H consists of the currency (notes and coins) issued by the Government and the banks to central bank. A part of the currency issued is held by the public, which we designate as C_p and a part is held by the banks as reserves which we designate as R.

A part of these currency reserves of the banks is held by them in their own cash vaults and a part is deposited in the banks to central bank in the Reserve Accounts which banks hold with banks. Accordingly, the high-powered money can be obtained as sum of currency held by the public and the part held by the banks as reserves. Thus,

$$H = C_p + R$$

Where,

- H = The amount of high-powered money.
- C_p = Currency held by the public.
- R = Cash Reserves of currency with the banks.

It is worth noting that banks to central bank and Government are producers of the high-powered money and the commercial banks do not have any role in producing this high-powered money (H). However, commercial banks are producers of demand deposits which are also used as money like currency.

But for producing demand deposits or credit, banks have to keep with themselves cash reserves of currency which have been denoted by R in equation ($H = C_p + R$) above. Since these cash reserves with the banks serve as a basis for the multiple creations of demand deposits which constitute an important part of total money supply in the economy, it provides high-powered-ness to the currency issued by Reserve Bank and Government.

A glance at equations ($M = C_p + D$) and ($H = C_p + R$) above will reveal that the difference in the two equations, one describing the total money supply and the other high-powered money, is that whereas in the former, demand deposits (D) are added to the currency held by the public, in the latter it is cash reserves (R) of the banks that are added to the currency held by the public.

In fact, it is against these cash reserves (R) that banks are able to create a multiple expansion of credit or demand deposits due to which there is large expansion in money supply in the economy. The theory of determination of money supply is based on the supply of and demand for high- powered money.

Some economists therefore call it 'The H Theory of Money Supply'. However, it is more popularly called 'Money-multiplier Theory of Money Supply' because it explains the determination of money supply as a certain multiple of the high- powered money. How the high-powered money (H) is related to the total money supply is graphically depicted in Figure.

The base of this figure shows the supply of high-powered money (H), while the top of the figure shows the total stock of money supply. It will be seen that the total stock of money supply (that is, the top) is determined by a multiple of the high-powered money (H). It will be further seen that whereas currency held by the public (C_p) uses the same amount of high-powered money, that is, there is one-to-one relationship between currency held by the public and the money supply.

In sharp contrast to this, bank deposits (D) are a multiple of the cash reserves (R) of the banks which are part of the supply of high-powered money. That is, one rupee of high- powered money kept as bank reserves gives rise to much more amount of demand deposits. Thus, the relationship between money supply and the high-powered money is determined by the money multiplier.

The money multiplier which we denote by m is the ratio of total money supply (M) to the stock of high-powered money, that is, m = M/H. The size of money multiplier depends on the preference of the public to hold currency relative to deposits, (that is, ratio of currency to deposits which we denote by K) and banks' desired cash reserves ratio to deposits which we call r. We explain below the precise multiplier relationship between high-powered money and the total stock of money supply.

In sharp contrast to this, bank deposits (D) are a multiple of the cash reserves (R) of the banks which are part of the supply of high-powered money. That is, one rupee of high- powered money kept as bank reserves gives rise to much more amount of demand deposits. Thus, the relationship between money supply and the high-powered money is determined by the money multiplier.

The money multiplier which we denote by m is the ratio of total money supply (M) to the stock of high-powered money, that is, m = M/H. The size of money multiplier depends on the preference of the public to hold currency relative to deposits, (that is, ratio of currency to deposits which we denote by K) and banks' desired cash reserves ratio to deposits which we call r. We explain below the precise multiplier relationship between high-powered money and the total stock of money supply.

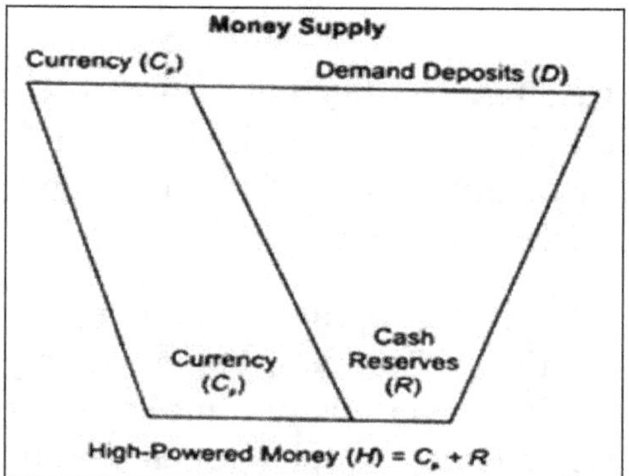

The high powered money and the stock of total money supply.

It follows from above that if there is increase in currency held by the public which is a part of the high-powered money with demand deposits remaining unchanged, there will be a direct increase in the money supply in the economy because this constitutes a part of the money supply.

If instead currency reserves held by the banks increase, this will not change the money supply immediately but will set in motion a process of multiple creation of demand deposits of the public in the banks. Although banks use these currency reserves held by the public which constitutes a part of the high- powered money to give more loans to the businessmen and thus create demand deposits, they do not affect either the amount of currency or the composition of high-powered money. The amount of high-powered money is fixed by banks by its past actions. Thus, changes in high-powered money are the result of decisions of banks to central bank or the Government which owns and controls it.

Money Multiplier

Money multiplier is the degree to which money supply is expanded as a result of the increase in high-powered money. Thus,

$$m = M/H$$

Rearranging we have, M = H.m.

Thus money supply is determined by the size of money multiplier (m) and the amount of high- powered money (H). If we know the value of money multiplier we can predict how much money will change when there is a change in the amount of high-powered money.

Change in the high-powered money is decided and controlled by banks to central bank, the money multiplier determines the extent to which decision by banks regarding the change in high-powered money will bring about change in the total money supply in the economy.

Size of Money Multiplier

Now, an important question is what determines the size of money multiplier. It is the cash or currency reserve ratio r of the banks (which determines deposit multiplier) and currency-deposit ratio of the public (which we denote by k) which together determines size of money multiplier. We derive below the expression for the size of multiplier.

From equation M = Cp + D above, we know that total money supply (M) consists of currency with the public (C_p) and demand deposits with the banks. Thus,

$$M = C_P + D$$

The public hold the amount of currency in a certain ratio of demand deposit with bank. Let this currency deposit ratio be devoted by k,

$$C_P = kD$$

Substituting kD for C_p in equation ($M = C_P + D$) we have,

$$M = kD + D = (k+1)D$$

Now take equation which defines high – powered money (H) as,

$$H = C_P + R$$

where R represent cash or currency reserve which banks keep as a certain ratio of their deposits and is called cash – reserve ratio and is denoted by r. Thus,

$$R = rD$$

Now substituting rD for R and kD for C_P in equation ($H = C_P + R$) we have,

$$H = kD + rD$$

$$H = (k+r)D$$

Now, money multiplier is ratio of total money supply to the high powered money, therefore we divide equation ($M = C_P + D$) by equation ($H = (k+r)D$), to get the value of multiplier, which we denoted by m. Thus,

$$m = \frac{M}{H} = \frac{(k+1)D}{(k+r)D} = \frac{k+1}{k+r}$$

Or, money multiplier $= \frac{M}{H} = \frac{I+k}{r+k}$

Or, $M = H = \frac{I+k}{r+k}$

Where,

- r = Cash-reserve ratio of the banks.
- k = Currency–deposit ratio of the public.

Where H is the high–powered money and $\frac{I+k}{r+k}$ is money multiplier.

From above it follows that money supply in the economy is determined by the following:

- H, that is, the amount of high-powered money, which is also called reserve money.
- r, that is, cash reserve ratio of banks (i. e., ratio of currency reserves to deposits of the banks). This cash reserve ratio of banks determines the magnitude of deposit multiplier.
- k, that is, currency-deposit ratio of the public.

From the equation $H = (k + r)D$ expressing the determinants of money supply, it follows that money supply will increase:

- When the supply of high-powered money (i.e., reserve money) H increases.
- When the currency-deposit ratio (k) of the public decreases.
- When the cash or currency reserves-deposit ratio of the banks (r) falls.

Cash Reserve Ratio of the Banks and the Deposit Multiplier

Because of fractional reserve system, with a small increase in cash reserves with the banks, they are able to create a multiple increase in total demand deposits which are an important part of money supply. The ratio of change in total deposits to a change in reserves is called the deposit multiplier which depends on cash reserve ratio.

The value of deposit multiplier is the reciprocal of cash reserve ratio, ($d_m = 1/r$) where d_m stands for deposit multiplier. If cash reserve ratio is 10 per cent of deposits, then $d_m = 1/0.10 = 10$. Thus deposit multiplier of 10 shows that for every Rs. 100 increase in cash reserves with the banks, there will be expansion in demand deposits of the banks by Rs. 1000 assuming that no leakage of cash to the public occurs during the process of deposit expansion by the banks.

Currency-Deposit Ratio of the Public and Money Multiplier

However, in the real world, with the increase in reserves of the banks, demand deposits and money supply do not increase to the full extent of deposit multiplier. This is for two reasons. First, the public does not hold all its money balances in the form of demand deposits with the banks.

When as a result of increase in cash reserves, banks start increasing demand deposits, the people may also like to have some more currency with them as money balances. This means during the process of creation of demand deposits by banks, some currency is leaked out from the banks to the people.

This drainage of currency to the people in the real world reduces the magnitude of expansion of demand deposit and therefore the size of money multiplier. Suppose the cash reserve ratio is 10 per cent and cash or currency of Rs. 100 is deposited in bank A. The bank A will lend out Rs. 90 and therefore create demand deposits of Rs. 90 and so the process will continue as the borrowers use these deposits for payment through cheques to others who deposit them in another bank B.

However, if borrower of bank A withdraws Rs. 10 in cash from the bank and issues cheques of the remaining borrowed amount of Rs. 80, then bank B will have only Rs. 80 as new deposits instead of Rs. 90 which it would have if cash of Rs. 10 was not withdrawn by the borrower. With these new deposits of Rs. 80, bank B will create demand deposits of Rs. 72, that is, it will lend out Rs. 72 and keep Rs. 8 as reserves with it ($80 \times 10/100 = 8$).

The drainage of currency may occur during all the subsequent stages of deposit expansion in the banking system. The greater the leakage of currency, the lower will be the money multiplier. We thus see that the currency-deposit ratio, which we denote by k, is an important determinant of the actual value of money multiplier.

It is important to note that deposit multiplier works both ways, positively when cash reserves with banks increase, and negatively when the cash reserves with the banks decline. That is, when there is a decrease in currency reserves with the banks, there will be multiple contraction in demand deposits with the banks.

Excess Reserves

In the explanation of the expansion of demand deposits or deposit multiplier we have assumed that banks do not keep currency reserves in excess of the required cash reserve ratio. The ratio r in the deposit multiplier is the required cash reserve ratio fixed.

However, banks may like to keep with themselves some excess reserves, the amount of which depends on the extent of liquidity (i.e. availability of cash with them) and profitability of making investment and rate of interest on loans advanced to business firms. Therefore, the desired reserve ratio is greater than the statutory minimum required reserve ratio. Obviously, the holding of excess reserves by the banks also reduces the value of deposit multiplier.

Interest Rate Determination

Interest Rate

An interest rate is the charge of borrowing money. Or if we view from other's perspective, it is the reimbursement for the service and risk of lending money. Without this incentive people would be unwilling to take risk and might be reluctant to lend or save money. Since interest rate is cost to the borrower and return to the lender, it affects the borrowing and lending, investment and saving, portfolio composition, selection of projects and their lives, capital-intensity of production techniques chosen, international capital flows, and distribution of income.

Marginal Productivity Theory

This theory simply states that the marginal productivity of capital determines the rate of interest. Interest is paid because capital is productive and is equal to the marginal product of capital. In the modern complex production system, the role of capital is very important as a producer can produce a much larger volume than what can be produced without capital.

Accordingly, the higher productivity of capital makes the interest higher. The converse is also true. So, a producer would employ capital up to that amount at which the rate of interest becomes equal to the value of the marginal product of capital.

However, like the marginal product of other factors, the marginal product of capital cannot be separately determined as every product is jointly produced by all the factors. Further-more the theory is one-sided as it emphasises only the demand side of capital for the determination of interest. Finally, the use of capital does not always increase total production as assumed in the theory.

Demand and Supply Theory

According to this theory, the demand for and the supply of capital jointly determine the rate of interest. The demand for capital is governed by its marginal product and the supply of capital by waiting or saving.

The rate of interest comes to the equilibrium position at the level at which the demand for capital becomes equal to its supply. But the theory is criticised on the ground that it assumes the existence of full employment which is a myth. Moreover, it fails to take into account the effect of changes in investment upon the level of income and savings.

Keynesian Theory

Demand for Money in a Two Asset Economy

In order to explain the DD for money and interest-rate determination, Keynes assumed an easy economy where there are two assets which people can retain in their in their portfolio balance. These two assets are: (1) money in the form of currency and demand deposits in the banks which earn no interest, (2) long term bonds. The interest rate and the bond prices are inversely related. When the bond prices go up, rate of interest rises and vice versa. The demand for money depends upon how they decide to balance their portfolios between money and bonds. This decision about the portfolio balance can be influenced by two factors.

First, the higher the level of nominal income in two asset economy people would want to hold more money in their portfolio balance. This happens because of transactions motive according to which at the high nominal income level, the purchases by the people of goods and services will be relatively high which require more money to be kept for transactions purposes.

Second, the higher the nominal rate of interest, lower the demand for money for speculative motive. This is firstly because a higher nominal rate of interest implies a higher opportunity cost for holding money. At higher rate of interest holders of money can earn more incomes by holding bonds instead of money. Secondly, if the current rate of interest is higher than what is expected in the future, the people would like to hold more bonds and less money in their portfolio. On the other hand, if the current rate of interest is low (in other words, if the bond prices are currently high), the people will be reluctant to hold larger quantity of bonds (and instead they could hold more money in their portfolio) for the fear that bond prices would fall in the future causing capital losses to them.

Money Demand Curve

It follows from the above that quantity of money demanded increases with the fall in the rate of interest or with the increase in the level of nominal income. At a given level of nominal income, we can draw a money demand curve showing the quantity of money demanded at various rates of interest. As demand for money is inversely related to the rate of interest, the money demand curve at a given level of income say will be downward sloping as shown by the curve LP_1 in Figure. When the level of money income increases, suppose from Y_1 to Y_2, the curve of demand for money shifts upward to the new position LP_2.

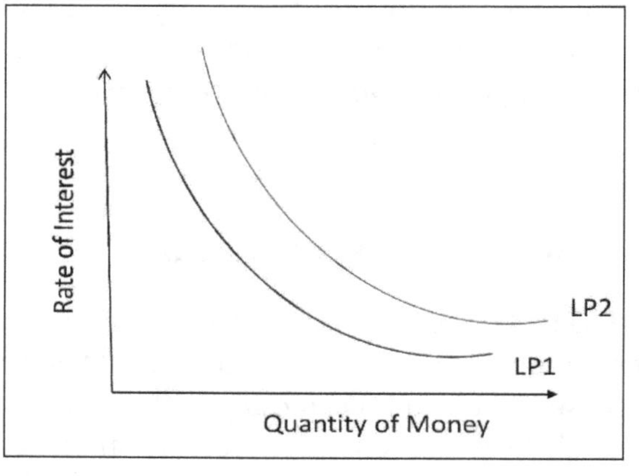

Determination of Rate of Interest: Equilibrium in the Money Market

The rate of interest, according to J.M. Keynes, is determined by DD for money (Liquidity Preference) and the SS of money. The factors which decide DD for money has been explained above. The supply of money, at a given time, is fixed by the monetary authority of the country.

In figure LP is the DD curve for money at a given level of nominal income. MS is the money supply curve which is a upright straight line showing that 200 cr. is the Fixed money supply by the authority. It will be seen that quantity demanded of money equals the given money supply at 10 % interest rate. Thus, the disequilibrium will arise if interest rate deviates from 10%.

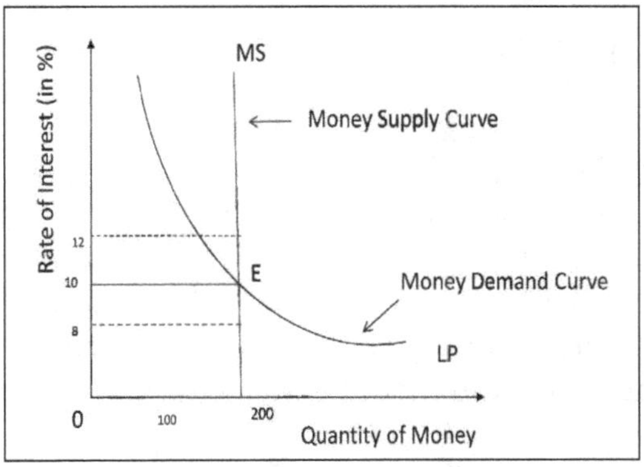

Let us also see the effect of change in money supply on the rate of interest. Suppose the money supply increases from ON to ON. With initial equilibrium at or, there emerges excess SS money as a result of this people would want to buy more bonds. As a result, the bond prices will go up which implies that the rate of interest will decline. Thus an increase in money supply leads to the fall in rate of interest.

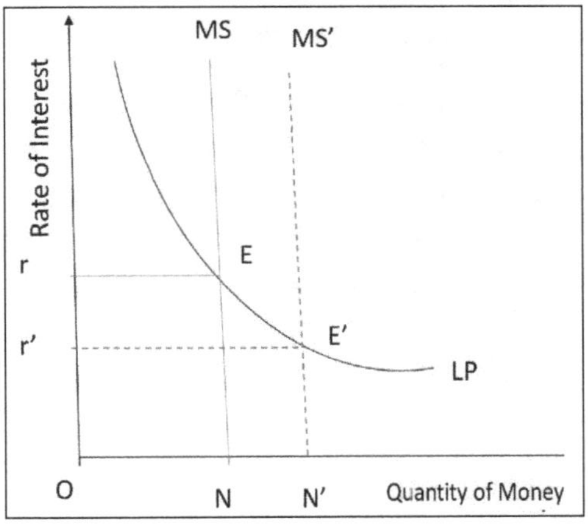

Loanable Funds Theory

The market for loanable funds consists of arrangements and procedures to carry out transactions between people who want to borrow money and people who want to lend money.

Demand

The demand for loanable funds originates from two basic units of the economy— consumers and business firms.

1. Consumers demand loanable funds because they prefer current goods to the same

amount of future goods. On average, people have a positive rate of time preference. This simply means that people subjectively value goods obtainable in the immediate or near future (including the present) more highly than goods obtained in the distant future. Most people would prefer to have a new television set today rather than the same or a better set after ten years.

There is nothing unusual about a positive rate of time preference. In a world characterised by uncertainty most people prefer the reality of current consumption to the uncertainty of some large amount (in physical or monetary terms) of future consumption. As the old saying goes: "A bird in hand is worth two in the bush." Consumers are also ready to pay interest for earlier availability of durable goods like cars or refrigerators. Thus, from consumers' point of view, interest is the cost of easier and earlier availability of goods.

2. Business firms or investors demand loanable funds because they are a form of capital (i.e., money capital). Capital is demanded because it is productive. Capital makes other factors more productive. In other words, investors demand loanable funds so that they can invest in capital goods and finance roundabout methods of production. Such methods of production are usually more productive than simple methods of production. Since roundabout methods of production often make it possible to produce a larger output at a lower cost, investors can gain, even if they pay interest to purchase the machines, buildings and other resources required by the production process.

Thus, an investor's demand for loanable funds arises due to the productivity of the capital investment. An increase in the rate of interest is, in essence, an increase in the cost of larger availability of consumption goods made possible by a machine. As Figure below shows, consumers and investors would borrow more at low rates of interest (or curtail their borrowings in response to increase in the rate of interest). Likewise, some investment projects that would now lead to gain at a lower interest rate will not be profitable at higher rates. Thus, the amount of loanable funds demanded varies inversely with the rate of interest.

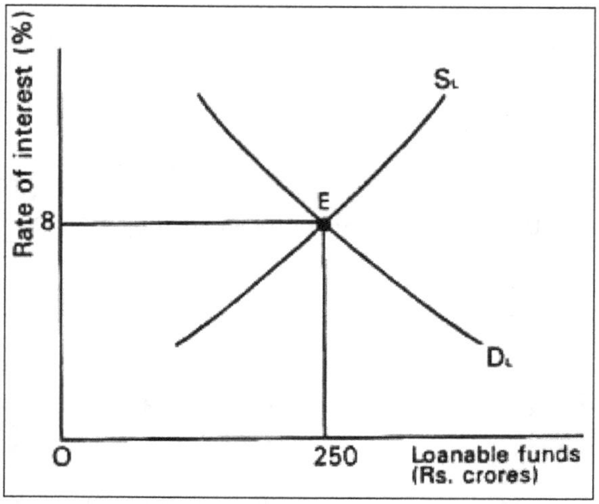

Interest rate determination.

Supply

Even though higher interest rates lead to a fall in the amount of borrowing by consumers and investors, they encourage lenders to make a larger volume of funds available to the market. Even individuals with a positive rate of time preference will curtail current consumption to supply more loanable funds in the market if the rate of interest is reasonably high or sufficiently attractive.

People, no doubt, prefer current (earlier) consumption to future (deferred) consumption. But they also prefer more goods to few goods. So they are ready to sacrifice current consumption if they expect to get more consumption goods in exchange at some future date.

A rise in the rate of interest increases the quantity of future goods available to people willing to sacrifice current consumption. This increase in the quantity of future goods that can be acquired for each rupee supplied can be showed on a supply curve that slopes upward from left to right.

In figure, the demand curve for loanable funds intersects the supply curve at point E and the equilibrium rate of interest (8%) is automatically determined (by market forces). The interest rate (8%) brings the plans of borrowers in harmony with the plans of lenders. In equilibrium, the quantity of funds demanded by borrowers is equal to the amount supplied by lenders ($250 millions) as figure shows.

Criticisms of Loanable Funds

Three major criticisms of the loanable funds are:

- The classical writers noted the effect of money on the rate of interest through the saving-investment process. Hence the loanable funds theory is not a new theory.
- Secondly, the loanable funds theory ignores certain real forces exerting influence on the rate of interest such as the marginal productivity of capital, the abstinence, and time preference.
- In most modern economics, the rate of interest is not determined by the market forces, i.e., by the forces of demand and supply. Instead, it is determined by institutional forces, i.e., by the policies and actions of the central bank and the government. Their policies exert the most important influence on the rate of interest by determining both the demand for and supply of loanable funds-in the country.
- Indeterminate rate of interest: The rate of interest, as pointed out by Keynes, remains indeterminate in the theory as the supply of loanable funds cannot be ascertained without knowing the level of income.
- Interest is not the reward of saving: Interest cannot be regarded as the reward for savings as savings in the form of idle cash balances do not bring any interest.

References

- Money-multiplier-and-reserve-ratio-in-us: economicshelp.org, Retrieved 20, April 2020
- Money-supply-importance-concepts-determinants-and-everything-else-10477: economicsdiscussion.net, Retrieved 07, August 2020
- Theories-for-determining-the-rate-of-interest-12646: economicsdiscussion.net, Retrieved 24, February 2020

4

Understanding Supply and Demand

The quantity of a product produced or producers wish to sell is known as supply. The quantity that consumers want to buy is known as demand. This chapter includes some aspects of supply and demand such as law of supply, law of demand, demand curve and economic equilibrium, etc. The topics elaborated in this chapter will help in gaining a better perspective about supply and demand.

In microeconomics, supply and demand is an economic model of price determination in a market. It concludes that in a competitive market, the unit price for a particular good, or other traded item such as labor or liquid financial assets, will vary until it settles at a point where the quantity demanded (at the current price) will equal the quantity supplied (at the current price), resulting in an economic equilibrium for price and quantity transacted.

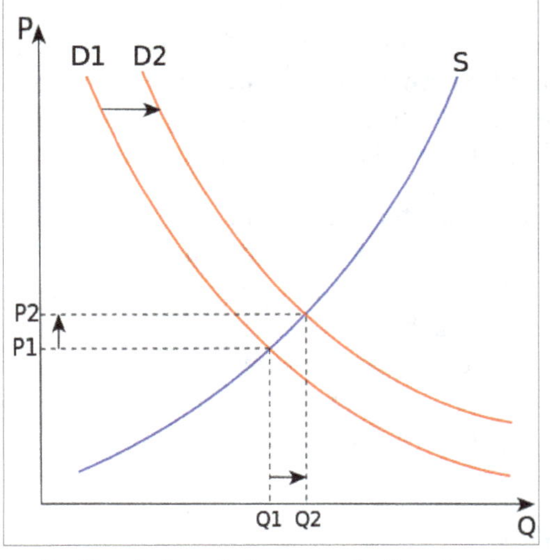

The price P of a product is determined by a balance between production at each price (supply S) and the desires of those with purchasing power at each price (demand D). The diagram shows a positive shift in demand from D_1 to D_2, resulting in an increase in price (P) and quantity sold (Q) of the product.

Graphical Representation of Supply and Demand

Although it is normal to regard the quantity demanded and the quantity supplied as functions of the price of the goods, the standard graphical representation, usually attributed to Alfred Marshall, has price on the vertical axis and quantity on the horizontal axis.

Since determinants of supply and demand other than the price of the goods in question are not explicitly represented in the supply-demand diagram, changes in the values of these variables are represented by moving the supply and demand curves (often described as "shifts" in the curves). By contrast, responses to changes in the price of the good are represented as movements along unchanged supply and demand curves.

Supply Schedule

A supply schedule is a table that shows the relationship between the price of a good and the quantity supplied. Under the assumption of perfect competition, supply is determined by marginal cost. That is, firms will produce additional output while the cost of producing an extra unit of output is less than the price they would receive.

A hike in the cost of raw goods would decrease supply, shifting costs up, while a discount would increase supply, shifting costs down and hurting producers as producer surplus decreases.

By its very nature, conceptualizing a supply curve requires the firm to be a perfect competitor (i.e. to have no influence over the market price). This is true because each point on the supply curve is the answer to the question "If this firm is *faced with* this potential price, how much output will it be able to and willing to sell?" If a firm has market power, its decision of how much output to provide to the market influences the market price, therefore the firm is not "faced with" any price, and the question becomes less relevant.

Economists distinguish between the supply curve of an individual firm and between the market supply curve. The market supply curve is obtained by summing the quantities supplied by all suppliers at each potential price. Thus, in the graph of the supply curve, individual firms' supply curves are added horizontally to obtain the market supply curve.

Economists also distinguish the short-run market supply curve from the long-run market supply curve. In this context, two things are assumed constant by definition of the short run: the availability of one or more fixed inputs (typically physical capital), and the number of firms in the industry. In the long run, firms have a chance to adjust their holdings of physical capital, enabling them to better adjust their quantity supplied at any given price. Furthermore, in the long run potential competitors can enter or exit the industry in response to market conditions. For both of these reasons, long-run market supply curves are generally flatter than their short-run counterparts.

The determinants of supply are:

1. Production costs: how much a goods costs to be produced. Production costs are the cost of the inputs; primarily labor, capital, energy and materials. They depend on the technology used in production, and/or technological advances.
2. Firms' expectations about future prices.
3. Number of suppliers.

Demand Schedule

A demand schedule, depicted graphically as the demand curve, represents the amount of some goods that buyers are willing and able to purchase at various prices, assuming all determinants of demand other than the price of the good in question, such as income, tastes and preferences, the price of substitute goods, and the price of complementary goods, remain the same. Following the law of demand, the demand curve is almost always represented as downward-sloping, meaning that as price decreases, consumers will buy more of the good.

Just like the supply curves reflect marginal cost curves, demand curves are determined by marginal utility curves. Consumers will be willing to buy a given quantity of a good, at a given price, if the marginal utility of additional consumption is equal to the opportunity cost determined by the price, that is, the marginal utility of alternative consumption choices. The demand schedule is defined as the *willingness* and *ability* of a consumer to purchase a given product in a given frame of time.

It is aforementioned, that the demand curve is generally downward-sloping, there may be rare examples of goods that have upward-sloping demand curves. Two different hypothetical types of goods with upward-sloping demand curves are Giffen goods (an inferior but staple good) and Veblen goods (goods made more fashionable by a higher price).

By its very nature, conceptualizing a demand curve requires that the purchaser be a perfect competitor—that is, that the purchaser has no influence over the market price. This is true because each point on the demand curve is the answer to the question "If this buyer is *faced with* this potential price, how much of the product will it purchase?" If a buyer has market power, so its decision of how much to buy influences the market price, then the buyer is not "faced with" any price, and the question is meaningless.

Like with supply curves, economists distinguish between the demand curve of an individual and the market demand curve. The market demand curve is obtained by summing the quantities demanded by all consumers at each potential price. Thus, in the graph of the demand curve, individuals' demand curves are added horizontally to obtain the market demand curve.

The determinants of demand are:

1. Income.
2. Tastes and preferences.
3. Prices of related goods and services.
4. Consumers' expectations about future prices and incomes that can be checked.
5. Number of potential consumers.

Microeconomics

Generally speaking, an equilibrium is defined to be the price-quantity pair where the quantity demanded is equal to the quantity supplied. It is represented by the intersection of the demand and supply curves. The analysis of various equilibria is a fundamental aspect of microeconomics:

Market Equilibrium: A situation in a market when the price is such that the quantity demanded by consumers is correctly balanced by the quantity that firms wish to supply. In this situation, the market clears.

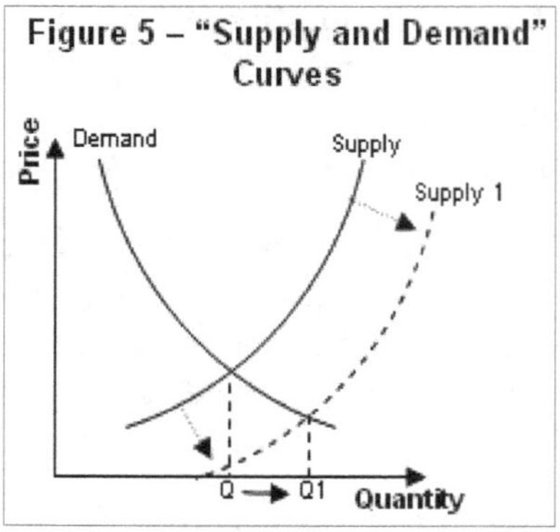

Equilibrium

Changes in market equilibrium: Practical uses of supply and demand analysis often center on the different variables that change equilibrium price and quantity, represented as shifts in the respective curves. Comparative statics of such a shift traces the effects from the initial equilibrium to the new equilibrium.

Demand Curve Shifts

When consumers increase the quantity demanded *at a given price*, it is referred to as an *increase in demand*. Increased demand can be represented on the graph as the curve being shifted to the right. At each price point, a greater quantity is demanded, as from the initial curve D1 to the new curve D2. In the diagram, this raises the equilibrium price from P1 to the higher P2. This raises the equilibrium quantity from Q1 to the higher Q2. A movement along the curve is described as a "change in the quantity demanded" to distinguish it from a "change in demand," that is, a shift of the curve. there has been an *increase* in demand which has caused an increase in (equilibrium) quantity. The increase in demand could also come from changing tastes and fashions, incomes, price changes in complementary and substitute goods, market expectations, and number of buyers. This would cause the entire demand curve to shift changing the equilibrium price and quantity. Note in the diagram that the shift of the demand curve, by causing a new equilibrium price to emerge, resulted in *movement along* the supply curve from the point (Q_1, P_1) to the point (Q_2, P_2).

If the *demand decreases*, then the opposite happens: a shift of the curve to the left. If the demand starts at D2, and *decreases* to D1, the equilibrium price will decrease, and the equilibrium quantity will also decrease. The quantity supplied at each price is the same as before the demand shift, reflecting the fact that the supply curve has not shifted; but the equilibrium quantity and price are different as a result of the change (shift) in demand.

Supply Curve Shifts

When technological progress occurs, the supply curve shifts. For example, assume that someone invents a better way of growing wheat so that the cost of growing a given quantity of wheat decreases. Otherwise stated, producers will be willing to supply more wheat at every price and this shifts the supply curve S1 outward, to S2—an *increase in supply*. This increase in supply causes the equilibrium price to decrease from P1 to P2. The equilibrium quantity increases from Q1 to Q2 as consumers move along the demand curve to the new lower price. As a result of a supply curve shift, the price and the quantity move in opposite directions. If the quantity supplied *decreases*, the opposite happens. If the supply curve starts at S2, and shifts leftward to S1, the equilibrium price will increase and the equilibrium quantity will decrease as consumers move along the demand curve to the new higher price and associated lower quantity demanded. The quantity demanded at each price is the same as before the supply shift, reflecting the fact that the demand curve has not shifted. But due to the change (shift) in supply, the equilibrium quantity and price have changed.

The movement of the supply curve in response to a change in a non-price determinant of supply is caused by a change in the y-intercept, the constant term of the supply equation. The supply curve shifts up and down the y axis as non-price determinants of demand change.

Partial Equilibrium

Partial equilibrium, as the name suggests, takes into consideration only a part of the market to attain equilibrium.

Jain proposes (attributed to George Stigler): "A partial equilibrium is one which is based on only a restricted range of data, a standard example is price of a single product, the prices of all other products being held fixed during the analysis."

The supply-and-demand model is a **partial equilibrium** model of economic equilibrium, where the clearance on the market of some specific goods is obtained independently from prices and quantities in other markets. In other words, the prices of all substitutes and complements, as well as income levels of consumers are constant. This makes analysis much simpler than in a general equilibrium model which includes an entire economy.

Here the dynamic process is that prices adjust until supply equals demand. It is a powerfully simple technique that allows one to study equilibrium, efficiency and comparative statics. The stringency of the simplifying assumptions inherent in this approach make the model considerably more tractable, but may produce results which, while seemingly precise, do not effectively model real world economic phenomena.

Partial equilibrium analysis examines the effects of policy action in creating equilibrium only in that particular sector or market which is directly affected, ignoring its effect in any other market or industry assuming that they being small will have little impact if any.

Hence this analysis is considered to be useful in constricted markets.

Léon Walras first formalized the idea of a one-period economic equilibrium of the general economic system, but it was French economist Antoine Augustin Cournot and English political economist Alfred Marshall who developed tractable models to analyze an economic system.

Other Markets

The model of supply and demand also applies to various specialty markets.

The model is commonly applied to wages, in the market for labor. The typical roles of supplier and demander are reversed. The suppliers are individuals, who try to sell their labor for the highest price. The demanders of labor are businesses, which try to buy the type of labor they need at the lowest price. The equilibrium price for a certain type of labor is the wage rate.

A number of economists (for example Pierangelo Garegnani, Robert L. Vienneau, and Arrigo Opocher & Ian Steedman), building on the work of Piero Sraffa, argue that this model of the labor market, even given all its assumptions, is logically incoherent. Michael Anyadike-Danes and Wyne Godley argue, based on simulation results, that little of the empirical work done with the textbook model constitutes a potentially falsifying test, and, consequently, empirical evidence hardly exists for that model.

This criticism of the application of the model of supply and demand generalizes, particularly to all markets for factors of production.

In both classical and Keynesian economics, the money market is analyzed as a supply-and-demand system with interest rates being the price. The money supply may be a vertical supply curve, if the central bank of a country chooses to use monetary policy to fix its value regardless of the interest rate; in this case the money supply is totally inelastic. On the other hand, the money supply curve is a horizontal line if the central bank is targeting a fixed interest rate and ignoring the value of the money supply; in this case the money supply curve is perfectly elastic. The demand for money intersects with the money supply to determine the interest rate.

Empirical Estimation

Demand and supply relations in a market can be statistically estimated from price, quantity, and other data with sufficient information in the model. This can be done with *simultaneous-equation methods of estimation* in econometrics. Such methods allow solving for the model-relevant "structural coefficients," the estimated algebraic counterparts of the theory. The *Parameter identification problem* is a common issue in "structural estimation." Typically, data on exogenous variables (that is, variables other than price and quantity, both of which are endogenous variables) are needed to perform such an estimation. An alternative to "structural estimation" is reduced-form estimation, which regresses each of the endogenous variables on the respective exogenous variables.

Macroeconomic Uses of Demand and Supply

Demand and supply have also been generalized to explain macroeconomic variables in a market economy, including the quantity of total output and the general price level. The Aggregate Demand-Aggregate Supply model may be the most direct application of supply and demand to macroeconomics, but other macroeconomic models also use supply and demand. Compared to microeconomic uses of demand and supply, different (and more controversial) theoretical considerations apply to such macroeconomic counterparts as aggregate demand and aggregate supply. Demand and supply are also used in macroeconomic theory to relate money supply and money demand to interest rates, and to relate labor supply and labor demand to wage rates.

History

According to Hamid S. Hosseini, the power of supply and demand was understood to some extent by several early Muslim scholars, such as fourteenth-century Syrian scholar Ibn Taymiyyah, who wrote: "If desire for goods increases while its availability decreases, its price rises. On the other hand, if availability of the good increases and the desire for it decreases, the price comes down."

> "If desire for goods increases while its availability decreases, its price rises. On the other hand, if availability of the good increases and the desire for it decreases, the price comes down."
>
> — *Ibn Taymiyyah*,

Adam Smith

John Locke's 1691 work *Some Considerations on the Consequences of the Lowering of Interest and the Raising of the Value of Money.* includes an early and clear description of supply and demand and their relationship. In this description demand is rent: "The price of any commodity rises or falls by the proportion of the number of buyer and sellers" and "that which regulates the price... [of goods] is nothing else but their quantity in proportion to their rent."

The phrase "supply and demand" was first used by James Denham-Steuart in his *Inquiry into the Principles of Political Economy*, published in 1767. Adam Smith used the phrase in his 1776 book *The Wealth of Nations*, and David Ricardo titled one chapter of his 1817 work *Principles of Political Economy and Taxation* "On the Influence of Demand and Supply on Price".

In *The Wealth of Nations*, Smith generally assumed that the supply price was fixed but that its "merit" (value) would decrease as its "scarcity" increased, in effect what was later called the law of demand also. Ricardo, in *Principles of Political Economy and Taxation*, more rigorously laid down the idea of the assumptions that were used to build his ideas of supply and demand. Antoine Augustin Cournot first developed a mathematical model of supply and demand in his 1838 *Researches into the Mathematical Principles of Wealth*, including diagrams.

During the late 19th century the marginalist school of thought emerged. This field mainly was started by Stanley Jevons, Carl Menger, and Léon Walras. The key idea was that the price was set by the most expensive price, that is, the price at the margin. This was a substantial change from Adam Smith's thoughts on determining the supply price.

In his 1870 essay "On the Graphical Representation of Supply and Demand", Fleeming Jenkin in the course of "introduc[ing] the diagrammatic method into the English economic literature" published the first drawing of supply and demand curves therein, including comparative statics from a shift of supply or demand and application to the labor market. The model was further developed and popularized by Alfred Marshall in the 1890 textbook *Principles of Economics*.

Criticisms

The philosopher Hans Albert has argued that the ceteris paribus conditions of the marginalist theory rendered the theory itself an empty tautology and completely closed to experimental testing. In essence, he argues, the supply and demand curves (theoretical functions which express the quantity of a product which would be offered or requested for a given price) are purely ontological.

Cambridge economist Joan Robinson attacked the theory in similar line, arguing that the concept is circular: "Utility is the quality in commodities that makes individuals want to buy them, and the fact that individuals want to buy commodities shows that they have utility" Robinson also point-ed out that because the theory assumes that preferences are fixed this means that utility is not a testable assumption. This is because if we take changes in peoples' behavior in relation to a change in prices or a change in the underlying budget constraint we can never be sure to what extent the change in behavior was due to the change in price or budget constraint and how much was due to a change in preferences.

Even in practical terms, neither cardinal nor ordinal utility is empirically observable in the real world. In the case of cardinal utility, it is impossible to measure the level of satisfaction "quantitatively" when someone consumes or purchases an apple. In case of ordinal utility, it is impossible to determine what choices were made when someone purchases, for example, an orange. Any act would involve preference over a vast set of choices (such as apple, orange juice, other vegetable, vitamin C tablets, exercise, not purchasing, etc.).

At least two assumptions are necessary for the validity of the standard model: first, that supply and demand are independent; second, that supply is "constrained by a fixed resource". If these conditions do not hold, then the Marshallian model cannot be sustained. Sraffa's critique focused on the inconsistency (except in implausible circumstances) of partial equilibrium analysis and the rationale for the upward slope of the supply curve in a market for a produced consumption good. The notability of Sraffa's critique is also demonstrated by Paul A. Samuelson's comments and engagements with it over many years, for example:

> "What a cleaned-up version of Sraffa (1926) establishes is how *nearly empty* are *all* of Marshall's partial equilibrium boxes. To a logical purist of Wittgenstein and Sraffa class, the *Marshallian partial* equilibrium box of *constant* cost is even more empty than the box of *increasing* cost.".

Aggregate excess demand in a market is the difference between the quantity demanded and the quantity supplied as a function of price. In the model with an upward-sloping supply curve and downward-sloping demand curve, the aggregate excess demand function only intersects the axis at one point, namely, at the point where the supply and demand curves intersect. The Sonnenschein–Mantel–Debreu theorem shows that the standard model cannot be rigorously derived in general from general equilibrium theory.

The model of prices being determined by supply and demand assumes perfect competition. But:

> "economists have no adequate model of how individuals and firms adjust prices in a competitive model. If all participants are price-takers by definition, then the actor who adjusts prices to eliminate excess demand is not specified".

Goodwin, Nelson, Ackerman, and Weisskopf write:

> "If we mistakenly confuse precision with accuracy, then we might be misled into thinking that an explanation expressed in precise mathematical or graphical terms is somehow more rigorous or useful than one that takes into account particulars of history, institutions or business strategy. This is not the case. Therefore, it is important not to put too much confidence in the apparent precision of supply and demand graphs. Supply and demand analysis is a useful precisely formulated conceptual tool that clever people have devised to help us gain an abstract understanding of a complex world. It does not—nor should it be expected to—give us in addition an accurate and complete description of any particular real world market."

E. F. Schumacher challenges the prevailing economic assumption that fulfilling demand is the purpose of economic activity, offering a framework of what he calls "Buddhist economics" in which wise demands, fulfilling genuine human needs, are distinguished from unwise demands, arising from the five intellectual impairments recognized by Buddhism:

The cultivation and expansion of needs is the antithesis of wisdom. It is also the antithesis of freedom and peace. Every increase of needs tends to increase one's dependence on outside forces over which one cannot have control, and therefore increases existential fear. Only by a reduction of needs can one promote a genuine reduction in those tensions which are the ultimate causes of strife and war.

Law of Supply

The **law of supply** is a fundamental principle of economic theory which states that, all else equal, an increase in price results in an increase in quantity supplied. In other words, there is a direct relationship between price and quantity: quantities respond in the same direction as price changes. This means that producers are willing to offer more products for sale on the market at higher prices y increasing production as a way of increasing profits.

In short, Law of Supply is a positive relationship between quantity supplied and price and is the reason for the upward slope of the supply curve. When the supply goes down, the price increases.

Mathematical Definition

In non-differentiable terms, the law of supply can be expressed as:

$$(p-p')(y-y')\geq 0,$$

where y is the amount that would be supplied at some price p, and y' is the amount that would be supplied at some other price p'. Thus for example if $p > p'$ then $y > y'$.

Law of Demand

In economics, the law of demand states that," all else being equal, as the price of a product increases **(↑)**, quantity demanded falls **(↓)**; likewise, as the price of a product decreases **(↓)**, quantity demanded increases **(↑)**". In simple terms, the law of demand describes an inverse relationship, and an elasticity, between price and quantity of demand. There is a negative relationship between the quantity demanded of a good and its price. The factors held constant in this relationship are the prices of other goods and the consumer's income. There are, however, some possible exceptions to the law of demand.

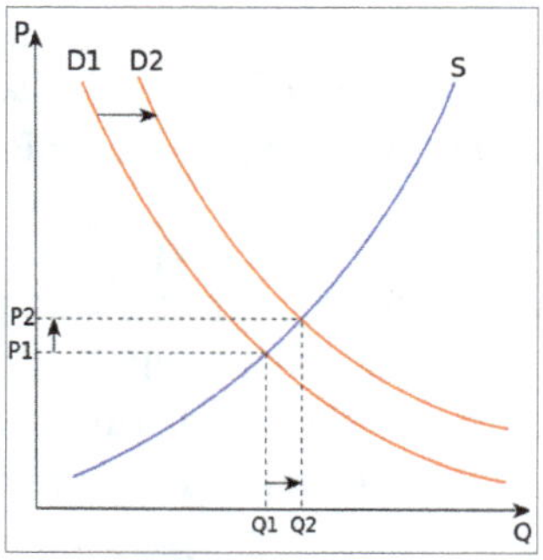

A demand curve, shown in red and shifting to the right, demonstrating the inverse relationship between price and quantity demanded (the curve slopes downwards from left to right; higher prices reduce the quantity demanded).

Mathematical Expression

Mathematically, the inverse relationship may be expressed as a causal relation:

$$Q_x = f(P_x), \quad f' < 0,$$

where Q_x is the quantity demanded of good x, P_x is the price of the good, f is the demand function, and f' is its derivative.

Here, P_x is the causal factor (independent variable) and Q_x Is the dependent variable.

Graphical Depiction

A demand curve is a graphical depiction that abides by the law of demand. It shows how the quantity demanded of some product during a specified period of time will change as the price of that product changes, holding all other determinants of the quantity demanded constant. Price is measured on the vertical axis and quantity demanded on the horizontal axis.

There are two important things to note about the demand curve:

- It is downward sloping indicating that between the price of a product and the quantity demanded a negative or inverse relationship exists. In other words, as the price declines the quantity demanded increases. This is indicated by a downward movement along the demand curve. An increase in price decreases the quantity demanded, and an upward movement along the demand curve occurs.

- The movement along a given demand curve due to a change in price is referred to as "change in quantity demanded". (i:e demand changes as only the price changes, and diagrammatically, there is only one demand curve,with the movement noticeable between points) the price changes, the quantity demanded changes. The term "change in demand" refers to a shift of the demand curve because of factors other than price(in the which case, prices, incomes of consumers, government policies,seasons and weather, tastes,reigning fashion, festivals etc and other non-price factors determine/cause the demand curve to shift.Diagrammatically, new curves are drawn to show the shifts, aside from the other curves/readers should note this important distinction).

Exceptions to The Law of Demand

Generally the amount demanded of a good increases with a decrease in price of the good and vice versa. In some cases, however, this may not be true. There are certain goods which do not follow this law. These include Veblen goods and Giffen goods. Further exception and details are given in the sections below.

Giffen Goods

Initially proposed by Sir Robert Giffen, economists disagree on the existence of Giffen goods in the market. A Giffen good describes an inferior good that as the price increases, demand for the product increases. As an example, during the Irish Potato Famine of the 19th century, potatoes were considered a Giffen good. Potatoes were the largest staple in the Irish diet, so as the price rose it had a large impact on income. People responded by cutting out on luxury goods such as meat and vegetables, and instead bought more potatoes. Therefore, as the price of potatoes increased, so did the quantity demanded.

Expectation of Change in The Price of Commodity

If an increase in the price of a commodity causes households to expect the price of a commodity to increase further, they may start purchasing a greater amount of the commodity even at the presently increased price. Similarly, if the household expects the price of the commodity to decrease, it may postpone its purchases. Thus, some argue that the law of demand is violated in such cases. In this case, the demand curve does not slope down from left to right; instead it presents a backward slope from the top right to down left. This curve is known as an exceptional demand curve.

Basic or Necessary Goods

The goods which people need no matter how high the price is are basic or necessary goods. Medicines covered by insurance are a good example. An increase or decrease in the price of such a good does not affect its quantity demanded. These goods have a perfectly inelastic relationship, in that any change in price does not change the quantity demanded.

The Law of Demand and Change in Demand

The law of demand states that, other things remaining same, the quantity demanded of a good increases when its price falls and decreases when the price rises. This is represented by movement along the demand curve, since the product's price is on the vertical axis.

The demand for goods changes as a consequence of changes in income, tastes etc. Since these factors are not on the axes of the demand curve diagram, such a change is reflected in a shift of the demand curve to a new location. A shift of the demand curve is referred to as a *change in demand*, in contrast to a movement along a fixed demand curve, which is referred to as a *change in the quantity demanded*.

Demand Curve

In economics, the **demand curve** is the graph depicting the relationship between the price of a certain commodity and the amount of it that consumers are willing and able to purchase at any given price. It is a graphic representation of a demand schedule. The demand curve for all consumers together follows from the demand curve of every individual consumer: the individual demands at each price are multiplied together.

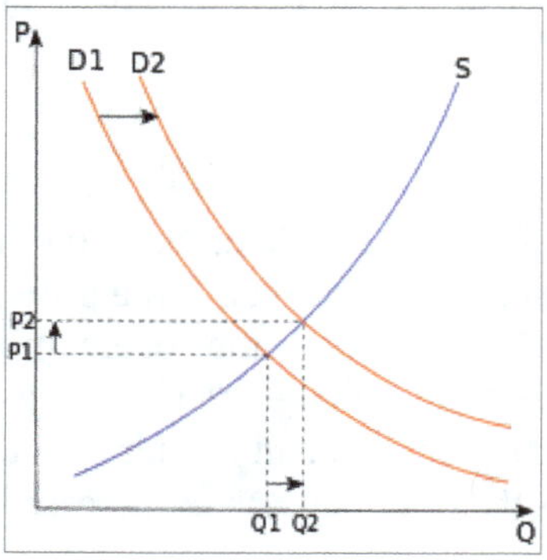

An example of a demand curve shifting. The shift from D1 To D2 means an increase in demand with consequences for the other variables.

Demand curves are used to estimate behaviors in competitive markets, and are often combined with supply curves to estimate the equilibrium price (the price at which sellers together are willing to sell the same amount as buyers together are willing to buy, also known as market clearing price) and the equilibrium quantity (the amount of that good or service that will be produced and bought without surplus/excess supply or shortage/excess demand) of that market. In a monopolistic market, the demand curve facing the monopolist is simply the market demand curve.

Demand curves are usually considered as theoretical structures that are expected to exist in the real world, but real world measurements of actual demand curves are difficult and rare.

Characteristics

According to convention, the demand curve is drawn with price on the vertical (y) axis and quantity on the horizontal (x) axis. The function actually plotted is the inverse demand function.

The demand curve usually slopes downwards from left to right; that is, it has a negative association. The negative slope is often referred to as the "law of demand", which means people will buy more of a service, product, or resource as its price falls.

The demand curve is related to the marginal utility curve, since the price one is willing to pay depends on the utility. However, the demand directly depends on the income of an individual while the utility does not. Thus it may change indirectly due to change in demand for other commodities.

Linear Demand Curve

The demand curve is often graphed as a straight line of the form Q = a – bP where a and b are parameters. The constant "a" embodies the effects of all factors other than price that affect demand. If income were to change, for example, the effect of the change would be represented by a change in the value of "a" and be reflected graphically as a shift of the demand curve. The constant "b" is the slope of the demand curve and shows how the price of the good affects the quantity demanded.

The graph of the demand curve uses the inverse demand function in which price is expressed as a function of quantity. The standard form of the demand equation can be converted to the inverse equation by solving for P or P = a/b – Q/b.

More plainly, in the equation P = a – bQ, "a" is the intercept where price is zero (where the demand curve intercepts the X-axis), "b" is the slope of the demand curve, "Q" is quantity and "P" is price.

Shift

The shift of a demand curve takes place when there is a change in any non-price determinant of demand, resulting in a new demand curve. Non-price determinants of demand are those things that will cause demand to change even if prices remain the same—in other words, the things whose changes might cause a consumer to buy more or less of a good even if the good's own price remained unchanged. Some of the more important factors are the prices of related goods (both substitutes and complements), income, population, and expectations. However, demand is the willingness and ability of a consumer to purchase a good *under the prevailing circumstances*; so, any circumstance that affects the consumer's willingness or ability to buy the good or service in question can be a non-price determinant of demand. As an example, weather could be a factor in the demand for beer at a baseball game.

When income increases, the demand curve for normal goods shifts outward as more will be demanded at all prices, while the demand curve for inferior goods shifts inward due to the increased attainability of superior substitutes. With respect to related goods, when the price of a good (e.g. a hamburger) rises, the demand curve for substitute goods (e.g. chicken) shifts out, while the demand curve for complementary goods (e.g. tomato sauce) shifts in (i.e. there is more demand for substitute goods as they become more attractive in terms of value for money, while demand for complementary goods contracts in response to the contraction of quantity demanded of the underlying good).

Demand Shifters

- Changes in disposable income, the magnitude of the shift also being related to the income elasticity of demand.
- Changes in tastes and preferences—tastes and preferences are assumed to be fixed in the

short-run. This assumption of fixed preferences is a necessary condition for aggregation of individual demand curves to derive market demand.

- Changes in expectations.
- Changes in the prices of related goods (substitutes and complements).
- Population size and composition.
- N.B. Whilst variations in the price of the actual product affects the overall quantity demanded, economists do not consider price to affect the demand curve.

Changes That Decrease Demand

Circumstances which can cause the demand curve to shift to the left include:

- Decrease in price of a substitute.
- Increase in price of a complement.
- Decrease in consumer income if the good is a normal good.
- Increase in consumer income if the good is an inferior good.

Factors Affecting Market Demand

Market or aggregate demand is the summation of individual demand curves. In addition to the factors which can affect individual demand there are three factors that can affect market demand (cause the market demand curve to shift):

- A change in the number of consumers,
- A change in the distribution of tastes among consumers,
- A change in the distribution of income among consumers with different tastes.

Some circumstances which can cause the demand curve to shift in include:

- Decrease in price of a substitute.
- Increase in price of a complement.
- Decrease in income if good is normal good.
- Increase in income if good is inferior good.

Movement Along A Demand Curve

There is movement *along* a demand curve when a change in price causes the quantity demanded to change. It is important to distinguish between movement along a demand curve, and a shift in a demand curve. Movements along a demand curve happen only when the price of the good changes. When a non-price determinant of demand changes the curve shifts. These "other variables" are part of the demand function. They are "merely lumped into intercept term of a simple linear demand function." Thus a change in a non-price determinant of demand is reflected in a change in the x-intercept causing the curve to shift along the x axis.

Discreteness of Amounts

If a commodity is sold in whole units, and these are valuable for a consumer, then the individual demand curve can hardly be approximated by a continuous curve. It is a set function of the price, defined by a price above which no unit is bought, a price range for which one is bought, etc.

Units of Measurement

If the local currency is dollars, for example, then the units of measurement of the variable "price" are "dollars per unit of the good" and the units of measurement of "quantity" are "units of the good per time (e.g., per week or per year). Thus quantity demanded is a flow variable.

Price Elasticity of Demand (PED)

PED is a measure of the sensitivity of the quantity variable, Q, to changes in the price variable, P. Elasticity answers the question of how much the quantity will change in percentage terms for a 1% change in the price, and is thus important in determining how revenue will change.

The elasticity of demand indicates how sensitive the demand for a good is to a price change. If the PED is between zero and 1, demand is said to be inelastic; if PED equals 1, the demand is unitary elastic; and if the Price elasticity of demand is greater than 1, demand is elastic. A low coefficient implies that changes in price have little influence on demand. A high elasticity indicates that consumers will respond to a price rise by buying a lot less of the good and that consumers will respond to a price cut by buying a lot more.

Taxes and Subsidies

A sales tax on the commodity does not directly change the demand curve, if the price axis in the graph represents the price including tax. Similarly, a subsidy on the commodity does not directly change the demand curve, if the price axis in the graph represents the price after deduction of the subsidy.

If the price axis in the graph represents the price before addition of tax and/or subtraction of subsidy then the demand curve moves inward when a tax is introduced, and outward when a subsidy is introduced.

Supply

In economics, **supply** is the amount of something that firms, consumers, laborers, providers of financial assets, or other economic agents are willing to provide to the marketplace. Supply is often plotted graphically with the quantity provided (the dependent variable) plotted horizontally and the price (the independent variable) plotted vertically.

In the goods market, supply is the amount of a product per unit of time that producers are willing to sell at various given prices when all other factors are held constant. In the labor market, the supply of labor is the amount of time per week, month, or year that individuals are willing to spend working, as a function of the wage rate. In the financial markets, the money supply is the amount of highly liquid assets available in the money market, which is either determined or influenced by a country's monetary authority.

The remainder of this article focuses on the supply of goods.

Supply Schedule

A supply schedule is a table which shows how much one or more firms will be willing to supply at particular prices under the existing circumstances. Some of the more important factors affecting supply are the good's own price, the prices of related goods, production costs, technology and expectations of sellers.

Factors Affecting Supply

Innumerable factors and circumstances could affect a seller's willingness or ability to produce and sell a good. Some of the more common factors are:

Good's own price: The basic supply relationship is between the price of a good and the quantity supplied. Although there is "Law of Supply", generally, the relationship is positive, meaning that an increase in price will induce an increase in the quantity supplied.

Prices of related goods: For purposes of supply analysis related goods refer to goods from which inputs are derived to be used in the production of the primary good. For example, Spam is made from pork shoulders and ham. Both are derived from pigs. Therefore pigs would be considered a related good to Spam. In this case the relationship would be negative or inverse. If the price of pigs goes up the supply of Spam would decrease (supply curve shifts left) because the cost of production would have increased. A related good may also be a good that can be produced with the firm's existing factors of production. For example, suppose that a firm produces leather belts, and that the firm's managers learn that leather pouches for smartphones are more profitable than belts. The firm might reduce its production of belts and begin production of cell phone pouches based on this information. Finally, a change in the price of a joint product will affect supply. For example beef products and anani sikim leather are joint products. If a company runs both a beef processing operation and a tannery an increase in the price of steaks would mean that more cattle are processed which would increase the supply of leather.

Conditions of production: The most significant factor here is the state of technology. If there is a technological advancement in one good's production, the supply increases. Other variables may also affect production conditions. For instance, for agricultural goods, weather is crucial for it may affect the production outputs.

Expectations: Sellers' concern for future market conditions can directly affect supply. If the seller believes that the demand for his product will sharply increase in the foreseeable future the firm owner may immediately increase production in anticipation of future price increases. The supply curve would shift out.

Price of inputs: Inputs include land, labor, energy and raw materials. If the price of inputs increases the supply curve will shift left as sellers are less willing or able to sell goods at any given price. For example, if the price of electricity increased a seller may reduce his supply of his product because of the increased costs of production.

Number of suppliers: The market supply curve is the horizontal summation of the individual supply curves. As more firms enter the industry the market supply curve will shift out driving down prices.

Government policies and regulations: Government intervention can have a signif-icant effect on supply. Government intervention can take many forms including environmental and health regulations, hour and wage laws, taxes, electrical and natural gas rates and zoning and land use regulations.

This list is not exhaustive. All facts and circumstances that are relevant to a seller's willingness or ability to produce and sell goods can affect supply. For example, if the forecast is for snow retail sellers will respond by increasing their stocks of snow sleds or skis or winter clothing or bread and milk.

Supply Function and Equation

The supply function is the mathematical expression of the relationship between supply and those factors that affect the willingness and ability of a supplier to offer goods for sale. An example would be the curve implied by $Q_s = f(P; P_{rg})$ where P is the price of the good and P_{rg} is the price of a related good. The semicolon means that the variables to the right are held constant when quantity supplied is plotted against the good's own price. The supply equation is the explicit mathematical expression of the functional relationship. A linear example is $Q_s = 325 + P - 30P_{rg}$.. Here 325 is the repository of all non-specified factors that affect supply for the product. The coefficient of P is positive following the general rule that price and quantity supplied are directly related. $P = f(Q)$. is the price of a related good. Typically its coefficient is negative because the related good is an input or a source of inputs.

Supply Curve

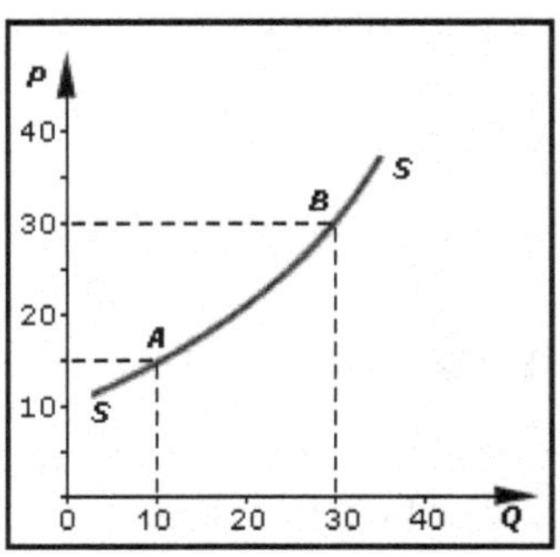

An example of a nonlinear supply curve.

The relationship of price and supply curve. The curve is generally positively sloped. The curve depicts the relationship between two variables only; price and quantity supplied. All other factors affecting supply are held constant. However, these factors are part of the supply equation and are implicitly present in the constant term.

Movements Versus Shifts

Movements along the curve occur only if there is a change in quantity supplied caused by a change in the good's own price. A shift in the supply curve, referred to as a change in supply, occurs only if a non-price determinant of supply changes. For example, if the price of an ingredient used to produce the good, a related good, were to increase, the supply curve would shift left.

Inverse Supply Equation

By convention in the context of supply and demand graphs, economists graph the dependent variable (quantity) on the horizontal axis and the independent variable (price) on the vertical axis. The *inverse supply equation* is the equation written with the vertical-axis variable isolated on the left side: $P = f(Q)$. As an example, if the supply equation is $Q = 40P - 2P_{rg}$ then the inverse supply equation would be $P = \frac{Q}{40} + \frac{P_{rg}}{20}$.

Marginal Costs and Short-run Supply Curve

A firm's short-run supply curve is the marginal cost curve above the shutdown point—the short-run marginal cost curve (SRMC) above the minimum average variable cost). The portion of the SRMC below the shutdown point is not part of the supply curve because the firm is not producing any output. The firm's long-run supply curve is that portion of the long-run marginal cost curve above the minimum of the long run average cost curve.

Shape of The Short-run Supply Curve

The Law of Diminishing Marginal Returns (LDMR) shapes the SRMC curve. The LDMR states that as production increases eventually a point (the point of diminishing marginal returns) will be reached after which additional units of output resulting from fixed increments of the labor input will be successively smaller. That is, beyond the point of diminishing marginal returns the marginal product of labor will continually decrease and hence a continually higher selling price would be necessary to induce the firm to produce more and more output.

From Firm to Market Supply Curve

The market supply curve is the horizontal summation of firm supply curves.

The Shape of The Market Supply Curve

There is no law of supply that "requires" that the market supply curve have a positive slope; the curve may slope down or up or be horizontal or vertical.

Elasticity

The price elasticity of supply (PES) measures the responsiveness of quantity supplied to changes in price, as the percentage change in quantity supplied induced by a one percent change in price. It is calculated for discrete changes as $\left(\frac{\Delta Q}{\Delta P}\right)\times\frac{P}{Q}$ and for smooth changes of differentiable supply functions as $\left(\frac{\partial Q}{\partial P}\right)\times\frac{P}{Q}$. Since supply is usually increasing in price, the price elasticity of supply is usually positive. For example, if the PES for a good is 0.67 a 1% rise in price will induce a two-thirds increase in quantity supplied.

Significant determinants include:

> Complexity of Production: Much depends on the complexity of the production process. Textile production is relatively simple. The labor is largely unskilled and production facilities are little more than buildings – no special structures are needed. Thus the PES for textiles is elastic. On the other hand, the PES for specific types of motor vehicles is relatively inelastic. Auto manufacture is a multi-stage process that requires specialized equipment, skilled labor, a large suppliers network and large R&D costs.
>
> Time to respond: The more time a producer has to respond to price changes the more elastic the supply. For example, a cotton farmer cannot immediately respond to an increase in the price of soybeans.
>
> Excess capacity: A producer who has unused capacity can quickly respond to price changes in his market assuming that variable factors are readily available.
>
> Inventories: A producer who has a supply of goods or available storage capacity can quickly respond to price changes.

Other elasticities can be calculated for non-price determinants of supply. For example, the percentage change the amount of the good supplied caused by a one percent increase in the price of a related good is an input elasticity of supply if the related good is an input in the production process. An example would be the change in the supply of cookies caused by a one percent increase in the price of sugar.

Elasticity Along Linear Supply Curves

The slope of a linear supply curve is constant; the elasticity is not. If the linear supply curve intersects the price axis PES will be infinitely elastic at the point of intersection. The coefficient of elasticity decreases as one moves "up" the curve. However, all points on the supply curve will have a coefficient of elasticity greater than one. If the linear supply curve intersects the quantity axis PES will equal zero at the point of intersection and will increase as one moves up the curve; however, all points on the curve will have a coefficient of elasticity less than 1. If the linear supply curve intersects the origin PES equals one at the point of origin and along the curve.

Market Structure and The Supply Curve

There is no such thing as a monopoly supply curve. Perfect competition is the only market structure for which a supply function can be derived. In a perfectly competitive market the price is given by the marketplace from the point of view of the supplier; a manager of a competitive firm can state what quantity of goods will be supplied for any price by simply referring to the firm's marginal cost curve. To generate his supply function the seller could simply initially hypothetically set the price equal to zero and then incrementally increase the price; at each price he could calculate the hypothetical quantity supplied using the marginal cost curve. Following this process the manager could trace out the complete supply function. A monopolist cannot replicate this process, because price is not imposed by the marketplace and hence is not an independent variable from the point of view of the firm; instead, the firm simultaneously chooses both the price and the quantity subject to the stipulation that together they form a point on the customers' demand curve. A change in demand can result in "changes in price with no changes in output, changes in output with no changes in price or both". There is simply not a one to one relationship between price and quantity supplied. There is no single function that relates price to quantity supplied.

Economic Equilibrium

In economics, economic equilibrium is a state where economic forces such as supply and demand are balanced and in the absence of external influences the (equilibrium) values of economic variables will not change. For example, in the standard textbook model of perfect competition, equilibrium occurs at the point at which quantity demanded and quantity supplied are equal. Market equilibrium in this case refers to a condition where a market price is established through competition such that the amount of goods or services sought by buyers is equal to the amount of goods or services produced by sellers. This price is often called the competitive price or market clearing price and will tend not to change unless demand or supply changes and the quantity is called "competitive quantity" or market clearing quantity. However, the concept of *equilibrium* in economics also applies to imperfectly competitive markets, where it takes the form of a Nash equilibrium.

Properties of Equilibrium

Three basic properties of equilibrium in general have been proposed by Huw Dixon. These are:

Equilibrium property P1: The behavior of agents is consistent.

Equilibrium property P2: No agent has an incentive to change its behavior.

Equilibrium Property P3: Equilibrium is the outcome of some dynamic process (stability).

Example: The Competitive Equilibrium

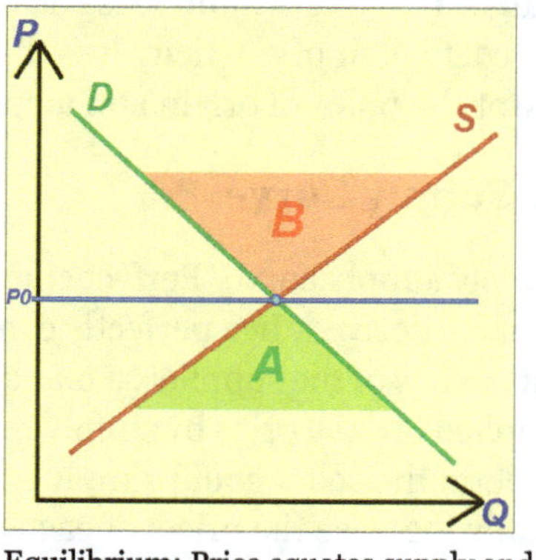

Competitive Equilibrium: Price equates supply and demand.

- P – price
- Q – quantity demanded and supplied
- S – supply curve
- D – demand curve
- P_0 – equilibrium price
- A – excess demand – when $P<P_0$
- B – excess supply – when $P>P_0$

In a competitive equilibrium, supply equals demand. Property P1 is satisfied, because at the equilibrium price the amount supplied is equal to the amount demanded. Property P2 is also satisfied. Demand is chosen to maximize utility given the market price: no one on the demand side has any incentive to demand more or less at the prevailing price. Likewise supply is determined by firms maximizing their profits at the market price: no firm will want to supply any more or less at the equilibrium price. Hence, agents on neither the demand side nor the supply side will have any incentive to alter their actions.

To see whether Property P3 is satisfied, consider what happens when the price is above the equilibrium. In this case there is an excess supply, with the quantity supplied exceeding that demanded. This will tend to put downward pressure on the price to make it return to equilibrium. Likewise where the price is below the equilibrium point there is a shortage in supply leading to an increase in prices back to equilibrium. Not all equilibria are "stable" in the sense of Equilibrium property P3. It is possible to have competitive equilibria that are unstable. However, if an equilibrium is unstable, it raises the question of how you might get there. Even if it satisfies properties P1 and P2, the absence of P3 means that the market can only be in the unstable equilibrium if it starts off there.

In most simple microeconomic stories of supply and demand a static equilibrium is observed in a market; however, economic equilibrium can be also dynamic. Equilibrium may also be economy-wide or general, as opposed to the partial equilibrium of a single market. Equilibrium can change if there is a change in demand or supply conditions. For example, an increase in supply will disrupt the equilibrium, leading to lower prices. Eventually, a new equilibrium will be attained in most markets. Then, there will be no change in price or the amount of output bought and sold until there is an exogenous shift in supply or demand (such as changes in technology or tastes). That is, there are no endogenous forces leading to the price or the quantity.

Example: Nash Equilibrium

The Nash equilibrium is widely used in economics as the main alternative to competitive equilibrium. It is used whenever there is a strategic element to the behavior of agents and the "price taking" assumption of competitive equilibrium is inappropriate. The first use of the Nash equilibrium was in the Cournot duopoly as developed by Antoine Augustin Cournot in his 1838 book. Both firms produce a homogenous product: given the total amount supplied by the two firms, the (single) industry price is determined using the demand curve. This determines the revenues of each firm (the industry price times the quantity supplied by the firm). The profit of each firm is then this revenue minus the cost of producing the output. Clearly, there is a *strategic interdependence* between the two firms. If one firm varies its output, this will in turn affect the market price and so the revenue and profits of the other firm. We can define the payoff function which gives the profit of each firm as a function of the two outputs chosen by the firms. Cournot assumed that each firm chooses its own output to maximize its profits given the output of the other firm. The Nash equilibrium occurs when both firms are producing the outputs which maximize their own profit given the output of the other firm.

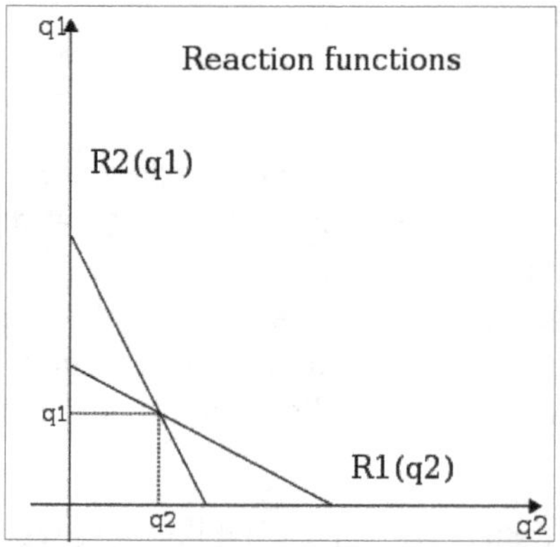

Equilibrium quantities as a solution to two reaction functions in Cournot duopoly. Firm 1's reaction function q1=R1(q2) gives its optimal output q1 to a given output q2 of firm 2. Likewise, firm 2's reaction function q2=R2(q1). The *Cournot-Nash equilibrium* occurs where the two reaction functions intersect and both firms are choosing the optimal output given the output of the other firm.

In terms of the equilibrium properties, we can see that P2 is satisfied: in a Nash equilibrium, neither firm has an incentive to deviate from the Nash equilibrium given the output of the other firm. P1 is satisfied since the payoff function ensures that the market price is consistent with the outputs supplied and that each firms profits equal revenue minus cost at this output.

Is the equilibrium stable as required by P3? Cournot himself argued that it was stable using the stability concept implied by best response dynamics. The reaction function for each firm gives the output which maximizes profits (best response) in terms of output for a firm in terms of a given output of the other firm. In the standard Cournot model this is downward sloping: if the other firm produces a higher output, your best response involves producing less. Best response dynamics involves firms starting from some arbitrary position and then adjusting output to their best-response to the previous output of the other firm. So long as the reaction functions have a slope of less than -1, this will converge to the Nash equilibrium. However, this stability story is open to much criticism. As Dixon argues: "*The crucial weakness is that, at each step, the firms behave myopically: they choose their output to maximize their current profits given the output of the other firm, but ignore the fact that the process specifies that the other firm will adjust its output...*". There are other concepts of stability that have been put forward for the Nash equilibrium, evolutionary stability for example.

Normative Evaluation

Most economists e.g., Paul Samuelson caution against attaching a normative meaning (value judgement) to the equilibrium price. For example, food markets may be in equilibrium at the same time that people are starving (because they cannot afford to pay the high equilibrium price). Indeed, this occurred during the Great Famine in Ireland in 1845–52, where food was exported though people were starving, due to the greater profits in selling to the English – the equilibrium price of the Irish-British market for potatoes was above the price that Irish farmers could afford, and thus (among other reasons) they starved.

Interpretations

In most interpretations, classical economists such as Adam Smith maintained that the free market would tend towards economic equilibrium through the price mechanism. That is, any excess supply (market surplus or glut) would lead to *price cuts*, which decrease the quantity supplied (by reducing the incentive to produce and sell the product) and increase the quantity demanded (by offering consumers bargains), automatically abolishing the glut. Similarly, in an unfettered market, any excess demand (or shortage) would lead to *price increases*, reducing the quantity demanded (as customers are priced out of the market) and increasing in the quantity supplied (as the incentive to produce and sell a product rises). As before, the disequilibrium (here, the shortage) disappears. This automatic abolition of non-market-clearing situations distinguishes markets from central planning schemes, which often have a difficult time getting prices right and suffer from persistent shortages of goods and services.

This view came under attack from at least two viewpoints. Modern mainstream economics points to cases where equilibrium does not correspond to market clearing (but instead to unemployment), as with the efficiency wage hypothesis in labor economics. In some ways parallel is the phenomenon of credit rationing, in which banks hold interest rates low to create an excess demand for loans, so they can pick and choose whom to lend to. Further, economic equilibrium can correspond with monopoly, where the monopolistic firm maintains an artificial shortage to prop up prices and to maximize profits. Finally, Keynesian macroeconomics points to underemployment equilibrium, where a surplus of labor (i.e., cyclical unemployment) co-exists for a long time with a shortage of aggregate demand.

Solving for The Competitive Equilibrium Price

To solve for the equilibrium price, one must either plot the supply and demand curves, or solve for their equations being equal.

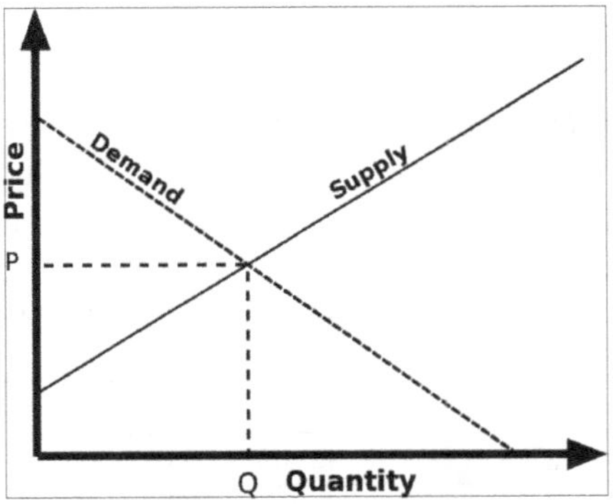

In the diagram, depicting simple set of supply and demand curves, the quantity demanded and supplied at price **P** are equal.

An example may be:

At any price above **P** supply exceeds demand, while at a price below **P** the quantity demanded exceeds that supplied. In other words, prices where demand and supply are out of balance are termed points of disequilibrium, creating shortages and oversupply. Changes in the conditions of demand or supply will shift the demand or supply curves. This will cause changes in the equilibrium price and quantity in the market.

Consider the following demand and supply schedule:

Price ($)	Demand	Supply
8.00	6,000	18,000
7.00	8,000	16,000
6.00	10,000	14,000
5.00	12,000	12,000
4.00	14,000	10,000
3.00	16,000	8,000
2.00	18,000	6,000
1.00	20,000	4,000

- The equilibrium price in the market is $5.00 where demand and supply are equal at 12,000 units.
- If the current market price was $3.00 – there would be excess demand for 8,000 units, creating a shortage.
- If the current market price was $8.00 – there would be excess supply of 12,000 units.

When there is a shortage in the market we see that, to correct this disequilibrium, the price of the good will be increased back to a price of $5.00, thus lessening the quantity demanded and increasing the quantity supplied thus that the market is in balance.

When there is an oversupply of a good, such as when price is above $6.00, then we see that producers will decrease the price to increase the quantity demanded for the good, thus eliminating the excess and taking the market back to equilibrium.

Influences Changing Price

A change in equilibrium price may occur through a change in either the supply or demand schedules. For instance, starting from the above supply-demand configuration, an increased level of disposable income may produce a new demand schedule, such as the following:

Price ($)	Demand	Supply
8.00	10,000	18,000
7.00	12,000	16,000
6.00	14,000	14,000
5.00	16,000	12,000

4.00	18,000	10,000
3.00	20,000	8,000
2.00	22,000	6,000
1.00	24,000	4,000

Here we see that an increase in disposable income would increase the quantity demanded of the good by 2,000 units at each price. This increase in demand would have the effect of shifting the demand curve rightward. The result is a change in the price at which quantity supplied equals quantity demanded. In this case we see that the two now equal each other at an increased price of $6.00. Note that a decrease in disposable income would have the exact opposite effect on the market equilibrium.

We will also see similar behaviour in price when there is a change in the supply schedule, occurring through technological changes, or through changes in business costs. An increase in technological usage or know-how or a decrease in costs would have the effect of increasing the quantity supplied at each price, thus reducing the equilibrium price. On the other hand, a decrease in technology or increase in business costs will decrease the quantity supplied at each price, thus increasing equilibrium price.

The process of comparing two static equilibria to each other, as in the above example, is known as comparative statics. For example, since a rise in consumers' income leads to a higher price (and a decline in consumers' income leads to a fall in the price — in each case the two things change in the same direction), we say that the comparative static effect of consumer income on the price is positive. This is another way of saying that the total derivative of price with respect to consumer income is greater than zero.

Dynamic Equilibrium

Whereas in a static equilibrium all quantities have unchanging values, in a dynamic equilibrium various quantities may all be growing at the same rate, leaving their ratios unchanging. For example, in the neoclassical growth model, the working population is growing at a rate which is exogenous (determined outside the model, by non-economic forces). In dynamic equilibrium, output and the physical capital stock also grow at that same rate, with output per worker and the capital stock per worker unchanging. Similarly, in models of inflation a dynamic equilibrium would involve the price level, the nominal money supply, nominal wage rates, and all other nominal values growing at a single common rate, while all real values are unchanging, as is the inflation rate.

The process of comparing two dynamic equilibria to each other is known as comparative dynamics. For example, in the neoclassical growth model, starting from one dynamic equilibrium based in part on one particular saving rate, a permanent increase in the saving rate leads to a new dynamic equilibrium in which there are permanently higher capital per worker and productivity per worker, but an unchanged growth rate of output; so it is said that in this model the comparative dynamic effect of the saving rate on capital per worker is positive but the comparative dynamic effect of the saving rate on the output growth rate is zero.

Disequilibrium

Disequilibrium characterizes a market that is not in equilibrium. Disequilibrium can occur extremely briefly or over an extended period of time. Typically in financial markets it either never occurs or only momentarily occurs, because trading takes place continuously and the prices of financial assets can adjust instantaneously with each trade to equilibrate supply and demand. At the other extreme, many economists view labor markets as being in a state of disequilibrium—specifically one of excess supply—over extended periods of time. Goods markets are somewhere in between: prices of some goods, while sluggish in adjusting due to menu costs, long term contracts, and other impediments, do not stay at disequilibrium levels indefinitely, and many goods markets such as commodity markets are highly organised and liquid and have essentially instantaneous adjustment of their prices to equilibrium levels.

Credit Markets

Disequilibrium credit rationing can occur for one of two reasons. In the presence of usury laws, if the equilibrium interest rate on loans is above the legally allowable rate, the market cannot clear and at the maximum allowable rate the quantity of credit demanded will exceed the quantity of credit supplied.

A more subtle source of credit rationing is that higher interest rates can increase the risk of default by the borrower, making the potential lender reluctant to lend at otherwise attractively high interest rates.

Labour Markets

Labour markets are prone to particular sources of price rigidity because the item being transacted is people, and laws or social constraints designed to protect those people may hinder market adjustments. Such constraints include restrictions on who or how many people can be laid off and when (which can affect both the number of layoffs and the number of people hired by firms that are concerned by the restrictions), restrictions on the lowering of wages when a firm experiences a decline in the demand for its product, and long-term labor contracts that pre-specify wages.

Spillovers between Markets

Disequilibrium in one market can affect demand or supply in other markets. Specifically, if an economic agent is constrained in one market, his supply or demand in another market may be changed from its unconstrained form, termed the *notional demand*, into a modified form known as *effective demand*. If this occurs systematically for a large number of market participants, market outcomes in the latter market for prices and quantities transacted (themselves either equilibrium or disequilibrium outcomes) will be affected.

Examples include:

- If the supply of mortgage credit to potential homebuyers is rationed, this will decrease the demand for newly built houses.
- If labourers cannot supply all the labor they wish to, they will have constrained income and their demand in the goods market will be lower.
- If employers cannot hire all the labor they wish to, they cannot produce as much output as they wish to, and supply in the market for their good will be diminished.

Elasticity

In economics, elasticity is the measurement of how responsive an economic variable is to a change in another. It gives answers to questions such as:

- "If I lower the price of a product, how much more will sell?"
- "If I raise the price of one good, how will that affect sales of this other good?"
- "If the market price of a product goes down, how much will that affect the amount that firms will be willing to supply to the market?"

An *elastic* variable (with elasticity value greater than 1) is one which responds more than proportionally to changes in other variables. In contrast, an *inelastic* variable (with elasticity value less than 1) is one which changes less than proportionally in response to changes in other variables. A variable can have different values of its elasticity at different starting points: for example, the quantity of a good supplied by producers might be elastic at low prices but inelastic at higher prices, so that a rise from an initially low price might bring on a more-than-proportionate increase in quantity supplied while a rise from an initially high price might bring on a less-than-proportionate rise in quantity supplied.

Elasticity can be quantified as the ratio of the percentage change in one variable to the percentage change in another variable, when the latter variable has a causal influence on the former. A more precise definition is given in terms of differential calculus. It is a tool for measuring the responsiveness of one variable to changes in another, causative variable. Elasticity has the advantage of being a unitless ratio, independent of the type of quantities being varied. Frequently used elasticities include price elasticity of demand, price elasticity of supply, income elasticity of demand, elasticity of substitution between factors of production and elasticity of intertemporal substitution.

Elasticity is one of the most important concepts in neoclassical economic theory. It is useful in understanding the incidence of indirect taxation, marginal concepts as they relate to the theory of the firm, and distribution of wealth and different types of goods as they relate to the theory of consumer choice. Elasticity is also crucially important in any discussion of welfare distribution, in particular consumer surplus, producer surplus, or government surplus.

In empirical work an elasticity is the estimated coefficient in a linear regression equation where both the dependent variable and the independent variable are in natural logs. Elasticity is a popular tool among empiricists because it is independent of units and thus simplifies data analysis.

A major study of the price elasticity of supply and the price elasticity of demand for US products was undertaken by Hendrik S. Houthakker and Lester D. Taylor.

Specific Elasticities

Elasticities of Supply

Price Elasticity of Supply

The price elasticity of supply measures how the amount of a good that a supplier wishes to supply changes in response to a change in price. In a manner analogous to the price elasticity of demand, it captures the extent of horizontal movement along the supply curve relative to the extent of vertical movement. If the price elasticity of supply is zero the supply of a good supplied is "totally inelastic" and the quantity supplied is fixed.

Elasticities of Scale

Elasticity of scale or *output elasticity* measures the percentage change in output induced by a collective percent change in the usages of all inputs. A production function or process is said to exhibit constant returns to scale if a percentage change in inputs results in an equal percentage in outputs (an elasticity equal to 1). It exhibits increasing returns to scale if a percentage change in inputs results in greater percentage change in output (an elasticity greater than 1). The definition of decreasing returns to scale is analogous.

Elasticities of Demand

Price Elasticity of Demand

Price elasticity of demand is a measure used to show the responsiveness, or elasticity, of the quantity demanded of a good or service to a change in its price. More precisely, it gives the percentage change in quantity demanded in response to a one percent change in price (ceteris paribus, i.e. holding constant all the other determinants of demand, such as income).

Cross-price Elasticity of Demand

Cross-price elasticity of demand is a measure of the responsiveness of the demand for one product to changes in the price of a different product. It is the ratio of percentage change in the former to the percentage change in the latter. If it is positive, the goods are called substitutes because a rise in the price of the other good causes consumers to substitute away from buying as much of the other good as before and into buying more of this good. If it is negative, the goods are called complements.

Applications

The concept of elasticity has an extraordinarily wide range of applications in economics. In particular, an understanding of elasticity is fundamental in understanding the response of supply and demand in a market.

Some common uses of elasticity include:

- Effect of changing price on firm revenue.
- Analysis of incidence of the tax burden and other government policies.
- Income elasticity of demand, used as an indicator of industry health, future consumption patterns and as a guide to firms' investment decisions.
- Effect of international trade and terms of trade effects.

- Analysis of consumption and saving behavior.
- Analysis of advertising on consumer demand for particular goods.

Variants

In some cases the discrete (non-infinitesimal) arc elasticity is used instead. In other cases, such as modified duration in bond trading, a percentage change in output is divided by a unit (not percentage) change in input, yielding a semi-elasticity instead.

Various Elasticities

Price Elasticity of Supply

Price elasticity of supply (PES or E_s) is a measure used in economics to show the responsiveness, or elasticity, of the quantity supplied of a good or service to a change in its price.

The elasticity is represented in numerical form, and is defined as the percentage change in the quantity supplied divided by the percentage change in price.

When the coefficient is less than one, the supply of the good can be described as *inelastic*; when the coefficient is greater than one, the supply can be described as *elastic*. An elasticity of zero indicates that quantity supplied does not respond to a price change: it is "fixed" in supply. Such goods often have no labor component or are not produced, limiting the short run prospects of expansion. If the coefficient is exactly one, the good is said to be *unitary elastic*.

The quantity of goods supplied can, in the short term, be different from the amount produced, as manufacturers will have stocks which they can build up or run down.

Determinants

Availability of Raw Materials:

> For example, availability may cap the amount of gold that can be produced in a country regardless of price. Likewise, the price of Van Gogh paintings is unlikely to affect their supply.

Length and Complexity of Production:

> Much depends on the complexity of the production process. Textile production is relatively simple. The labor is largely unskilled and production facilities are little more than buildings – no special structures are needed. Thus the PES for textiles is elastic. On the other hand, the PES for specific types of motor vehicles is relatively inelastic. Auto manufacture is a multi-stage process that requires specialized equipment, skilled labor, a large suppliers network and large R&D costs.

Mobility of Factors:

> If the factors of production are easily available and if a producer producing one good can

switch their resources and put it towards the creation of a product in demand, then it can be said that the PES is relatively elastic. The inverse applies to this, to make it relatively inelastic.

Time to Respond:

The more time a producer has to respond to price changes the more elastic the supply. Supply is normally more elastic in the long run than in the short run for produced goods, since it is generally assumed that in the long run all factors of production can be utilised to increase supply, whereas in the short run only labor can be increased, and even then, changes may be prohibitively costly. For example, a cotton farmer cannot immediately (i.e. in the short run) respond to an increase in the price of soybeans because of the time it would take to procure the necessary land.

Inventories:

A producer who has a supply of goods or available storage capacity can quickly increase supply to market.

Spare/Excess Production Capacity:

A producer who has unused capacity can (and will) quickly respond to price changes in his market assuming that variable factors are readily available. The existence of spare capacity within a firm, would be indicative of more proportionate response in quantity supplied to changes in price (hence suggesting price elasticity). It indicates that the producer would be able to utilise spare factor markets (factors of production) at its disposal and hence respond to changes in demand to match with supply. The greater the extent of spare production capacity, the quicker suppliers can respond to price changes and hence the more price elastic the good/service would be.

Various research methods are used to calculate price elasticities in real life, including analysis of historic sales data, both public and private, and use of present-day surveys of customers' preferences to build up test markets capable of modelling elasticity such changes. Alternatively, conjoint analysis (a ranking of users' preferences which can then be statistically analysed) may be used.

Graphical Representation

It is important to note that elasticity and slope are, for the most part, unrelated. Thus, when supply is represented linearly, regardless of the slope of the supply line, the coefficient of elasticity of any linear supply curve that passes through the origin is 1 (unit elastic). The coefficient of elasticity of any linear supply curve that cuts the y-axis is greater than 1 (elastic), and the coefficient of elasticity of any linear supply curve that cuts the x-axis is less than 1 (inelastic). Likewise, for any given supply curve, it is likely that PES will vary along the curve.

Selected Supply Elasticities

- Heating Oil: 1.57 (Short Run)
- Gasoline: 1.61 (Short Run)

- Tobacco: 7.0 (Long Run)
- Housing: 1.6–3.7 (Long Run)
- Cotton:
    - 0.3 (Short Run)
    - 1.0 (Long Run)
- Steel: 1.2 (Long Run, from Minimills)
- Land: 0, except when land reclamation is taking place

Price Elasticity of Demand

Price elasticity of demand (**PED** or $\mathbf{E_d}$) is a measure used in economics to show the responsiveness, or elasticity, of the quantity demanded of a good or service to a change in its price, ceteris paribus. More precisely, it gives the percentage change in quantity demanded in response to a one percent change in price (ceteris paribus)

Price elasticities are almost always negative, although analysts tend to ignore the sign even though this can lead to ambiguity. Only goods which do not conform to the law of demand, such as Veblen and Giffen goods, have a positive PED. In general, the demand for a good is said to be *inelastic* (or *relatively inelastic*) when the PED is less than one (in absolute value): that is, changes in price have a relatively small effect on the quantity of the good demanded. The demand for a good is said to be *elastic* (or *relatively elastic*) when its PED is greater than one (in absolute value): that is, changes in price have a relatively large effect on the quantity of a good demanded.

Revenue is maximized when price is set so that the PED is exactly one. The PED of a good can also be used to predict the incidence (or "burden") of a tax on that good. Various research methods are used to determine price elasticity, including test markets, analysis of historical sales data and conjoint analysis.

Definition

It is a measure of responsiveness of the quantity of a raw good or service demanded to changes in its price. The formula for the coefficient of price elasticity of demand for a good is:

$$e_{\langle p \rangle} = \frac{\mathrm{d}Q / Q}{\mathrm{d}P / P}$$

The above formula usually yields a negative value, due to the inverse nature of the relationship between price and quantity demanded, as described by the "law of demand". For example, if the price increases by 5% and quantity demanded decreases by 5%, then the elasticity at the initial price and quantity = −5%/5% = −1. The only classes of goods which have a PED of greater than 0 are Veblen and Giffen goods. Although the PED is negative for the vast majority of goods and services, economists often refer to price elasticity of demand as a positive value (i.e., in absolute value terms).

This measure of elasticity is sometimes referred to as the *own-price* elasticity of demand for a good, i.e., the elasticity of demand with respect to the good's own price, in order to distinguish it from the elasticity of demand for that good with respect to the change in the price of some other good, i.e., a complementary or substitute good. The latter type of elasticity measure is called a *cross*-price elasticity of demand.

As the difference between the two prices or quantities increases, the accuracy of the PED given by the formula above *decreases* for a combination of two reasons. First, the PED for a good is not necessarily constant; as explained below, PED can vary at different points along the demand curve, due to its percentage nature. Elasticity is not the same thing as the slope of the demand curve, which is dependent on the units used for both price and quantity. Second, percentage changes are not symmetric; instead, the percentage change between any two values depends on which one is chosen as the starting value and which as the ending value. For example, if quantity demanded increases *from* 10 units *to* 15 units, the percentage change is 50%, i.e., (15 – 10) ÷ 10 (converted to a percentage). But if quantity demanded decreases *from* 15 units *to* 10 units, the percentage change is –33.3%, i.e., (10 – 15) ÷ 15.

Two alternative elasticity measures avoid or minimise these shortcomings of the basic elasticity formula: *point-price elasticity* and *arc elasticity*.

Point-price Elasticity of Demand

Point elasticity of demand method is used to determine change in demand within same demand curve, basically a very small amount of change in demand is measured through point elasticity. (Maharjan, R.) One way to avoid the accuracy problem described above is to minimise the difference between the starting and ending prices and quantities. This is the approach taken in the definition of *point-price* elasticity, which uses differential calculus to calculate the elasticity for an infinitesimal change in price and quantity at any given point on the demand curve:

$$E_d = \frac{P}{Q_d} \times \frac{dQ_d}{dP}$$

In other words, it is equal to the absolute value of the first derivative of quantity with respect to price (dQ_d/dP) multiplied by the point's price (P) divided by its quantity (Q_d).

In terms of partial-differential calculus, point-price elasticity of demand can be defined as follows: let $x(p, w)$ be the demand of goods $x_1, x_2, \ldots, x_L$ as a function of parameters price and wealth, and let $x_l(p, w)$ be the demand for good l. The elasticity of demand for good $x_l(p, w)$ with respect to price p_k is:

$$E_{x_l, p_k} = \frac{\partial x_l(p, w)}{\partial p_k} \cdot \frac{p_k}{x_l(p, w)} = \frac{\partial \log x_l(p, w)}{\partial \log p_k}$$

However, the point-price elasticity can be computed only if the formula for the demand function, $Q_d = f(P)$, is known so its derivative with respect to price, dQ_d / dP, can be determined.

Arc Elasticity

A second solution to the asymmetry problem of having a PED dependent on which of the two given points on a demand curve is chosen as the "original" point will and which as the "new" one is to compute the percentage change in P and Q relative to the *average* of the two prices and the *average* of the two quantities, rather than just the change relative to one point or the other. Loosely speaking, this gives an "average" elasticity for the section of the actual demand curve—i.e., the *arc* of the curve—between the two points. As a result, this measure is known as the *arc elasticity*, in this case with respect to the price of the good. The arc elasticity is defined mathematically as:

$$E_d = \frac{\frac{P_1 + P_2}{2}}{\frac{Q_{d_1} + Q_{d_2}}{2}} \times \frac{\Delta Q_d}{\Delta P} = \frac{P_1 + P_2}{Q_{d_1} + Q_{d_2}} \times \frac{\Delta Q_d}{\Delta P}$$

This method for computing the price elasticity is also known as the "midpoints formula", because the average price and average quantity are the coordinates of the midpoint of the straight line between the two given points. This formula is an application of the midpoint method. However, because this formula implicitly assumes the section of the demand curve between those points is linear, the greater the curvature of the actual demand curve is over that range, the worse this approximation of its elasticity will be.

History

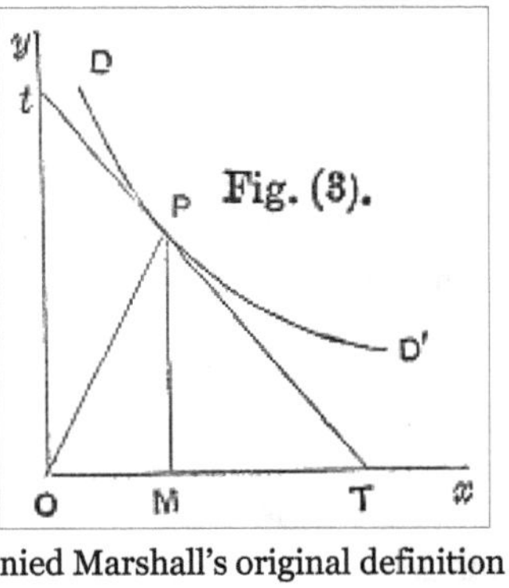

The illustration that accompanied Marshall's original definition of PED, the ratio of PT to Pt.

Together with the concept of an economic "elasticity" coefficient, Alfred Marshall is credited with defining PED ("elasticity of demand") in his book *Principles of Economics*, published in 1890. He described it thus: "And we may say generally:— the elasticity (or responsiveness) of demand in a market is great or small according as the amount demanded increases much or little for a given fall in price, and diminishes much or little for a given rise in price". He reasons this since "the only universal law as to a person's desire for a commodity is that it diminishes... but this diminution may be slow or rapid. If it is slow... a small fall in price will cause a comparatively large increase in his purchases. But if it is rapid, a small fall in price will cause only a very small increase in his purchases. In the former case... the elasticity of his wants, we may say, is great. In the latter case... the elasticity of his demand is small." Mathematically, the Marshallian PED was based on a point-price definition, using differential calculus to calculate elasticities.

Determinants

The overriding factor in determining PED is the willingness and ability of consumers after a price change to postpone immediate consumption decisions concerning the good and to search for substitutes ("wait and look"). A number of factors can thus affect the elasticity of demand for a good:

Availability of Substitute Goods:

The more and closer the substitutes available, the higher the elasticity is likely to be, as people can easily switch from one good to another if an even minor price change is made; There is a strong substitution effect. If no close substitutes are available, the substitution effect will be small and the demand inelastic.

Breadth of Definition of A Good:

The broader the definition of a good (or service), the lower the elasticity. For example, Company X's fish and chips would tend to have a relatively high elasticity of demand if a significant number of substitutes are available, whereas food in general would have an extremely low elasticity of demand because no substitutes exist.

Percentage of Income:

The higher the percentage of the consumer's income that the product's price represents, the higher the elasticity tends to be, as people will pay more attention when purchasing the good because of its cost; The income effect is substantial. When the goods represent only a negligible portion of the budget the income effect will be insignificant and demand inelastic,

Necessity:

The more necessary a good is, the lower the elasticity, as people will attempt to buy it no matter the price, such as the case of insulin for those who need it.

Duration:

For most goods, the longer a price change holds, the higher the elasticity is likely to be, as more and more consumers find they have the time and inclination to search for substitutes. When fuel prices increase suddenly, for instance, consumers may still fill up their empty tanks in the short run, but when prices remain high over several years, more consumers will reduce their demand for fuel by switching to carpooling or public transportation, investing in vehicles with greater fuel economy or taking other measures. This does not hold for consumer durables such as the cars themselves, however; eventually, it may become necessary for consumers to replace their present cars, so one would expect demand to be less elastic.

Brand Loyalty:

An attachment to a certain brand—either out of tradition or because of proprietary barriers—can override sensitivity to price changes, resulting in more inelastic demand.

Who Pays:

> Where the purchaser does not directly pay for the good they consume, such as with corporate expense accounts, demand is likely to be more inelastic.

Interpreting Values of Price Elasticity Coefficients

Elasticities of demand are interpreted as follows:

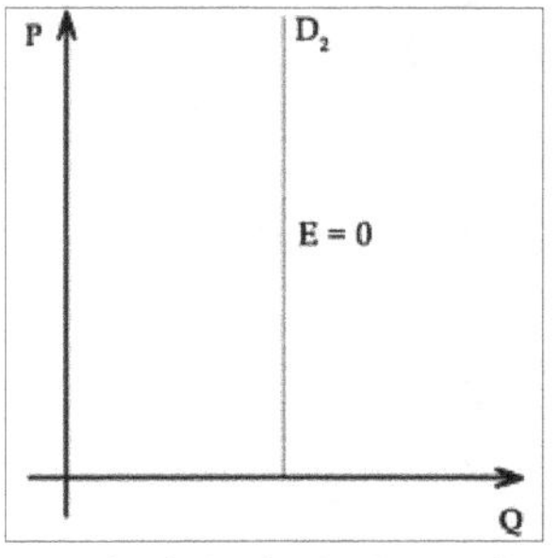

Perfectly inelastic demand.

A decrease in the price of a good normally results in an increase in the quantity demanded by consumers because of the law of demand, and conversely, quantity demanded decreases when price rises. As summarized in the table above, the PED for a good or service is referred to by different descriptive terms depending on whether the elasticity coefficient is greater than, equal to, or less than −1. That is, the demand for a good is called:

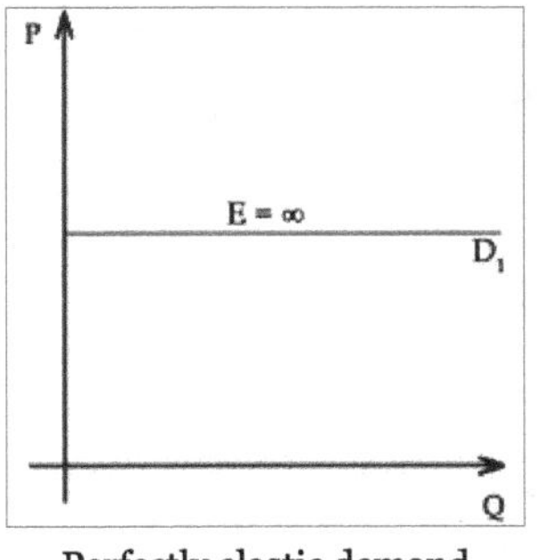

Perfectly elastic demand.

- *relatively inelastic* when the percentage change in quantity demanded is *less than* the percentage change in price (so that $E_d > -1$);
- *unit elastic, unit elasticity, unitary elasticity,* or *unitarily elastic* demand when the percentage change in quantity demanded is *equal to* the percentage change in price (so that $E_d = -1$); and
- *relatively elastic* when the percentage change in quantity demanded is *greater than* the percentage change in price (so that $E_d < -1$).

As the two accompanying diagrams show, *perfectly elastic* demand is represented graphically as a horizontal line, and *perfectly inelastic* demand as a vertical line. These are the *only* cases in which the PED and the slope of the demand curve ($\Delta P/\Delta Q$) are *both* constant, as well as the *only* cases in which the PED is determined solely by the slope of the demand curve (or more precisely, by the *inverse* of that slope).

Relation to Marginal Revenue

The following equation holds:

$$R' = P\left(1 - \frac{1}{E_d}\right)$$

where R' is the marginal revenue P is the price Proof: TR = Total Revenue

$$R' = \frac{\partial TR}{\partial Q} = \frac{\partial}{\partial Q}(PQ) = P + Q\frac{\partial P}{\partial Q}$$

$$E_d = -\frac{\partial Q}{\partial P} \cdot \frac{P}{Q} \Rightarrow -E_d \cdot \frac{Q}{P} = \frac{\partial Q}{\partial P} \Rightarrow -\frac{P}{E_d \cdot Q} = \frac{\partial P}{\partial Q}$$

$$R' = P + Q \cdot -\frac{P}{E_d \cdot Q} = P\left(1 - \frac{1}{E_d}\right)$$

On a graph with both a demand curve and a marginal revenue curve, demand will be elastic at all quantities where marginal revenue is positive. Demand is unit elastic at the quantity where marginal revenue is zero. Demand is inelastic at every quantity where marginal revenue is negative.

Effect on Total Revenue

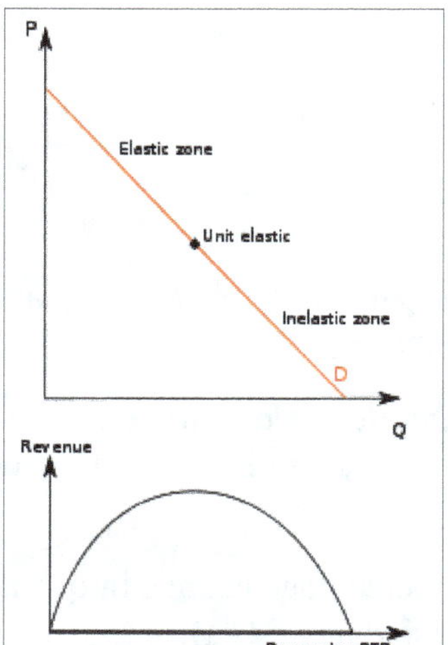

A set of graphs shows the relationship between demand and total revenue (TR) for a linear demand curve. As price decreases in the elastic range, TR increases, but in the inelastic range, TR decreases. TR is maximised at the quantity where PED = 1.

A firm considering a price change must know what effect the change in price will have on total revenue. Revenue is simply the product of unit price times quantity:

$$R' = P\left(1 - \frac{1}{E_d}\right)$$

Generally any change in price will have two effects:

The price effect:

> For inelastic goods, an increase in unit price will tend to increase revenue, while a decrease in price will tend to decrease revenue. (The effect is reversed for elastic goods.)

The quantity effect:

> An increase in unit price will tend to lead to fewer units sold, while a decrease in unit price will tend to lead to more units sold.

For inelastic goods, because of the inverse nature of the relationship between price and quantity demanded (i.e., the law of demand), the two effects affect total revenue in opposite directions. But in determining whether to increase or decrease prices, a firm needs to know what the net effect will be. Elasticity provides the answer: The percentage change in total revenue is approximately equal to the percentage change in quantity demanded plus the percentage change in price. (One change will be positive, the other negative.) The percentage change in quantity is related to the percentage change in price by elasticity: hence the percentage change in revenue can be calculated by knowing the elasticity and the percentage change in price alone.

As a result, the relationship between PED and total revenue can be described for any good:

- When the price elasticity of demand for a good is *perfectly inelastic* ($E_d = 0$), changes in the price do not affect the quantity demanded for the good; raising prices will always cause total revenue to increase. Goods necessary to survival can be classified here; a rational person will be willing to pay anything for a good if the alternative is death. For example, a person in the desert weak and dying of thirst would easily give all the money in his wallet, no matter how much, for a bottle of water if he would otherwise die. His demand is not contingent on the price.

- When the price elasticity of demand for a good is *relatively inelastic* ($-1 < E_d < 0$), the percentage change in quantity demanded is smaller than that in price. Hence, when the price is raised, the total revenue increases, and vice versa.

- When the price elasticity of demand for a good is *unit (or unitary) elastic* ($E_d = -1$), the percentage change in quantity demanded is equal to that in price, so a change in price will not affect total revenue.

- When the price elasticity of demand for a good is *relatively elastic* ($-\infty < E_d < -1$), the percentage change in quantity demanded is greater than that in price. Hence, when the price is raised, the total revenue falls, and vice versa.

- When the price elasticity of demand for a good is *perfectly elastic* (E_d is $-\infty$), any increase in the price, no matter how small, will cause the quantity demanded for the good to drop to zero. Hence, when the price is raised, the total revenue falls to zero. This situation is typical for goods that have their value defined by law (such as fiat currency); if a 5 dollar bill were sold for anything more than 5 dollars, nobody would buy it, so demand is zero.

Hence, as the accompanying diagram shows, total revenue is maximized at the combination of price and quantity demanded where the elasticity of demand is unitary.

It is important to realize that price-elasticity of demand is *not* necessarily constant over all price ranges. The linear demand curve in the accompanying diagram illustrates that changes in price also change the elasticity: the price elasticity is different at every point on the curve.

References

- Marshall, Alfred . Principles of Economics. Library of Economics and Liberty. ISBN 0-256-01547-3. Retrieved 5, March 2020
- Paul A. Samuelson , Foundations of Economic Analysis, Harvard University Press. ISBN 0-674-31301-1
- Taylor, John B. (1 February 2006). Economics. Cengage Learning. ISBN 978-0-618-64085-0. Retrieved 5, March 2020
- Mas-Colell, Andreu; Winston, Michael D.; Green, Jerry R. Microeconomic Theory. New York: Oxford University Press. ISBN 1-4288-7151-9
- Mankiw, N. Gregory. Principles of Economics, Wall Street Journal Edition. Dryden Press, San Diego. pp . 71 –73. ISBN 0-03-098238-3
- Ritter, Lawrence S.; Silber, William L.; Udell, Gregory F. (2000). Principles of Money, Banking, and Financial Markets (10th ed.). Addison-Wesley, Menlo Park C. pp. 431–438, 465–476. ISBN 0-321-37557 2
- O'Sullivan, Arthur; Sheffrin, Steven M. (2003). Economics: Principles in Action. Upper Saddle River, New Jersey 07458: Pearson Prentice Hall. p. 104. ISBN 0-13-063085-3
- Gillespie, Andrew (1 March 2007). Foundations of Economics. Oxford University Press. ISBN 978-0-19-929637-8. Retrieved 28, February 2020
- Gwartney, James D.; Stroup, Richard L.; Sobel, Russell S.; David MacPherson (14 January 2008). Economics: Private and Public Choice. Cengage Learning. ISBN 978-0-324-58018-1. Retrieved 28, February 2020
- Jain, T.R. (2006–2007). Microeconomics and Basic Mathematics. New Delhi: VK Publications. p. 28. ISBN 81-87140-89-5
- O'Sullivan, Arthur; Steven M. Sheffrin (2003). Economics: Principles in action. Upper Saddle River, New Jersey 07458: Pearson Prentice Hall. pp. 81–82. ISBN 0-13-063085-3
- Goodwin, N, Nelson, J; Ackerman, F & Weisskopf, T: Microeconomics in Context 2d ed. Sharpe 2009 ISBN 978-0-7656-2301-0

5

Diverse Economic Models

Economic models are a simplified representation of economic processes which helps in observing and making predictions about economic behavior. Some of the models explained in this chapter are econometric and macroeconomic model, Brander-Spencer model, big push model and Mundell-Fleming model. This chapter discusses in detail these models related to economics.

Econometric Model

Econometric models are statistical models used in econometrics. An econometric model specifies the statistical relationship that is believed to hold between the various economic quantities pertaining to a particular economic phenomenon under study. An econometric model can be derived from a deterministic economic model by allowing for uncertainty, or from an economic model which itself is stochastic. However, it is also possible to use econometric models that are not tied to any specific economic theory.

A simple example of an econometric model is one that assumes that monthly spending by consumers is linearly dependent on consumers' income in the previous month. Then the model will consist of the equation:

$$C_t = a + bY_{t-1} + e_t,$$

where C_t is consumer spending in month t, Y_{t-1} is income during the previous month, and e_t is an error term measuring the extent to which the model cannot fully explain consumption. Then one objective of the econometrician is to obtain estimates of the parameters a and b; these estimated parameter values, when used in the model's equation, enable predictions for future values of consumption to be made contingent on the prior month's income.

Formal Definition

In econometrics, as in statistics in general, it is presupposed that the quantities being analyzed can be treated as random variables. An econometric model then is a set of joint probability distributions to which the true joint probability distribution of the variables under study is supposed to belong. In the case in which the elements of this set can be indexed by a finite number of real-valued *parameters*, the model is called a parametric model; otherwise it is a nonparametric or semiparametric model. A large part of econometrics is the study of methods for selecting models, estimating them, and carrying out inference on them.

The most common econometric models are structural, in that they convey causal and counterfactual information, and are used for policy evaluation. For example, an equation modeling consumption spending based on income could be used to see what consumption would be contingent on any of various hypothetical levels of income, only one of which (depending on the choice of a fiscal policy) will end up actually occurring.

Basic Models

Some of the common econometric models are:

- Linear regression
- Generalized linear models
- Probit
- Logit
- Tobit
- ARIMA
- Vector Autoregression
- Cointegration
- Hazard

Use in Policy-making

Comprehensive models of macroeconomic relationships are used by central banks and governments to evaluate and guide economic policy. One famous econometric model of this nature is the Federal Reserve Bank econometric model.

Major Econometric Models

Vector Autoregression

Vector auto regression (VAR) is an econometric model used to capture the linear inter dependencies among multiple time series. VAR models generalize the univariate autoregressive model (AR model) by allowing for more than one evolving variable. All variables in a VAR enter the model in the same way: each variable has an equation explaining its evolution based on its own lags and the lags of the other model variables. VAR modeling does not require as much knowledge about the forces influencing a variable as do structural models with simultaneous equations: The only prior knowledge required is a list of variables which can be hypothesized to affect each other intertemporally.

Specification

Definition

A VAR model describes the evolution of a set of k variables (called *endogenous variables*) over the same sample period ($t = 1, \ldots, T$) as a linear function of only their past values. The variables are collected in a $k \times 1$ vector y_t, which has as the ith element, $y_{i,t}$, the observation at time "t" of the ith variable. For example, if the ith variable is GDP, then $y_{i,t}$ is the value of GDP at time t.

A *p-th order VAR*, denoted VAR(p), is

$$y_t = c + A_1 y_{t-1} + A_2 y_{t-2} + \cdots + A_p y_{t-p} + e_t,$$

where the l-periods back observation y_{t-1} is called the l-th *lag* of y, c is a $k \times 1$ vector of constants (intercepts), A_i is a time-invariant $k \times k$ matrix and e_t is a $k \times 1$ vector of error terms satisfying,

1. $\mathrm{E}(e_t) = 0$ — every error term has mean zero;
2. $\mathrm{E}(e_t e_{t'}) = \Omega$ — the contemporaneous covariance matrix of error terms is Ω (a $k \times k$ positive-semidefinite matrix);
3. $\mathrm{E}(e_t e_{t-k}') = 0$ for any non-zero k — there is no correlation across time; in particular, no serial correlation in individual error terms.

A pth-order VAR is also called a VAR with p lags. The process of choosing the maximum lag p in the VAR model requires special attention because inference is dependent on correctness of the selected lag order.

use VAR in time series data when data not stationary on first difference.(by chashman)

Order of Integration of The Variables

Note that all variables have to be of the same order of integration. The following cases are distinct:

- All the variables are I(0) (stationary): one is in the standard case, i.e. a VAR in level.
- All the variables are I(d) (non-stationary) with $d > 0$:
    - The variables are cointegrated: the error correction term has to be included in the VAR. The model becomes a Vector error correction model (VECM) which can be seen as a restricted VAR.
    - The variables are not cointegrated: the variables have first to be differenced d times and one has a VAR in difference.

Concise Matrix Notation

One can stack the vectors in order to write a VAR(p) with a concise matrix notation:

$$Y = BZ + U$$

Details of the matrices are in a separate page.

Example

For a general example of a VAR(p) with k variables, see General matrix notation of a VAR(p).

A VAR(1) in two variables can be written in matrix form (more compact notation) as,

$$\begin{bmatrix} y_{1,t} \\ y_{2,t} \end{bmatrix} = \begin{bmatrix} c_1 \\ c_2 \end{bmatrix} + \begin{bmatrix} A_{1,1} & A_{1,2} \\ A_{2,1} & A_{2,2} \end{bmatrix} \begin{bmatrix} y_{1,t-1} \\ y_{2,t-1} \end{bmatrix} + \begin{bmatrix} e_{1,t} \\ e_{2,t} \end{bmatrix},$$

(in which only a single A matrix appears because this example has a maximum lag p equal to 1), or, equivalently, as the following system of two equations,

$$y_{1,t} = c_1 + A_{1,1}y_{1,t-1} + A_{1,2}y_{2,t-1} + e_{1,t}$$

$$y_{2,t} = c_2 + A_{2,1}y_{1,t-1} + A_{2,2}y_{2,t-1} + e_{2,t}.$$

Each variable in the model has one equation. The current (time t) observation of each variable depends on its own lagged values as well as on the lagged values of each other variable in the VAR.

Writing VAR(p) as VAR(1)

A VAR with p lags can always be equivalently rewritten as a VAR with only one lag by appropriately redefining the dependent variable. The transformation amounts to stacking the lags of the VAR(p) variable in the new VAR(1) dependent variable and appending identities to complete the number of equations.

For example, the VAR(2) model,

$$y_t = c + A_1 y_{t-1} + A_2 y_{t-2} + e_t$$

can be recast as the VAR(1) model,

$$\begin{bmatrix} y_t \\ y_{t-1} \end{bmatrix} = \begin{bmatrix} c \\ 0 \end{bmatrix} + \begin{bmatrix} A_1 & A_2 \\ I & 0 \end{bmatrix} \begin{bmatrix} y_{t-1} \\ y_{t-2} \end{bmatrix} + \begin{bmatrix} e_t \\ 0 \end{bmatrix},$$

where I is the identity matrix.

The equivalent VAR(1) form is more convenient for analytical derivations and allows more compact statements.

Structural Vs. Reduced Form

Structural VAR

A *structural VAR with p lags* (sometimes abbreviated SVAR) is,

$$B_0 y_t = c_0 + B_1 y_{t-1} + B_2 y_{t-2} + \cdots + B_p y_{t-p} + \epsilon_t,$$

where c_0 is a $k \times 1$ vector of constants, B_i is a $k \times k$ matrix (for every $i = 0, \ldots, p$) and ε_t is a $k \times 1$ vector of error terms. The main diagonal terms of the B_0 matrix (the coefficients on the ith variable in the ith equation) are scaled to 1.

The error terms ε_t (*structural shocks*) satisfy the conditions (1) - (3) in the definition above, with the particularity that all the elements off the main diagonal of the covariance matrix $\mathrm{E}(\epsilon_t \epsilon_{t'}) = \Sigma$ are zero. That is, the structural shocks are uncorrelated.

For example, a two variable structural VAR(1) is:

$$\begin{bmatrix} 1 & B_{0;1,2} \\ B_{0;2,1} & 1 \end{bmatrix} \begin{bmatrix} y_{1,t} \\ y_{2,t} \end{bmatrix} = \begin{bmatrix} c_{0;1} \\ c_{0;2} \end{bmatrix} + \begin{bmatrix} B_{1;1,1} & B_{1;1,2} \\ B_{1;2,1} & B_{1;2,2} \end{bmatrix} \begin{bmatrix} y_{1,t-1} \\ y_{2,t-1} \end{bmatrix} + \begin{bmatrix} \epsilon_{1,t} \\ \epsilon_{2,t} \end{bmatrix},$$

where

$$\Sigma = \mathrm{E}(\epsilon_t \epsilon_{t'}) = \begin{bmatrix} \sigma_1^2 & 0 \\ 0 & \sigma_2^2 \end{bmatrix};$$

that is, the variances of the structural shocks are denoted $\mathrm{var}(\epsilon_i) = \sigma_i^2$ (i = 1, 2) and the covariance is $\mathrm{cov}(\epsilon_1, \epsilon_2) = 0$.

Writing the first equation explicitly and passing $y_{2,t}$ to the right hand side one obtains,

$$y_{1,t} = c_{0;1} - B_{0;1,2} y_{2,t} + B_{1;1,1} y_{1,t-1} + B_{1;1,2} y_{2,t-1} + \epsilon_{1,t}$$

Note that $y_{2,t}$ can have a contemporaneous effect on $y_{1,t}$ if $B_{0;1,2}$ is not zero. This is different from the case when B_0 is the identity matrix (all off-diagonal elements are zero — the case in the initial definition), when $y_{2,t}$ can impact directly $y_{1,t+1}$ and subsequent future values, but not $y_{1,t}$.

Because of the parameter identification problem, ordinary least squares estimation of the structural VAR would yield inconsistent parameter estimates. This problem can be overcome by rewriting the VAR in reduced form.

From an economic point of view, if the joint dynamics of a set of variables can be represented by a VAR model, then the structural form is a depiction of the underlying, "structural", economic relationships. Two features of the structural form make it the preferred candidate to represent the underlying relations:

1. *Error terms are not correlated.* The structural, economic shocks which drive the dynamics of the economic variables are assumed to be independent, which implies zero correlation between error terms as a desired property. This is helpful for separating out the effects of economically unrelated influences in the VAR. For instance, there is no reason why an oil price shock (as an example of a supply shock) should be related to a shift in consumers' preferences towards a style of clothing (as an example of a demand shock); therefore one would expect these factors to be statistically independent.

2. *Variables can have a contemporaneous impact on other variables.* This is a desirable feature especially when using low frequency data. For example, an indirect tax rate increase would not affect tax revenues the day the decision is announced, but one could find an effect in that quarter's data.

Reduced-form VAR

By premultiplying the structural VAR with the inverse of B_0,

$$y_t = B_0^{-1}c_0 + B_0^{-1}B_1 y_{t-1} + B_0^{-1}B_2 y_{t-2} + \cdots + B_0^{-1}B_p y_{t-p} + B_0^{-1}\epsilon_t,$$

and denoting,

$$B_0^{-1}c_0 = c, \quad B_0^{-1}B_i = A_i \text{ for } i = 1,\ldots,p \text{ and } B_0^{-1}\epsilon_t = e_t$$

one obtains the *p*th order reduced VAR,

$$y_t = c + A_1 y_{t-1} + A_2 y_{t-2} + \cdots + A_p y_{t-p} + e_t$$

Note that in the reduced form all right hand side variables are predetermined at time *t*. As there are no time *t* endogenous variables on the right hand side, no variable has a *direct* contemporaneous effect on other variables in the model.

However, the error terms in the reduced VAR are composites of the structural shocks $e_t = B_0^{-1}\varepsilon_t$. Thus, the occurrence of one structural shock $\varepsilon_{i,t}$ can potentially lead to the occurrence of shocks in all error terms $e_{j,t}$, thus creating contemporaneous movement in all endogenous variables. Consequently, the covariance matrix of the reduced VAR

$$\Omega = \mathrm{E}(e_t e_{t'}) = \mathrm{E}(B_0^{-1}\epsilon_t \epsilon_{t'} (B_0^{-1})') = B_0^{-1}\Sigma(B_0^{-1})'$$

can have non-zero off-diagonal elements, thus allowing non-zero correlation between error terms.

Estimation

Estimation of The Regression Parameters

Starting from the concise matrix notation:

$$Y = BZ + U$$

- The multivariate least squares (MLS) approach for estimating B yields:

$$\hat{B} = YZ(ZZ)^{-1}.$$

This can be written alternatively as:

$$\mathrm{Vec}(\hat{B}) = ((ZZ)^{-1}Z \otimes I_k)\,\mathrm{Vec}(Y)$$

where ⊗ denotes the Kronecker product and Vec the vectorization of the indicated matrix.

This estimator is consistent and asymptotically efficient. It is furthermore equal to the conditional maximum likelihood estimator.

- As the explanatory variables are the same in each equation, the multivariate least squares estimator is equivalent to the ordinary least squares estimator applied to each equation separately.

Estimation of The Covariance Matrix of The Errors

As in the standard case, the maximum likelihood estimator (MLE) of the covariance matrix differs from the ordinary least squares (OLS) estimator.

MLE estimator: $\hat{\Sigma} = \frac{1}{T}\sum_{t=1}^{T}\hat{\epsilon}_t\hat{\epsilon}_t'$

OLS estimator: $\hat{\Sigma} = \frac{1}{T-kp-1}\sum_{t=1}^{T}\hat{\epsilon}_t\hat{\epsilon}_t'$ for a model with a constant, k variables and p lags.

In a matrix notation, this gives:

$$\hat{\Sigma} = \frac{1}{T-kp-1}(Y-\hat{B}Z)(Y-\hat{B}Z)'.$$

Estimation of The Estimator's Covariance Matrix

The covariance matrix of the parameters can be estimated as

$$\widehat{\mathrm{Cov}}(\mathrm{Vec}(\hat{B})) = (ZZ')^{-1} \otimes \hat{\Sigma}.$$

Degrees of Freedom

Vector autoregression models often involve the estimation of many parameters. For example, with seven variables and four lags, each matrix of coefficients for a given lag length is 7 by 7, and the vector of constants has 7 elements, so a total of 49×4 + 7 = 203 parameters are estimated, substantially lowering the degrees of freedom of the regression (the number of data points minus the number of parameters to be estimated). This can hurt the accuracy of the parameter estimates and hence of the forecasts given by the model.

Interpretation of Estimated Model

Properties of the VAR model are usually summarized using structural analysis using Granger causality, impulse responses, and forecast error variance decompositions.

Impulse Response

Consider the first-order case (i.e., with only one lag), with equation of evolution,

$$y_t = Ay_{t-1} + e_t,$$

for evolving (state) vector y and vector e of shocks. To find, say, the effect of the j-th element of the vector of shocks upon the i-th element of the state vector 2 periods later, which is a particular impulse response, first write the above equation of evolution one period lagged:

$$y_{t-1} = Ay_{t-2} + e_{t-1}.$$

Use this in the original equation of evolution to obtain,

$$y_t = A^2 y_{t-2} + Ae_{t-1} + e_t;$$

then repeat using the twice lagged equation of evolution, to obtain,

$$y_t = A^3 y_{t-3} + A^2 e_{t-2} + Ae_{t-1} + e_t.$$

From this, the effect of the *j*-th component of e_{t-2} upon the *i*-th component of y_t is the *i*, *j* element of the matrix A^2.

It can be seen from this induction process that any shock will have an effect on the elements of *y* infinitely far forward in time, although the effect will become smaller and smaller over time assuming that the AR process is stable — that is, that all the eigenvalues of the matrix *A* are less than 1 in absolute value.

Forecasting Using An Estimated Var Model

An estimated VAR model can be used for forecasting, and the quality of the forecasts can be judged, in ways that are completely analogous to the methods used in univariate autoregressive modelling.

Applications

Christopher Sims advocated VAR models, criticizing the claims and performance of earlier modeling in macroeconomic econometrics. He recommended VAR models, which had previously appeared in time series statistics and in system identification, a statistical specialty in control theory. Sims advocated VAR models as providing a theory-free method to estimate economic relationships, thus being an alternative to the "incredible identification restrictions" in structural models.

Software

- R: there is a package called vars which deals with VAR models.
- Python: PyFlux has support for VARs and Bayesian VARs.
- SAS: VARMAX
- Stata: "var"
- EViews: "VAR"
- Gretl: "var"
- Regression analysis of time series: "SYSTEM"
- LDT

Autoregressive Integrated Moving Average

In statistics and econometrics, and in particular in time series analysis, an autoregressive integrated moving average (ARIMA) model is a generalization of an autoregressive moving average (ARMA) model. Both of these models are fitted to time series data either to better understand the data or to predict future points in the series (forecasting). ARIMA models are applied in some cases where data show evidence of non-stationarity, where an initial differencing step (corresponding to the "integrated" part of the model) can be applied to reduce the non-stationarity.

The AR part of ARIMA indicates that the evolving variable of interest is regressed on its own lagged (i.e., prior) values. The MA part indicates that the regression error is actually a linear combination of error terms whose values occurred contemporaneously and at various times in the past. The I (for "integrated") indicates that the data values have been replaced with the difference between their values and the previous values (and this differencing process may have been performed more than once). The purpose of each of these features is to make the model fit the data as well as possible.

Non-seasonal ARIMA models are generally denoted ARIMA(p,d,q) where parameters p, d, and q are non-negative integers, p is the order (number of time lags) of the autoregressive model, d is the degree of differencing (the number of times the data have had past values subtracted), and q is the order of the moving-average model. Seasonal ARIMA models are usually denoted ARIMA(p,d,q)(P,D,Q)$_m$, where m refers to the number of periods in each season, and the uppercase P,D,Q refer to the autoregressive, differencing, and moving average terms for the seasonal part of the ARIMA model.

When two out of the three terms are zeros, the model may be referred to based on the non-zero parameter, dropping "AR", "I" or "MA" from the acronym describing the model. For example, ARIMA (1,0,0) is AR(1), ARIMA(0,1,0) is I(1), and ARIMA(0,0,1) is MA(1).

ARIMA models can be estimated following the Box-Jenkins approach.

Definition

Given a time series of data X_t where t is an integer index and the X_t are real numbers, an ARMA(p,q) model is given by,

$$X_t - \alpha_1 X_{t-1} - \cdots - \alpha_{p'} X_{t-p'} = \varepsilon_t + \theta_1 \varepsilon_{t-1} + \cdots + \theta_q \varepsilon_{t-q},$$

or equivalently by,

$$\left(1 - \sum_{i=1}^{p'} \alpha_i L^i\right) X_t = \left(1 + \sum_{i=1}^{q} \theta_i L^i\right) \varepsilon_t$$

where L is the lag operator, the α_i are the parameters of the autoregressive part of the model, the θ_i are the parameters of the moving average part and the ε_t are error terms. The error terms are generally assumed to be independent, identically distributed variables sampled from a normal distribution with zero mean.

Assume now that the polynomial $\left(1-\sum_{i=1}^{p'}\alpha_i L^i\right)$ has a unit root (a factor $(1-L)$) of multiplicity d. Then it can be rewritten as:

$$\left(1-\sum_{i=1}^{p'}\alpha_i L^i\right)=\left(1-\sum_{i=1}^{p'\,d}\phi_i L^i\right)(1-L) \ .$$

An ARIMA(p,d,q) process expresses this polynomial factorisation property with $p=p'-d$, and is given by:

$$\left(1-\sum_{i=1}^{p'}\alpha_i L^i\right)=\left(1-\sum_{i=1}^{p'-d}\phi_i L^i\right)(1-L)^d .$$

and thus can be thought as a particular case of an ARMA($p+d,q$) process having the autoregressive polynomial with d unit roots. (For this reason, no ARIMA model with $d>0$ is wide sense stationary.)

The above can be generalized as follows.

$$\left(1-\sum_{i=1}^{p}\phi_i L^i\right)(1-L)^d X_t=\delta+\left(1+\sum_{i=1}^{q}\theta_i L^i\right)\varepsilon_t .$$

This defines an ARIMA(p,d,q) process with drift $\delta/(1-\Sigma\varphi_i)$.

Other Special Forms

The explicit identification of the factorisation of the autoregression polynomial into factors as above, can be extended to other cases, firstly to apply to the moving average polynomial and secondly to include other special factors. For example, having a factor $\left(1-L^s\right)$ in a model is one way of including a non-stationary seasonality of period s into the model; this factor has the effect of re-expressing the data as changes from s periods ago. Another example is the factor $\left(1-\sqrt{3}L+L^2\right)$, which includes a (non-stationary) seasonality of period 2. The effect of the first type of factor is to allow each season's value to drift separately over time, whereas with the second type values for adjacent seasons move together.

Identification and specification of appropriate factors in an ARIMA model can be an important step in modelling as it can allow a reduction in the overall number of parameters to be estimated, while allowing the imposition on the model of types of behaviour that logic and experience suggest should be there.

Differencing

Differencing in statistics refers to a transformation applied to time-series data in order to make it stationary. A stationary time series' properties do not depend on the time at which the series is observed.

In order to difference the data, the difference between consecutive observations is computed. Mathematically, this is shown as,

$$y_t' = y_t - y_{t-1}$$

Differencing removes the changes in the level of a time series, eliminating trend and seasonality and consequently stabilizing the mean of the time series.

Sometimes it may be necessary to difference the data a second time to obtain a stationary time series, which is referred to as second order differencing:

$$y_t^* = yt - yt - 1$$

$$= (y_t - y_{t-1}) - (y_{t-1} - y_{t-2})$$

$$= y_t - 2y_{t-1} + y_{t-2}$$

Another method of differencing data is seasonal differencing, which involves computing the difference between an observation and the corresponding observation in the previous year. This is shown as:

$$yt = y_t - y_{t-m} \quad \text{where} \quad m = \text{number of seasons.}$$

The differenced data is then used for the estimation of an ARMA model.

Forecasts Using ARIMA Models

The ARIMA model can be viewed as a "cascade" of two models. The first is non-stationary:

$$Y_t = (1-L)^d X_t$$

while the second is wide-sense stationary:

$$\left(1 - \sum_{i=1}^{p} \phi_i L^i\right) Y_t = \left(1 + \sum_{i=1}^{q} \theta_i L^i\right) \varepsilon_t.$$

Now forecasts can be made for the process Y_t, using a generalization of the method of autoregressive forecasting.

Forecast Intervals

The forecast intervals (confidence intervals for forecasts) for ARIMA models are based on assumptions that the residuals are uncorrelated and normally distributed. If either of these assumptions does not hold, then the forecast intervals may be incorrect. For this reason, researchers plot the ACF and histogram of the residuals to check the assumptions before producing forecast intervals.

95% forecast interval: $\hat{y}_{T+h|T} \pm 1.96\sqrt{v_{T+h|T}}$, where $v_{T+h|T}$ is the variance of $y_{T+h} \mid y_1, \ldots, y_T$.

For $h = 1$, $v_{T+h|T} = \hat{\sigma}^2$ for all ARIMA models regardless of parameters and orders.

For ARIMA(0,0,q), $y_t = e_t + \sum_{i=1}^{q} \theta_i e_{t-i}$.

$$v_{T+h|T} = \hat{\sigma}^2 [1 + \sum_{i=1}^{h-1} \theta_i e_{t-i}], \text{ for h=2,3,....}$$

In general, forecast intervals from ARIMA models will increase as the forecast horizon increases.

Examples

Some well-known special cases arise naturally or are mathematically equivalent to other popular forecasting models. For example:

- An ARIMA(0,1,0) model (or I(1) model) is given by $X_t = X_{t-1} + \varepsilon_t$ — which is simply a random walk.
- An ARIMA(0,1,0) with a constant, given by $X_t = c + X_{t-1} + \varepsilon_t$ — which is a random walk with drift.
- An ARIMA(0,0,0) model is a white noise model.
- An ARIMA(0,1,2) model is a Damped Holt's model.
- An ARIMA(0,1,1) model without constant is a Basic Exponential Smoothing.
- An ARIMA(0,2,2) model is given by $X_t = 2X_{t-1} - X_{t-2} + (\alpha + \beta - 2)\varepsilon_{t-1} + (1-\alpha)\varepsilon_{t-2} + \varepsilon_t$ — which is equivalent to Holt's linear method with additive errors, or Double exponential smoothing.

Information Criteria

To determine the order of a non-seasonal ARIMA model, a useful criterion is the Akaike information criterion (AIC) . It is written as,

$$AIC = -2\log(L) + 2(p+q+k+1),$$

where *L* is the likelihood of the data, *p* is the order of the autoregressive part and *q* is the order of the moving average part. The parameter *k* in this criterion is defined as the number of parameters in the model being fitted to the data. For AIC, if *k* = 1 then *c* ≠ 0 and if *k* = 0 then *c* = 0.

The corrected AIC for ARIMA models can be written as,

$$AICc = AIC + (2(p+q+k+1)(p+q+k+2))/(T-p-q-k-2).$$

The Bayesian Information Criterion can be written as,

$$BIC = AIC + (\log(T) - 2)(p+q+k+1).$$

The objective is to minimize the AIC, AICc or BIC values for a good model. The lower the value of one of these criteria for a range of models being investigated, the better the model will suit the data. It should be noted however that the AIC and the BIC are used for two completely different purposes. Whilst the AIC tries to approximate models towards the reality of the situation, the BIC attempts to find the perfect fit. The BIC approach is often criticized as there never is a perfect fit to real-life complex data; however, it is still a useful method for selection as it penalizes models more heavily for having more parameters than the AIC would.

AICc can only be used to compare ARIMA models with the same orders of differencing. For ARIMAs with different orders of differencing, RMSE can be used for model comparison.

Variations and Extensions

A number of variations on the ARIMA model are commonly employed. If multiple time series are used then the can be thought of as vectors and a VARIMA model may be appropriate. Sometimes a seasonal effect is suspected in the model; in that case, it is generally better to use a SARIMA (seasonal ARIMA) model than to increase the order of the AR or MA parts of the model. If the time-series is suspected to exhibit long-range dependence, then the *d* parameter may be allowed to have non-integer values in an autoregressive fractionally integrated moving average model, which is also called a Fractional ARIMA (FARIMA or ARFIMA) model.

Software Implementations

Various packages that apply methodology like Box-Jenkins parameter optimization are available to find the right parameters for the ARIMA model.

- EViews: has extensive ARIMA and SARIMA capabilities.
- Julia: contains an ARIMA implementation in the TimeModels package
- Mathematica: includes ARIMAProcess function.
- MATLAB: the Econometrics Toolbox includes ARIMA models and regression with ARIMA errors.
- NCSS: includes several procedures for ARIMA fitting and forecasting.
- Python: the "statsmodels" package includes models for time series analysis - univariate time series analysis: AR, ARIMA - vector autoregressive models, VAR and structural VAR - descriptive statistics and process models for time series analysis.
- R: the standard R *stats* package includes an *arima* function, which is documented in "ARIMA Modelling of Time Series". Besides the *ARIMA(p,d,q)* part, the function also includes seasonal factors, an intercept term, and exogenous variables (*xreg*, called "external regressors"). The CRAN task view on Time Series is the reference with many more links. The "forecast" package in R can automatically select an ARIMA model for a given time series with the auto.arima() function. The package can also simulate seasonal and non-seasonal ARIMA models with its simulate.Arima() function. It also has a function Arima(), which is a wrapper for the arima from the "stats" package.
- Ruby: the "statsample-timeseries" gem is used for time series analysis, including ARIMA models and Kalman Filtering.

- SAFE TOOLBOXES: includes ARIMA modelling and regression with ARIMA errors.
- SAS: includes extensive ARIMA processing in its Econometric and Time Series Analysis system: SAS/ETS.
- IBM SPSS: includes ARIMA modeling in its Statistics and Modeler statistical packages. The default Expert Modeler feature evaluates a range of seasonal and non-seasonal autoregressive (p), integrated (d), and moving average (q) settings and seven exponential smoothing models. The Expert Modeler can also transform the target time-series data into its square root or natural log. The user also has the option to restrict the Expert Modeler to ARIMA models, or to manually enter ARIMA nonseasonal and seasonal p, d, and q settings without Expert Modeler. Automatic outlier detection is available for seven types of outliers, and the detected outliers will be accommodated in the time-series model if this feature is selected.
- SAP: the APO-FCS package in SAP ERP from SAP allows creation and fitting of ARIMA models using the Box-Jenkins methodology.
- SQL Server Analysis Services: from Microsoft includes ARIMA as a Data Mining algorithm.
- Stata includes ARIMA modelling (using its arima command) as of Stata 9.

Macroeconomic Model

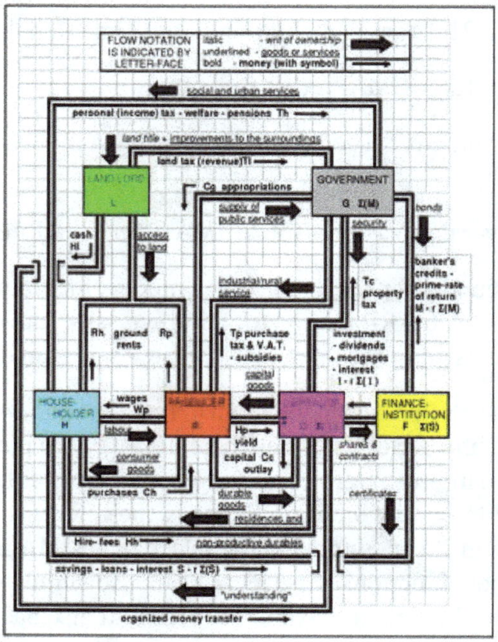

A macroeconomic model is an analytical tool designed to describe the operation of the economy of a country or a region. These models are usually designed to examine the dynamics of aggregate quantities such as the total amount of goods and services produced, total income earned, the level of employment of productive resources, and the level of prices.

Macroeconomic models may be logical, mathematical, and/or computational; the different types of macroeconomic models serve different purposes and have different advantages and disadvantages. Macroeconomics models may be used to clarify and illustrate basic theoretical principles; they may be used to test, compare, and quantify different macroeconomic theories; they may be used to produce "what if" scenarios (usually to predict the effects of changes in monetary, fiscal, or other macroeconomic policies); and they may be used to generate economic forecasts. Thus, macroeconomic models are widely used in academia, teaching and research, and are also widely used by international organizations, national governments and larger corporations, as well as by economics consultants and think tanks.

Types of Macroeconomic Models

Simple Theoretical Models

Simple text book descriptions of the macroeconomy involving a small number of equations or diagrams are often called 'models'. Examples include the IS-LM model and Mundell–Fleming model of Keynesian macroeconomics, and the Solow model of neoclassical growth theory. These models share several features. They are based on a few equations involving a few variables, which can often be explained with simple diagrams. Many of these models are static, but some are dynamic, describing the economy over many time periods. The variables that appear in these models often represent macroeconomic aggregates (such as GDP or total employment) rather than individual choice variables, and while the equations relating these variables are intended to describe economic decisions, they are not usually derived directly by aggregating models of individual choices. They are simple enough to be used as illustrations of theoretical points in introductory explanations of macroeconomic ideas; but therefore quantitative application to forecasting, testing, or policy evaluation is usually impossible without substantially augmenting the structure of the model.

Empirical Forecasting Models

In the 1940s and 1950s, as governments began accumulating national income and product accounting data, economists set out to construct quantitative models to describe the dynamics observed in the data. These models estimated the relations between different macroeconomic variables using (mostly linear) time series analysis. Like the simpler theoretical models, these empirical models described relations between aggregate quantities, but many addressed a much finer level of detail (for example, studying the relations between output, employment, investment, and other variables in many different industries). Thus, these models grew to include hundreds or thousands of equations describing the evolution of hundreds or thousands of prices and quantities over time, making computers essential for their solution. While the choice of which variables to include in each equation was partly guided by economic theory (for example, including past income as a determinant of consumption, as suggested by the theory of adaptive expectations), variable inclusion was mostly determined on purely empirical grounds.

Dutch economist Jan Tinbergen developed the first comprehensive national model, which he built for the Netherlands in 1936. He later applied the same modeling structure to the economies of the United States and the United Kingdom. The first global macroeconomic model, Wharton Econometric Forecasting Associates' LINK project, was initiated by Lawrence Klein. The model was cited in 1980 when Klein, like Tinbergen before him, won the Nobel Prize. Large-scale empirical models of this type, including the Wharton model, are still in use today, especially for forecasting purposes.

The Lucas Critique of Empirical Forecasting Models

Econometric studies in the first part of the 20th century showed a negative correlation between inflation and unemployment called the Phillips curve. Empirical macroeconomic forecasting models, being based on roughly the same data, had similar implications: they suggested that unemployment could be permanently lowered by permanently increasing inflation. However, in 1968, Milton Friedman and Edmund Phelps argued that this apparent tradeoff was illusory. They claimed that the historical relation between inflation and unemployment was due to the fact that past inflationary episodes had been largely unexpected. They argued that if monetary authorities permanently raised the inflation rate, workers and firms would eventually come to understand this, at which point the economy would return to its previous, higher level of unemployment, but now with higher inflation too. The stagflation of the 1970s appeared to bear out their prediction.

In 1976, Robert Lucas, Jr., published an influential paper arguing that the failure of the Phillips curve in the 1970s was just one example of a general problem with empirical forecasting models. He pointed out that such models are derived from observed relationships between various macroeconomic quantities over time, and that these relations differ depending on what macroeconomic policy regime is in place. In the context of the Phillips curve, this means that the relation between inflation and unemployment observed in an economy where inflation has usually been low in the past would differ from the relation observed in an economy where inflation has been high. Furthermore, this means one cannot predict the effects of a new policy regime using an empirical forecasting model based on data from previous periods when that policy regime was not in place. Lucas argued that economists would remain unable to predict the effects of new policies unless they built models based on economic fundamentals (like preferences, technology, and budget constraints) that should be unaffected by policy changes.

Dynamic Stochastic General Equilibrium Models

Partly as a response to the Lucas critique, economists of the 1980s and 1990s began to construct microfounded macroeconomic models based on rational choice, which have come to be called dynamic stochastic general equilibrium (DSGE) models. These models begin by specifying the set of agents active in the economy, such as households, firms, and governments in one or more countries, as well as the preferences, technology, and budget constraint of each one. Each agent is assumed to make an optimal choice, taking into account prices and the strategies of other agents, both in the current period and in the future. Summing up the decisions of the different types of agents, it is possible to find the prices that equate supply with demand in every market. Thus these models embody a type of equilibrium self-consistency: agents choose optimally given the prices, while prices must be consistent with agents' supplies and demands.

DSGE models often assume that all agents of a given type are identical (i.e. there is a 'representative household' and a 'representative firm') and can perform perfect calculations that forecast the future correctly on average (which is called rational expectations). However, these are only simplifying assumptions, and are not essential for the DSGE methodology; many DSGE studies aim for greater realism by considering heterogeneous agents or various types of adaptive expectations. Compared with empirical forecasting models, DSGE models typically have fewer variables and equations, mainly because DSGE models are harder to solve, even with the help of computers. Simple theoretical DSGE models, involving only a few variables, have been used to analyze the forces that drive business cycles; this empirical work has given rise to two main competing frameworks called the real business cycle model and the New Keynesian DSGE model. More elaborate DSGE models are used to predict the effects of changes in economic policy and evaluate their impact on social welfare. However, economic forecasting is still largely based on more traditional empirical models, which are still widely believed to achieve greater accuracy in predicting the impact of economic disturbances over time.

DSGE Versus CGE Models

A closely related methodology that pre-dates DSGE modeling is computable general equilibrium (CGE) modeling. Like DSGE models, CGE models are often microfounded on assumptions about preferences, technology, and budget constraints. However, CGE models focus mostly on long-run relationships, making them most suited to studying the long-run impact of permanent policies like the tax system or the openness of the economy to international trade. DSGE models instead emphasize the dynamics of the economy over time (often at a quarterly frequency), making them suited for studying business cycles and the cyclical effects of monetary and fiscal policy.

Agent-based Computational Macroeconomic Models

Another modeling methodology which has developed at the same time as DSGE models is Agent-based computational economics (ACE), which is a variety of Agent-based modeling. Like the DSGE methodology, ACE seeks to break down aggregate macroeconomic relationships into microeconomic decisions of individual agents. ACE models also begin by defining the set of agents that make up the economy, and specify the types of interactions individual agents can have with each other or with the market as a whole. Instead of defining the preferences of those agents, ACE models often jump directly to specifying their strategies. Or sometimes, preferences are specified, together with an initial strategy and a learning rule whereby the strategy is adjusted according to its past success. Given these strategies, the interaction of large numbers of individual agents (who may be very heterogeneous) can be simulated on a computer, and then the aggregate, macroeconomic relationships that arise from those individual actions can be studied.

Strengths and Weaknesses of DSGE and ACE Models

DSGE and ACE models have different advantages and disadvantages due to their different underlying structures. DSGE models may exaggerate individual rationality and foresight, and understate the importance of heterogeneity, since the rational expectations, representative agent case remains the simplest and thus the most common type of DSGE model to solve. Also, unlike ACE models, it may be difficult to study local interactions between individual agents in DSGE models, which instead focus mostly on the way agents interact through aggregate prices. On the other hand, ACE models may exaggerate errors in individual decision-making, since the strategies assumed in ACE models may be very far from optimal choices unless the modeler is very careful. A related issue is that ACE models which start from strategies instead of preferences may remain vulnerable to the Lucas critique: a changed policy regime should generally give rise to changed strategies.

Brander–Spencer Model

The Brander–Spencer model is an economic model in international trade originally developed by James Brander and Barbara Spencer in the early 1980s. The model illustrates a situation where, under certain assumptions, a government can subsidize domestic firms to help them in their competition against foreign producers and in doing so enhances national welfare. This conclusion stands in contrast to results from most international trade models, in which government non-interference is socially optimal.

The basic model is a variation on the Stackelberg–Cournot "leader and follower" duopoly game. Alternatively, the model can be portrayed in game theoretic terms as initially a game with multiple Nash equilibria, with government having the capability of affecting the payoffs to switch to a game with just one equilibrium. Although it is possible for the national government to increase a country's welfare in the model through export subsidies, the policy is of beggar thy neighbor type. This also means that if all governments simultaneously attempt to follow the policy prescription of the model, all countries would wind up worse off.

The model was part of the "New Trade Theory" that was developed in the late 1970s and early 1980s, which incorporated then recent developments from literature on industrial organization into theories of international trade. In particular, like in many other New Trade Theory models, economies of scale (in this case, in the form of fixed entry costs) play an important role in the Brander–Spencer model.

Entry Game Version

A simplified version of the model was popularized by Paul Krugman in the 1990s in his book *Peddling Prosperity*. In this set up there are two firms, one foreign and one domestic which are considering entering a new export market in a third country (or possibly the whole world). The demand in the export market is such that if only one firm enters, it will make a profit, but if they both enter each will make a loss, perhaps because of initial set up, infrastructure, product development, marketing or other fixed costs of entry. The matrix below presents a stylized example of the game that the two firms are engaged in.

	Enter	Stay Out
Enter	−10, −10	50, 0
Stay Out	0, 50	0, 0

Fig. 1: Entry game with multiple equilibria

	Enter	Stay Out
Enter	10, −10	70, 0
Stay Out	0, 50	0, 0

Fig. 2: Entry game with subsidy, single equilibrium

The available choices of the domestic firms are given on the left, while those of the foreign firm are on top. The first number in each cell denotes the payoff to the domestic firm while the second number is the payoff to the foreign firm.

The game with no government subsidy to the domestic firm is shown in Figure 1 on the left. If both firms enter, they each suffer a loss of 10 million dollars and if they both stay out of the market neither firm makes a profit or a loss. If only one firm enters however, that firm will realize a profit of 50 million dollars while the other firm will make nothing. The two Nash equilibria of this game (marked in purple) are the situations in which only one firm enters – but which firm, domestic or foreign, is indeterminate. In such a situation if the foreign firm has a slight initial advantage over the domestic firm (perhaps because it began product development earlier) the domestic firm will stay out and the foreign firm will enter.

The game changes however if the government credibly promises to subsidize the domestic firm if it enters the market, as illustrated in Figure 2. Suppose the government promises a subsidy of twenty million, regardless of whether the foreign firm also enters or not. In that case, if the foreign firm enters the domestic firm will lose ten million from entry costs but will be more than compensated by the government subsidy, ending up with a net payoff of ten million. If the foreign firm does not enter of course, it is still profitable for the domestic firm to enter. As a result, regardless of the action of the foreign firm, the domestic firm's incentive is to enter the market. Anticipating this, the foreign firm will stay out of the market itself, since otherwise it would incur a loss.

From the point of view of the domestic country, the subsidy is welfare improving. The 20 million subsidy is a transfer from the government to the firm hence it has no effect on national welfare (ignoring costs of taxation; as long as these are not too large the basic insight of the model goes through). Additionally the domestic firm gains 50 million which would have otherwise gone to the foreign firm.

Stackelberg–cournot Version

The original Brander and Spencer paper presented the game in the framework of a Cournot competition model.

Letting x denote the output of the domestic firm and y denote the output of the foreign firm, the inverse demand function (price as a function of total quantity) is given by $p(x+y)$. Hence the profit function for the domestic firm is $\pi^h = xp(x+y) - c(x) + sx$ where $xp(x+y)$ is total revenue, $c(x)$ is total cost of producing x units, and s is per unit subsidy provided by the government. The profit function for the foreign firm is similar except that it does not include a subsidy, $\pi^f = yp(x+y) - c(y)$.

Each firm chooses the quantity to supply in order to maximize profits, taking the other's choice as given. The (first order) conditions for profit maximization are $xp_x + p - c_x + s = 0$ for the domestic firm and $yp_y + p - c_y = 0$ for the foreign firm, where subscripted variables denote partial derivatives. Solving these for y implicitly defines a best response function for each firm; $y = R1(x; s)$ and $y = R2(x)$. These are illustrated in the figure below, with the domestic firm's output on the x axis and foreign firm's output on the y axis.

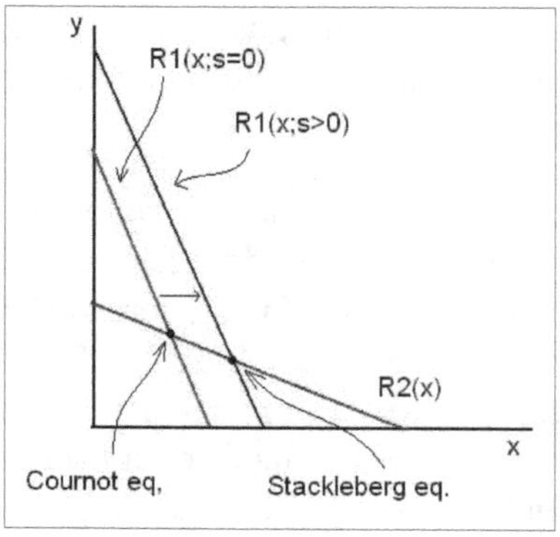

With no government subsidy (s=o) the resulting equilibrium will be the standard Cournot outcome, as shown in the graph by the intersection of the best response functions. A subsidy however has the effect of shifting the domestic firm's best response function to the right. Because its output is subsidized, the domestic firm increases production. This in turn means that the foreign firm's best response is to cut output, although not proportionally (hence, the market price falls). In the new equilibrium domestic firm produces more and foreign firm produces less.

In the model, domestic social welfare can be defined as the home firm's profit net of the subsidy (the model can be extended so that social welfare includes the firm's monopoly profit as well as the wages paid to the firm's workers; the results are qualitatively the same). It can be shown that the profit function evaluated at equilibrium quantity levels is concave in s and eventually negatively sloped. As a result, there is an "optimal subsidy" which maximizes the domestic firm's profits and hence domestic social welfare. As it turns out, if the government sets the subsidy exactly at the optimal level, the resulting equilibrium is the same as that of the "leader and follower" Stackelberg model. In that case one of the firms (in this case the domestic firm) has the ability to choose its output first. This creates the ability to credibly commit to a particular action, resulting in "first mover advantage". In the Brender–Spencer model, the government's subsidy creates this credible commitment even when the private firm does not have that ability.

Extensions

Domestic Consumption of Export Good

In standard models of international trade a fall in the price of a country's export good – a deterioration in its terms of trade – generally decreases the home country's welfare. In the Brander–Spencer model however the opposite is true. This is because in this model the markets are not perfectly competitive and the revenue from the expanded quantity sold compensates the firm for the revenue lost from the lower export price. If the good produced by the firm is also consumed domestically however the result is a bit more complicated. In the case where the firm is able to separate the home and export market (charge different prices in each with no possibility of third party arbitrage) then the level of the optimal subsidies will depend on whether marginal costs of production are constant, increasing or decreasing. The optimal subsidy level is either the same, higher or lower, respectively, compared to the level with no domestic consumption. This underscores the need on the part of the government for very precise information on industry structure and firm's cost functions.

In the more general case where the firm cannot price discriminate between domestic and foreign consumers the effects of a subsidy are less clear since both an expansion of exports and deterioration of terms of trade are present. However, Brender and Spencer show that starting out from the position of no subsidy, introducing a small subsidy can improve a country's welfare.

Extended Government Game

The basic model can be extended to incorporate a supra-game played by the governments of the respective countries. In this case, each government chooses the level of subsidy it will provide to its firm, taking the other government's action as given, and anticipating the reaction of the firms (in terms of quantity produced) to the subsidy. Brander and Spencer show that in the resulting Nash equilibrium the governments choose a level of subsidy that is too high and hence they do not manage to maximize social welfare. In fact, if the good produced is not consumed domestically, then the optimal level of subsidy is negative – an export tax. This is because the total quantity produced in the Cournot and the Stackelberg equilibrium is higher than the profit maximizing collusive monopoly level of output. Since both the home and foreign firm are producing for a third market, an export tax could reduce the total quantity produced down to the monopoly level, thus increasing both firms' profits. In that way the governments can effect a collusive outcome between their firms, at the expanse of the third country which imports the good.

Policy Applications and Applied Work

General Difficulties

As pointed out by Paul Krugman, the Brander–Spencer model, due to the sensitivity of the results to its assumptions, does not establish a generally applicable policy prescription in favor of government subsidies. Rather, it provides an example for when such intervention may be justifiable and points to some conditions which may favor it.

Paul Krugman popularized the model, but was also critical of it being misapplied to industries which did not meet the model's criteria.

A general difficulty with the application of the model, like many game theoretic models, is that it does not easily lend itself to econometric testing and parameter estimation. As a result, the two avenues of empirical research that have been pursued in subsequent literature have been estimates of a "conjectural variation" parameter for particular industries, and calibration of the models using behavioral parameters from other studies. The former approach assumes that firms have a "conjecture" as to how the other firms will react to their own choice of output and base their decision on this belief. However, the approach is problematic, both from an analytical (it is not internally consistent) and an empirical point of view (there's no guarantee that the parameter, even if it makes conceptual sense, remains stable when a new policy – the government's subsidy – is introduced). Calibrations of models of industry structure on the other hand have generally found that most industry are neither Cournot (in which case the Brander–Spencer policy prescription would be an export subsidy) nor Bertrand (in which case the optimal policy is an export tax). As a result, it is hard to say in which industries exactly the Brander–Spencer policy prescription may apply.

Agriculture

Marie Thursby has used an extended version of the model to examine international trade in wheat, 60% of which is produced by the United States and Canada. Thursby includes marketing boards, possibility of a monopsony, and a variety of government policies in the analysis. She finds that while there are significant economies of scale in the industry, the barriers to entry are not high and regardless of the extent of market power that US firms have in the industry, the optimal policy is actually an export tax, rather than a subsidy.

Aircraft

In his book which presented the model to the general public, Paul Krugman used the example of the aircraft industry, with the two players being Airbus and Boeing. In fact, Krugman and Baldwin examined the industry for wide bodied aircraft in the context of the model in a 1988 paper. The authors calibrate an extended version of the model in order to examine the effect of a subsidy to Airbus by European governments, and its presence in a market which can only support two firms at most, worldwide. They find that the subsidy had an unambiguously negative effect on welfare of the United States and a positive effect on rest of the world, which benefits from lower prices. The result for Europe hinges on price elasticity of demand; for relatively inelastic demand the net effect of subsidy is positive with most of the benefits accruing to European consumers, but for elastic demand, social welfare in Europe goes down. Importantly, unlike in the baseline Brander and Spencer model, Krugman and Baldwin find that the changes to consumer surplus resulting from the subsidy and entry, dominate the effect of changes in firm profits in social welfare calculations.

Gernot Klepper, in an analysis similar to Krugman and Baldwin, has also used the Brander Spencer and other models to analyze the effects of entry into the transport aircraft industry. He included the effects of learning during the production process which depends on the scale of production. His calibrated model suggested that per unit production costs can fall by as much as 20% if total production is doubled. In that case, the entry of another firm (in this case, Airbus) into the market would decrease per firm output and reduce the learning and scale effects. In his analysis, the entry of Airbus would cause an increase in consumer surplus, but this would be smaller than the resulting loss in producer surplus.

Criticism

In general, like with many of the New Trade Theory models, the results of the Brander Spencer model and the policy prescriptions it generates are very sensitive to the underlying assumptions on the nature of the industry in question, the information available to the national government, its ability to credibly commit to an action and the likely response of foreign governments. Some of these criticisms were already noted by Brander and Spencer in their paper, where they advised caution.

Further work on the model has shown that a slight difference in assumptions can produce completely different results. For example, Eaton and Grossmann showed that if the firms compete in prices rather in quantities (Bertrand competition rather than Cournot) then the optimal policy is an export tax rather a subsidy – a policy rarely used in practice, politically unpopular and contrary to protectionist sentiment which generally touted New Trade Theory models as an argument for their favored policies.

Influence

The 1985 paper "Export Subsidies and International Market Share Rivalry", which presented the original version of the model, was the most cited paper in the *Journal of International Economics* since the inception of the journal in 1971 (as of 2000).

Big Push Model

The big push model is a concept in development economics or welfare economics that emphasizes that a firm's decision whether to industrialize or not depends on its expectation of what other firms will do. It assumes economies of scale and oligopolistic market structure and explains when industrialization would happen.

The originator of this theory was Paul Rosenstein-Rodan in 1943. Further contributions were made later on by Murphy, Shleifer and Robert W. Vishny in 1989. Analysis of this economic model ordinarily involves using game theory.

The theory of the model emphasizes that underdeveloped countries require large amounts of investments to embark on the path of economic development from their present state of backwardness. This theory proposes that a 'bit by bit' investment programme will not impact the process of growth as much as is required for developing countries. In fact, injections of small quantities of investments will merely lead to a wastage of resources. Paul Rosenstein-Rodan approvingly quotes a Massachusetts Institute of Technology study in this regard, "There is a minimum level of resources that must be devoted to... a development programme if it is to have any chance of success. Launching a country into self-sustaining growth is a little like getting an airplane off the ground. There is a critical ground speed which must be passed before the craft can become airborne...."

Rosenstein-Rodan argued that the entire industry which is intended to be created should be treated and planned as a massive entity (a firm or trust). He supports this argument by stating that the social marginal product of an investment is always different from its private marginal product, so when a group of industries are planned together according to their social marginal products, the rate of growth of the economy is greater than it would have otherwise been.

The Three Indivisibilities

According to Rosenstein-Rodan, there exist three indivisibilities in underdeveloped countries. These indivisibilities are responsible for external economies and thus justify the need for a big push. The externalities are as follows-

1. Indivisibility in production function.
2. Indivisibility of demand.
3. Indivisibility in the supply of savings.

Indivisibility in Production Function

Indivisibilities in the production function may be with respect to any of the following:

- Inputs
- Processes
- Outputs

These lead to increasing returns (i.e., economies of scale), and may require a high optimum size of a firm. This can be achieved even in developing countries since at least one optimum scale firm can be established in many industries. But investment in social overhead capital comprises investment in all basic industries (like power, transport or communications) which must necessarily come before directly productive investment activities. Investment in social overhead capital is 'lumpy' in nature. Such capital requirements cannot be imported from other nations. Therefore, heavy initial investment necessarily needs to be made in social overhead capital (this is approximated to be about 30 to 40 percent of the total investment undertaken by underdeveloped countries). Social overhead capital is further characterized by four indivisibilities:

1. *Irreversibility in time*: It must precede other directly productive investments.
2. *Minimum durability of equipment*: Any lesser level of durability is either impossible due to technical reasons or much less efficient.
3. *Long gestation periods*: The investment in social overhead capital takes time to generate returns and its impact in the economy is not immediately or directly visible.
4. *Irreducible minimum social overhead capital–industry mix*: Investment needs to be of a certain minimum magnitude and spread across a mix of industries, without which it will not significantly impact the process of growth.

Indivisibility (Or Complementarity) of Demand

Developing countries are characterized by low per-capita income and purchasing power. Markets in these countries are therefore small. In a closed economy, modernization and increased efficiency in a single industry has no impact on the economy as a whole since the output of that industry will fail to find a market. A large number of industries need to be set up simultaneously so that people employed in one industry consume the output of other industries and thus create complementary demand.

To illustrate this, Rosenstein Rodan gives the example of a shoe industry. If a country makes large investments in the shoe industry, all the disguisedly employed labor from the other industries find work and a source of income, leading to a rise in production of shoes and their own incomes. This increased income will not be expended only on buying shoes. It is conceivable that the increased incomes will lead to increased spending on other products too. However, there is no corresponding supply of these products to satisfy this increased demand for the other goods. Following the basic market forces of demand and supply, the prices of these commodities will rise. To avoid such a situation, investment must be spread out amongst different industries.

The situation may be different in an open economy as the output of the new industry may replace former imports or possibly find its market by way of exports. But even if the world market acts as a substitute for domestic demand, a big push is still needed (though its required size may now be reduced due to the presence of international trade).

Indivisibility in The Supply of Savings

High levels of investment require a corresponding high level of savings. We cannot always rely on foreign aid as the huge levels of investments in the different sectors need to be made not only once, but multiple number of times. Hence domestic savings are a must. But in an underdeveloped economy,this is a challenge due to the low income levels.Marginal rate of savings needs to be increased following the rise in incomes due to higher investment.

How The Big Push Works

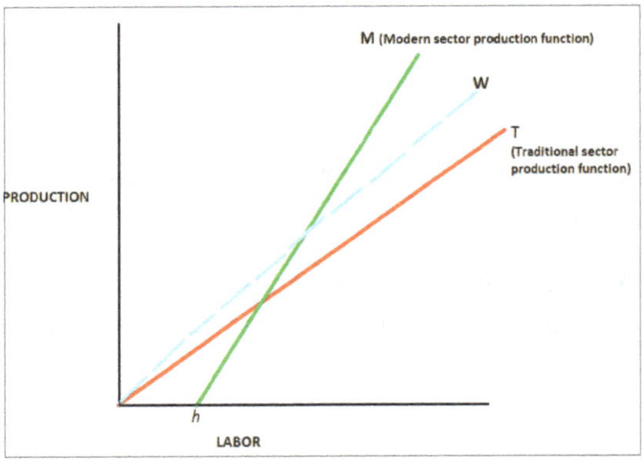

Fig.1

Consider a country whose economy is characterized by a large number sectors which are so small that any increase in the productivity of one sector has no impact on the economy as a whole. Each sector can either rely on traditional methods or switch to modern methods of production which would increase its efficiency. Let us assume that there are l workers in the economy and n sectors. Each sector therefore has l / n workers.

Using traditional technology, a sector would produce l/n amount of output, with each worker producing one unit of the commodity.

Using modern technology a sector would produce more as the productivity would be greater than one unit per worker. However, a modern sector would require some of the workers (say h) to perform administrative tasks.

In figure 1, the x-axis represents the labor employed and the y-axis represents the level of production. The production in the traditional sector is given by the curve T and the production in the modern sector is given by M. The curve M has a positive intercept on the x-axis, implying that even with zero production, there is a minimum level of h workers who still remain employed for carrying out administrative activities. With our assumption of l/n workers in the economy, the modern sector will have a higher level of productivity than the traditional sector. The production function of the modern sector is steeper than that of the traditional sector because of the higher productivity of workers in the former. The slope of both production functions is $1/m$, where m is the marginal labor required to produce an additional unit of output. This level of m is lower for the modern sector than it is for the traditional sector.

Assume that the traditional sector pays workers one unit of output which is subsequently spent equally by them in all sectors. The modern sector pays higher wages to workers. If all the workers are employed by the traditional sector, then the demand generated for the output of each sector is $D_1 = 1/n$. Government intervention in a manner that investment is carried out on those industries that have higher forward and backward linkages. We have two possible cases:

- *Wages are low* – When low wages are prevalent in the economy, say w_1, a firm which faces demand D_1 will need to employ l^* workers if it wants to modernize. This will cost the firm $w_1 l^*$.

  Now, wages are low. Therefore,

  $$w_1 l^* < D_1.$$

  This implies that costs (given by $w_1 l^*$) are lower than the earnings (given by D_1). So the firm makes a profit and will choose to modernize (even if other firms do not).

- *Wages are high* – When high wages are prevalent in the economy, say w_2, a firm which faces demand D_1 will make losses if no other firms choose to modernize.

  This is because,

  $$w_2 l^* > D_1.$$

  This implies that costs (given by $w_2 l^*$) are higher than the earnings (given by D_1).

  However, if all the other firms have modernized, the firm faces a higher demand D_2, arising out of higher income levels of workers of these modernized firms. The firm will hence choose to modernize as well so that it makes profits:

$$w_2 l^* < D_2 ..$$

Indivisibilities and External Economies

The concept of externalities is relevant for the Industrialization of underdeveloped countries, where decisions are to be made regarding distribution of savings among alternative investment opportunities. These arise from the interdependence in market economies.

Pecuniary economies are external economies transmitted through the price system, as prices are the signalling device (under conditions of perfect competition in a market economy). They arise in an industry (say industry X) due to internal economies of overcoming technical indivisibilities. This reduces the price of its product, which will benefit another industry (say industry Y) which use this output as an input or a factor of production. Subsequently, the profits of industry Y will rise, leading to its expansion and generating demand for the output of industry X. As a result, industry X's production and profits also expand.

However in underdeveloped countries, conditions of perfect competition are not present due to the decentralized and differentiated nature of the market. Prices fail to act as a signalling system in the following ways:

- Prices express the situation as it is and do not predict future economic situations
- Prices can decide present productive activities but cannot determine investments which would be appropriate for developing countries
- The response of the private sector to price signals is inadequate and imperfect due to the differentiation and decentralisation in developing countries

This justifies the need for centralized pan-industry planning of investment in Developing countries, as the private sector cannot undertake such planning.

Enlargement of the market size is another important externality which arises from the complementarity of industries. There exists an incentive to expand the scale of operations because the employees of one industry become the customers of another industry. In terms of products too (as in the above example of industries X and Y), one industry generates demand for the output of the other when the scale of operations increase.

Marshallian economies also accrue to a firm within a growing industry, resulting from agglomeration of industrial districts or clusters in a particular area. These occur due to the following advantages of agglomeration identified by Alfred Marshall:

1. Spillover of information.
2. Specialization and division of labor.
3. Development of a market for skilled labor.

Availability of skilled labour is an externality which arises when industrialization occurs, as workers acquire better training and skills. This is not achievable by mere establishment of a few industries, but requires a large program of industrial growth. It is one of the most important external economies because absence of skilled labor is a strong impediment to industrialization.

Role of The State

The large-scale programme of industrialization advocated by this model requires huge investments which are beyond the means of the private sector. The investment in infrastructure and basic industries (like power, transport and communications) is 'lumpy' and has long gestation periods. The role of the state in this theory is therefore critical for investment in social overhead capital. Even if the private sector had the requisite resources to invest in such a programme, it would not do so since it is driven by profit motives. Many investments are profitable in terms of social marginal net product but not in terms of private marginal net product. Due to this there is no incentive for individual entrepreneurs to invest and take advantage of external economies.

Criticisms

The theory has been criticized by Hla Myint and Celso Furtado, among others, primarily on the grounds of the massive effort required to be taken by underdeveloped countries to move along the path of industrialization. Some of the major criticisms are as follows.

- *Difficulties in execution and implementation*: The execution of related projects during the course of industrialization may involve unexpected or unavoidable changes due to revisions of plans, delays and deviations from the planned process. Hla Myint notes that the various departments and agencies involved in the process of development need to coordinate closely and evaluate and revise plans continuously. This is a challenging task for the governments of developing countries.
- *Lack of absorptive capacity*: The implementation of industrialization programmes may be constrained by ineffective disbursement,short-term bottlenecks, macroeconomic problems and volatility, loss of competitiveness and weakening of institutions. Credit is often utilized at low rates or after long time lags. There is often a loss of competitiveness due to the Dutch disease effect.
- *Historical inaccuracy*: When viewed in light of historical experience of countries over the last two centuries, no country displayed any evidence of development due to massive industrialization programmes. Stationary economies do not develop simply by making large-scale investment in social overhead capital.
- *Problems in mixed economies*: In a mixed economy, where the private and public sectors co-exist, the environment for growth may not be a conducive one. Unless there is a complementarity between the sectors, there is bound to arise competition between them, with the government departments keeping their plans confidential out of fear of speculative activities by the private sector. The private sector's activities are simultaneously inhibited due to lack of information of government policies and the general economic situation.
- *Neglect of methods of production*: Rather than capital formation, it is productive techniques which determine the success of a country in economic development. The big push model ignores productive techniques in its support for capital formation and industrialisation.

- *Shortage of resources in underdeveloped countries*: Eugenio Gudin criticizes the theory of the big push on the grounds that underdeveloped countries lack the capital required to provide the big push required for rapid development. If an underdeveloped nation had ample capital supply and scarce factors, it would not be classified as *underdeveloped* at all. Limited resource availability is the first impediment to such countries. Though this problem may be overcome by foreign aids, industrialization may not take off as expected if the aid flows are volatile.

- *Ignores the agricultural sector*: With its heavy emphasis on industry, the model finds no place for agriculture. This is a gaping flaw in the theory, as in most underdeveloped countries it is this sector which is large and has labor surplus. Investments in agriculture need to go hand-in-hand with those in industry so as to stimulate the industrial sector by providing a market for industrial goods. If neglected, it would be difficult to meet the food requirements of the nation in the short run and to significantly expand the size of the market in the long run.

- *Inflationary pressures*: It follows from the neglect of the agricultural sector that food shortages are likely to occur with industrialization. Though it would take time for investments in social overhead capital to yield returns, the demand would increase immediately, thus imposing inflationary pressures on the economy. Cost escalations may even cause projects to be postponed and the development process in general to slow down.

- *Dependence on indivisibilities*: The emphasis of this theory on indivisibility of processes is too much, as investments need not necessarily be on such a large scale to be economic. Social reforms are ignored, which are vital if a country is to grow on the basis of its own resources and initiatives. Development is bound to intensify if social reform is a part of the industrialization process.

Mundell–Fleming Model

The Mundell–Fleming model, also known as the IS-LM-BoP model (or IS-LM-BP model), is an economic model first set forth (independently) by Robert Mundell and Marcus Fleming. The model is an extension of the IS-LM Model. Whereas the traditional IS-LM Model deals with economy under autarky (or a closed economy), the Mundell–Fleming model describes a small open economy. Mundell's paper suggests that the model can be applied to Zurich, Brussels and so on.

The Mundell–Fleming model portrays the short-run relationship between an economy's nominal exchange rate, interest rate, and output (in contrast to the closed-economy IS-LM model, which focuses only on the relationship between the interest rate and output). The Mundell–Fleming model has been used to argue that an economy cannot simultaneously maintain a fixed exchange rate, free capital movement, and an independent monetary policy. This principle is frequently called the "impossible trinity," "unholy trinity," "irreconcilable trinity," "inconsistent trinity" or the "Mundell–Fleming trilemma."

Basic Set Up

Assumptions

Basic assumptions of the model are as follows:

- Spot and forward exchange rates are identical, and the existing exchange rates are expected to persist indefinitely.
- Fixed money wage rate, unemployed resources and constant returns to scale are assumed. Thus domestic price level is kept constant, and the supply of domestic output is elastic.
- Taxes and saving increase with income.
- The balance of trade depends only on income and the exchange rate.
- Capital mobility is perfect and all securities are perfect substitutes. Only risk neutral investors are in the system. The demand for money therefore depends only on income and the interest rate, and investment depends on the interest rate.
- The country under consideration is so small that the country can not affect foreign incomes or the world level of interest rates.

Variables

This model uses the following variables:

- Y is GDP.
- C is consumption.
- I is physical investment.
- G is government spending (an exogenous variable).
- M is the nominal money supply.
- P is the price level.
- i is the nominal interest rate.
- L is liquidity preference (real money demand).
- T is taxes.
- NX is net exports.

Equations

The Mundell–Fleming model is based on the following equations.

The IS curve:

$$Y = C + I + G + NX$$

where *NX* is net exports.

The LM curve:

$$\frac{M}{P} = L(i, Y)$$

A higher interest rate or a lower income (GDP) level leads to lower money demand.

The BoP (Balance of Payments) Curve:

$$BoP = CA + KA$$

where BoP is the balance of payments surplus, *CA* is the current account surplus, and *KA* is the capital account surplus.

IS Components

$$C = C(Y - T(Y), i - E(\pi))$$

where $E(\pi)$ is the expected rate of inflation. Higher disposable income or a lower real interest rate (nominal interest rate minus expected inflation) leads to higher consumption spending.

$$I = I(i - E(\pi), Y_{-1})$$

where Y_{-1} is GDP in the previous period. Higher lagged income or a lower real interest rate leads to higher investment spending.

$$NX = NX(e, Y, Y^*)$$

where *NX* is net exports, *e* is the nominal exchange rate (the price of domestic currency in terms of units of the foreign currency), *Y* is GDP, and *Y** is the combined GDP of countries that are foreign trading partners. Higher domestic income (GDP) leads to more spending on imports and hence lower net exports; higher foreign income leads to higher spending by foreigners on the country's exports and thus higher net exports. A higher *e* leads to lower net exports.

Balance of Payments (BOP) Components

- $CA = NX$
  - where *CA* is the current account and *NX* is net exports. That is, the current account is viewed as consisting solely of imports and exports.
- $KA = z(i - i^*) + k$
  - where i^* is the foreign interest rate, *k* is the exogenous component of financial capital flows, *z* is the interest-sensitive component of capital flows, and the derivative

of the function z is the degree of capital mobility (the effect of differences between domestic and foreign interest rates upon capital flows KA).

Variables Determined by The Model

After the subsequent equations are substituted into the first three equations above, one has a system of three equations in three unknowns, two of which are GDP and the domestic interest rate. Under flexible exchange rates, the exchange rate is the third endogenous variable while BoP is set equal to zero. In contrast, under fixed exchange rates e is exogenous and the balance of payments surplus is determined by the model.

Under both types of exchange rate regime, the nominal domestic money supply M is exogenous, but for different reasons. Under flexible exchange rates, the nominal money supply is completely under the control of the central bank. But under fixed exchange rates, the money supply in the short run (at a given point in time) is fixed based on past international money flows, while as the economy evolves over time these international flows cause future points in time to inherit higher or lower (but pre-determined) values of the money supply.

Mechanics of The Model

The model's workings can be described in terms of an IS-LM-BoP graph with the domestic interest rate plotted vertically and real GDP plotted horizontally. The IS curve is downward sloped and the LM curve is upward sloped, as in the closed economy IS-LM analysis; the BoP curve is upward sloped unless there is perfect capital mobility, in which case it is horizontal at the level of the world interest rate.

In this graph, under less than perfect capital mobility the positions of both the IS curve and the BoP curve depend on the exchange rate (as discussed below), since the IS-LM graph is actually a two-dimensional cross-section of a three-dimensional space involving all of the interest rate, income, and the exchange rate. However, under perfect capital mobility the BoP curve is simply horizontal at a level of the domestic interest rate equal to the level of the world interest rate.

Under A Flexible Exchange Rate Regime

In a system of flexible exchange rates, central banks allow the exchange rate to be determined by market forces alone.

Changes in The Money Supply

An increase in money supply shifts the LM curve to the right. This directly reduces the local interest rate relative to the global interest rate. A decrease in the money supply causes the exact opposite process.

Changes in Government Spending

An increase in government expenditure shifts the IS curve to the right. The shift causes both the local interest rate and income (GDP) to rise. A decrease in government expenditure reverses the process.

Changes in The Global Interest Rate

An increase in the global interest rate shifts the BoP curve upward and causes capital flows out of the local economy. This depreciates the local currency and boosts net exports, shifting the IS curve to the right. Under less than perfect capital mobility, the depreciated exchange rate shifts the BoP curve somewhat back down.Under perfect capital mobility, the BoP curve is always horizontal at the level of the world interest rate. When the latter goes up, the BoP curve shifts upward by the same amount, and stays there. The exchange rate changes enough to shift the IS curve to the location where it crosses the new BoP curve at its intersection with the unchanged LM curve; now the domestic interest rate equals the new level of the global interest rate.

A decrease in the global interest rate causes the reverse to occur.

Under A Fixed Exchange Rate Regime

In a system of fixed exchange rates, central banks announce an exchange rate (the parity rate) at which they are prepared to buy or sell any amount of domestic currency. Thus net payments flows into or out of the country need not equal zero; the exchange rate *e* is exogenously given, while the variable BoP is endogenous.

Under the fixed exchange rate system, the central bank operates in the foreign exchange market to maintain a specific exchange rate. If there is pressure to depreciate the domestic currency's exchange rate because the supply of domestic currency exceeds its demand in foreign exchange markets, the local authority buys domestic currency with foreign currency to decrease the domestic currency's supply in the foreign exchange market. This keeps the domestic currency's exchange rate at its targeted level. If there is pressure to appreciate the domestic currency's exchange rate because the currency's demand exceeds its supply in the foreign exchange market, the local authority buys foreign currency with domestic currency to increase the domestic currency's supply in the foreign exchange market. Again,this keeps the exchange rate at its targeted level.

Changes in The Money Supply

In the very short run the money supply is normally predetermined by the past history of international payments flows. If the central bank is maintaining an exchange rate that is consistent with a balance of payments surplus, over time money will flow into the country and the money supply will rise (and vice versa for a payments deficit). If the central bank were to conduct open market operations in the domestic bond market in order to offset these balance-of-payments-induced changes in the money supply — a process called sterilization, it would absorb newly arrived money by decreasing its holdings of domestic bonds (or the opposite if money were flowing out of the country). But under perfect capital mobility, any such sterilization would be met by further offsetting international flows.

Changes in Government Expenditure

Increased government expenditure shifts the IS curve to the right. The shift results in an incipient rise in the interest rate, and hence upward pressure on the exchange rate (value of the domestic currency) as foreign funds start to flow in, attracted by the higher interest rate. However, the exchange rate is controlled by the local monetary authority in the framework of a fixed exchange rate system. To maintain the exchange rate and eliminate pressure on it, the monetary authority purchases foreign currency using domestic funds in order to shift the LM curve to the right. In the end, the interest rate stays the same but the general income in the economy increases. In the IS-LM-BoP graph, the IS curve has been shifted exogenously by the fiscal authority, and the IS and BoP curves determine the final resting place of the system; the LM curve merely passively reacts.

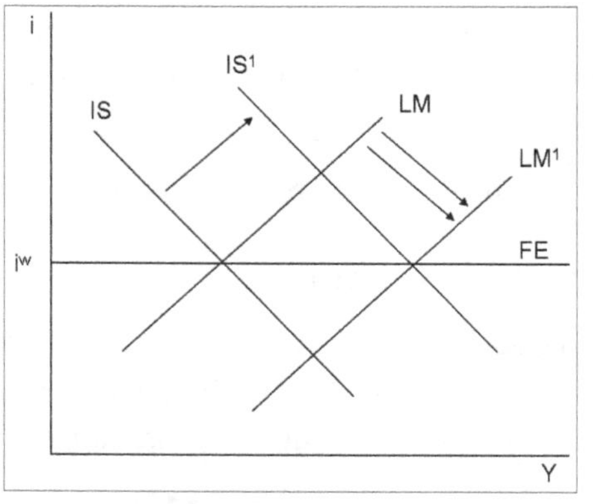

An increase in government spending forces the monetary authority to supply the market with local currency to keep the exchange rate unchanged. Shown here is the case of perfect capital mobility, in which the BoP curve (or, as denoted here, the FE curve) is horizontal.

The reverse process applies when government expenditure decreases.

Changes in The Global Interest Rate

To maintain the fixed exchange rate, the central bank must accommodate the capital flows (in or out) which are caused by a change of the global interest rate, in order to offset pressure on the exchange rate.

If the global interest rate increases, shifting the BoP curve upward, capital flows out to take advantage of the opportunity. This puts pressure on the home currency to depreciate, so the central bank must buy the home currency — that is, sell some of its foreign currency reserves — to accommodate this outflow. The decrease in the money supply resulting from the outflow, shifts the LM curve to the left until it intersect the IS and BoP curves at their intersection. Once again, the LM curve plays a passive role, and the outcomes are determined by the IS-BoP interaction.

Under perfect capital mobility, the new BoP curve will be horizontal at the new world interest rate, so the equilibrium domestic interest rate will equal the world interest rate.

If the global interest rate declines below the domestic rate, the opposite occurs. The BoP curve shifts down, foreign money flows in and the home currency is pressured to appreciate, so the central bank offsets the pressure by selling domestic currency (equivalently, buying foreign currency). The inflow of money causes the LM curve to shift to the right, and the domestic interest rate becomes lower (as low as the world interest rate if there is perfect capital mobility).

Differences from IS-LM

It is worth noting that some of the results from this model differ from those of the IS-LM model because of the open economy assumption. Results for a large open economy, on the other hand, can be consistent with those predicted by the IS-LM model. The reason is that a large open economy has the characteristics of both an autarky and a small open economy. In particular, it may not face perfect capital mobility, thus allowing internal policy measures to affect the domestic interest rate, and it may be able to sterilize balance-of-payments-induced changes in the money supply (as discussed above).

In the IS-LM model, the domestic interest rate is a key component in keeping both the money market and the goods market in equilibrium. Under the Mundell–Fleming framework of a small economy facing perfect capital mobility, the domestic interest rate is fixed and equilibrium in both markets can only be maintained by adjustments of the nominal exchange rate or the money supply (by international funds flows).

Example

The Mundell–Fleming model applied to a small open economy facing perfect capital mobility, in which the domestic interest rate is exogenously determined by the world interest rate, shows stark differences from the closed economy model.

Consider an exogenous increase in government expenditure. Under the IS-LM model, the IS curve shifts upward, with the LM curve intact, causing the interest rate and output to rise. But for a small open economy with perfect capital mobility and a flexible exchange rate, the domestic interest rate is predetermined by the horizontal BoP curve, and so by the LM equation given previously there is exactly one level of output that can make the money market be in equilibrium at that interest rate. Any exogenous changes affecting the IS curve (such as government spending changes) will be exactly offset by resulting exchange rate changes, and the IS curve will end up in its original position, still intersecting the LM and BoP curves at their intersection point.

The Mundell–Fleming model under a fixed exchange rate regime also has completely different implications from those of the closed economy IS-LM model. In the closed economy model, if the central bank expands the money supply the LM curve shifts out, and as a result income goes up and the domestic interest rate goes down. But in the Mundell–Fleming open economy model with perfect capital mobility, monetary policy becomes ineffective. An expansionary monetary policy resulting in an incipient outward shift of the LM curve would make capital flow out of the economy. The central bank under a fixed exchange rate system would have to instantaneously intervene by selling foreign money in exchange for domestic money to maintain the exchange rate. The accommodated monetary outflows exactly offset the intended rise in the domestic money supply, completely offsetting the tendency of the LM curve to shift to the right, and the interest rate remains equal to the world rate of interest.

Criticism

Exchange Rate Expectations

One of the assumptions of the Mundell–Fleming model is that domestic and foreign securities are perfect substitutes. Provided the world interest rate i^* is given, the model predicts the domestic rate will become the same level of the world rate by arbitrage in money markets. However, in reality, the world interest rate is different from the domestic rate. Rüdiger Dornbusch considered how exchange rate expectations made an effect on the exchange rate. Given the approximate formula:

$$i = i^* + \frac{e'}{e} - 1$$

and if the elasticity of expectations σ, is less than unity, then we have,

$$\frac{di}{de} = \sigma - 1 < 0 \quad .$$

Since domestic output is $y = E(i, y) + T(e, y)$, the differentiation of income with regard to the exchange rate becomes,

$$\frac{dy}{de} = \frac{\partial E}{\partial i}\frac{di}{de} + \frac{\partial E}{\partial y}\frac{dy}{de} + \frac{\partial T}{\partial e} + \frac{\partial T}{\partial y}\frac{dy}{de}$$

$$\frac{dy}{de} = \frac{1}{1 - E_y - T_y}\left(E_i \frac{di}{de} + T_e\right).$$

The standard IS-LM theory gives us the following basic relations:

$$E_i < 0, \quad E_y = 1 - s > 0$$

$$T_e > 0, \quad T_y = -m < 0.$$

Investment and consumption increase as the interest rates decrease, and currency depreciation improves the trade balance.

$$\frac{dy}{de} = \frac{1}{s+m}\left(E_i \frac{di}{de} + T_e\right)$$

$$\frac{dy}{de} = \frac{1}{s+m}\left(E_i(\sigma - 1) + T_e\right).$$

Then the total differentiations of trade balance and the demand for money are derived.

$$dT = \frac{\partial T}{\partial e}de + \frac{\partial T}{\partial y}dy = T_e de + T_y dy$$

$$dL = \frac{\partial L}{\partial i}di + \frac{\partial L}{\partial y}dy = L_i di + L_y dy$$

$$L_i < 0, \quad L_y > 0$$

and then, it turns out that,

$$\frac{dT}{dL} = \frac{T_e(s+m) + T_y(E_i(\sigma - 1) + T_e)}{L_i(\sigma - 1)(s+m) + L_y(E_i(\sigma - 1) + T_e)}$$

$$\frac{dT}{dL} = \frac{T_e s + T_y E_i(\sigma - 1)}{L_i(\sigma - 1)(s+m) + L_y(E_i(\sigma - 1) + T_e)}.$$

The denominator is positive, and the numerator is positive or negative. Thus, a monetary expansion, in the short run, does not necessarily improve the trade balance. This result is not compatible with what the Mundell-Fleming predicts. This is a consequence of introducing exchange rate expectations which the MF theory ignores. Nevertheless, Dornbusch concludes that monetary policy is still effective even if it worsens a trade balance, because a monetary expansion pushes down interest rates and encourages spending. He adds that, in the short run, fiscal policy works because it raises interest rates and the velocity of money.

References

- A.N. Agarwala, S.P. Singh , The Economics of Underdevelopment, Oxford University Press India, pp. 303–4, ISBN 978-0-19-560674-4
- Andrew Abel and Ben Bernanke , Macroeconomics, 2nd ed., Ch. 11.1, pp. 355-362. Addison-Wesley, ISBN 0-201-54392-3
- Hyndman, Rob J; Athanasopoulos, George. "8.9 Seasonal ARIMA models". Forecasting: principles and practice. oTexts. Retrieved 19, May 2020
- Edmund S. Phelps, ed., Microeconomic Foundations of Employment and Inflation Theory. New York, Norton and Co. ISBN 0-393-09326-3
- George W. Evans and Seppo Honkapohja (2001), Learning and Expectations in Macroeconomics. Princeton University Press, ISBN 0-691-04921-1
- Klein, Lawrence R., ed. Comparative Performance of US Econometric Models. Oxford University Press. ISBN 0-19-505772-4
- Woodford, Michael (2003). Interest and Prices: Foundations of a Theory of Monetary Policy. Princeton University Press. ISBN 0-691-01049-8
- Pearl, J. (2000). Causality: Models, Reasoning, and Inference. New York: Cambridge University Press. ISBN 0521773628
- S. K. Misra; V. K. Puri (2010). Economics Of Development And Planning — Theory And Practice (12th ed.). Himalaya Publishing House. pp. 217–222. ISBN 81-8488-829-5
- Hoover, Kevin D."Econometrics and the Analysis of Policy". The New Classical Macroeconomics. Oxford: Basil Blackwell. pp. 167–209. ISBN 0-631-14605-9

6

Significant Theories in Macroeconomics

The branch of economics which is concerned with the structure, decision making, behavior and performance of an economy is known as macroeconomics. This chapter elucidates topics such as induced innovation, supply-side and demand-side economics, modern monetary theory, recursive competitive equilibrium, etc. All the theories related to macroeconomics have been carefully analyzed in this chapter.

Diluted Property Rights Theory

The main argument of the Property Right Theory is that besides the value of good itself, the value of the Property Right is to be considered, that is:

- The right to use (usus).
- The right to change (abusus).
- The right to make profit or losses (usus fructus).
- The right to transfer.

The optimum economic design is achieved by dilution and concentration of these Property-Rights through transactions.

Coases (1988) agues that "in order to carry out a market transaction, it is necessary to discover who it is that one wishes to deal with, to inform people that one wishes to deal and on what terms, to conduct negotiations leading up to a bargain, to draw up the contract, to undertake the inspections needed to make sure that the terms of the contract are being observed, and so on. These operations are often extremely costly, sufficiently costly at any rate to prevent many transactions that would be carried out in a world in which the pricing system worked without cost."

These costs are the Transaction Costs. Thus, transaction costs are costs incurred in the determination, transference and implementation of Property-Rights.

The control of Property Rights can be hard, for example, how to quantify the value of a innovative research and development department, how to detect who in a group made each task, or who parked in a parking area – usus, who caused environmental damages – abusus, who made private telephone calls in the company phone – usus fructus, etc.

These examples also implied the impact of Property Right by third parties, i.e. by agents who were not involved in the transaction process. For example, the team member who really did the work is not receiving the adequate benefits, or the society has to carry the environmental costs of pollution. This impact is termed Externalities. There are positive and negative externalities: the former refers to situations where the utility of the social utility is higher than the individual utility, in this case, the institutional boundary provides less protection to the private property; the latter, in contrary, the social utility is lower than the private.

Agents tend to avoid Externalities, increasing the control over the Property Right, and consequently, the Transaction Cost. However, this will only make sense if the Transaction Costs incurred in controlling the property are lower than the losses caused by Externalities. Moreover, as organisations are mainly seeking for the individual maximisation of utility, the costs of externalities vary according to the institutional and social control.

According to this theory, the economical structures are a consequence of a balance between the distribution of Property Right and the consequent Transaction Costs and Externalities incurred. According to this perspective, there is a tendency to automatically form an efficient allocation of the Property Right within certain institutional bounders.

Property Right and the Design of Companies

In general, this theory argues that the relationships should be based on systems that are as legal and well-defined as transaction cost permit. It is argued that higher the dilution of the Property Right lead to higher degrees of control, but also to higher the Transaction Costs and lower the utility. Organisations can dilute and concentrate Property Rights in order to develop a more efficient organisation. Property Rights are diluted by:

- By conferring agents not all rights mentioned above,
- By dividing these among several agents, and
- Through constraints posed by the institutions (and legal systems) on the use of these rights.

The modularisation of companies is one strategy to concentrate the property rights. This strategy is based on the centralisation of usus, absus, usus frut und transference of properties in diverse independent "islands" in the company, that have to relate to each other through well defined "contracts". This is interesting, as it approximates competences and authority to make decisions, and improve management and supervision of tasks. Thus, this concentration of property right inside of the company enables the division of work as proposed by Taylor in a world of difficult control, uncertainty and asymmetric information.

Induced Innovation

A change in the relative prices of the factors of production is itself a spur to invention, and to invention of a particular kind—directed to economizing the use of a factor which has become relatively expensive", which suggests that an increase in real energy price will induce energy-saving innovation.

The induced innovation is related to not only real energy prices but also usefulness of existing knowledge. Patent citations from 1950 to 1994 were used to construct a weighted series of "knowledge stocks" of 11 energy sectors, with which he formulated the model. The results showed that both the energy prices and knowledge stocks have a strongly positive impact on new technological change, which implies that we can encourage more energy-saving.

However, some theoretical researchers indicate that it is not the real price but relative factor share we should take into consideration. Since the patent regressand is a proportion of total patents of each year, we should also look at the impact of other factors such as labor, so that we may get a more valid model to use.

Theoretical Specification and Popp Model

Popp used a log–log model to describe the relationship between the successful patent applications and energy prices, a knowledge stock and other variables such as the government R&D expenditure. In this kind of model, the coefficients estimated could be interpreted usefully as elasticities of the explanatory variables, which is a good tool for the policy makers. What should be noted is that as for the energy prices and government R&D he took an adaptive expectations model with distributed lags which is more realistic and sophisticated than using the raw data of energy prices and government expenditures, considering the real world situation. The Popp model is shown as follows:

$$\log\left(\frac{EPAT_{i,t}}{TOTPAT_t}\right) = \phi_i + \gamma(1-\lambda)\log P^*_{E,t} + \theta\log K_{i,t-1}$$
$$+\eta(1-\lambda)\log Z^*_{i,t} + \lambda^t\mu^0 + \varepsilon_{it},$$
$$i = 1,\ldots,11;\ t = 1,\ldots,20$$

where,

$$P^*_{E,t} = P_{E,t} + \lambda P_{E,t-1} + \lambda^2 P_{E,t-2} + \ldots + \lambda^{t-1} P_{E,1},$$

and

$$Z^*_{i,t} = Z_{i,t} + \lambda Z_{i,t-1} + \lambda^2 Z_{i,t-2} + \ldots + \lambda^{t-1} P_{i,1}.$$

$EPAT_{i,t}$ represents the number of successful nongovernment U.S. patent applications for technology field *i* in year $_t$, and TOTPAT$_t$, represents the total number of successful nongovernment U.S. patent applications in the same year. $P_{E,t}$ is the price of energy in that year. The variable $K_{i,t-1}$ represents the stock of knowledge that had accumulated by the previous year, and should be thought of as the knowledge available to the researcher at time *t*. Values for this stock will be introduced later. *Z* is a vector of the other independent variables such as R&D spending by the U.S. Department of energy.

The interpretation of parameters is consistent with the theory of Koyck approach. As we can see, the energy price is using an adaptive expectations model where λ s known as the coefficient of expectation, which stands for the weight put on the past observations. Note that $0 < \lambda \leq 1$. The term $\gamma(1 - \lambda)$ represents the short-run price elasticity of energy technological change where γ is the long-run elasticity and $(1 - \lambda)$ could be seen as weight without all past impacts. And μ^o is the truncation remainder.

Popp's model is ground-breaking. Since Hicks researchers have struggled to establish empirical relations on policy-induced development of technological change with respect to the process per se. Hence most models on the policy have taken technology as exogenous. Popp did a good job on induced innovation hypothesis. He successfully quantified knowledge to take knowledge endogenously as explanatory variable. However, theoretical researchers suggest that other explanatory variables should be built into the model in order to be valid.

From the theoretical model of Acemoglu we can get equations mentioned below, for different factors L and Z:

$$\dot{N}_L = \eta_L N_L^{(1+\delta)/2} N_Z^{(1-\delta)/2} S_L,$$

and

$$\dot{N}_Z = \eta_Z N_L^{(1-\delta)/2} N_Z^{(1+\delta)/2} S_Z,$$

where $\delta \leq 1$ is the degree of state independence, η_L and η_Z are positive parameters, and S_L and S_Z are investment levels for factors *L* and *Z* respectively. When $\delta = 0$, it implies N_L and N_Z create spillovers, with the same weight of 0.5, for the current research in both sectors. In contrast, when $\delta = 1$, then the research in factor *L* is irrelative with factor *Z*, which suggests that there are no spillovers between sectors. We can transform these equations into time series model according to the work of Hart. And we can see the links between the two expressions. The term K_a corresponds to N_L while K_b corresponds to N_Z. Ia is the investment of factor a which is equal to S_L in Equation 4, and the same applied for I_b and S_Z. Note that $\sigma = 1-\delta$. And the coefficients $\eta_L = r_a^{-1}$ and $\eta_Z = r_b^{-1}$.

$$K_{at+1} - K_{at} = K_{at}^{1-\frac{\sigma}{2}} K_{bt}^{\frac{\sigma}{2}} I_{at+1}^{\phi} / r_a,$$

and

$$K_{bt+1} - K_{bt} = K_{bt}^{1-\frac{\sigma}{2}} K_{at}^{\frac{\sigma}{2}} I_{bt+1}^{\phi} / r_b.$$

Here K_{at} and K_{bt} are current knowledge level at period *t + 1* of factor *a* and *b* respectively, I_a and I_b are inputs, r_a and r_a are positive parameters, and ϕ, σ are both parameters between 0 and 1. The term φ generalized the situation of investment, where in Acemoglu's model $\phi = 1$ is the special case. These functions imply that general knowledge of one factor based on its input can be augmented by both knowledge inside this factor and spillovers. They also suggest that we can build up a relationship between technological change and previous knowledge stocks and also the factor input. If we take the ratio of above two equation, we will derive such relation as follows:

$$\frac{K_{at+1} - K_{at}}{K_{bt+1} - K_{bt}} = A\left(\frac{I_{at+1}}{I_{bt+1}}\right)^{\phi}\left(\frac{K_{at}}{K_{bt}}\right)^{1-\sigma}$$

In equation below, we can see that it is similar to Popp's model, in which $EPAT_{i,t}$ could be represented by a and $TOTPAT_t$ is replaced by b, and other determinants such as government R&D are omitted for simplification,

and we also define that,

$$S = \frac{I_a}{I_b} = \frac{P_a Q_a}{P_b Q_b},$$

where *S* is the relative factor share of *a* and *b*, or, the ratio of factor share of *a* and *b*. The size of *S* is determined by the price and quantity of both factor *a* and *b*. Then we take the log of $\frac{K_{at+1} - K_{at}}{K_{bt+1} - K_{bt}} = A\left(\frac{I_{at+1}}{I_{bt+1}}\right)^{\phi}\left(\frac{K_{at}}{K_{bt}}\right)^{1-\sigma}$ and replace I_a/I_b with *S*. The derived equation gives our primary model of this thesis:

$$\log\left(\frac{K_{at} - K_{at-1}}{K_{bt} - K_{bt-1}}\right) \alpha + \phi \log S_t + \theta_1 \log K_{a,t-1} + \theta_2 \log K_{b,t-1} + \ldots$$

Note that θ_1 and θ_2 in the above equation are basically the same parameters with the absolute value of $(1 - \sigma)$ and opposite signs.

From figure we can get intuitive information about the patent activity and the other two explanatory variables we use in this thesis. They are all normalized to be 1 in the year 1970. The curve of relative factor share is defined by SE/SL which is the ratio of energy factor share and labor factor share. We can observe that curves of relative factor share and energy price are fundamentally following the same shape at the beginning, but diverge at around 1976. One of the reasons could be the denominator of the ratio of factor share which is the factor share of labor, is increasing over time. So that it brings down the trend of relative factor share compared to the trend of energy price. Another could be the quantity of energy is decreasing due to the energy-saving innovations. Both of the impacts make the trend of factor shares increase more slowly than the trend of real energy prices.

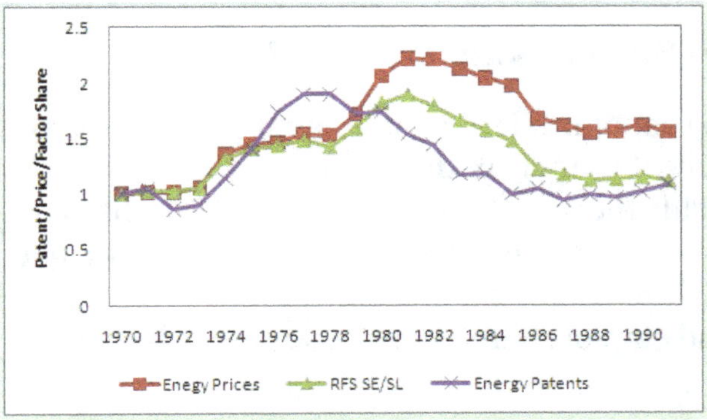

Energy Patents, Energy Prices and Relative factor Share

The figure suggests that if energy prices can explain the variation of patent activity, then factor share can be a good explanatory variable too, if not even better. Note that the patenting activity peaked at around 1977 while energy prices kept increasing until 1981. Popp explains that this is because there exists diminishing returns to knowledge. Hence the knowledge begins declining before the prices start to fall. However, if Popp is correct about the diminishing returns, and also the coefficient of energy prices is significantly positive in his model as he demonstrated, then it cannot be explained that when the real prices decreased after 1981, the patents did not decline even faster. Moreover, when the real prices stayed relative constant in the last few years, the patents did not keep declining but leveled off. So we can make some guess that Popp's model might not reflect the reality.

Supply-side Economics

Supply-side economics is a relatively new term which came into use in the mid-1970s as a result of the failure of Keynesian demand-side policies in the US economy which led to stagflation. The term is new but its basic principles are to be found in the works of the classical economists. According to J.B. Say, supply creates its own demand.

The very act of supplying goods implies a demand for them. If there is an imbalance between demand and supply, it is corrected automatically by changes in prices and wages and the economy always tends toward full employment.

The main emphasis of the classical economists was on economic growth for which they advocated non-interference with the market mechanism. It was the "invisible hand" which led to the maximisation of national wealth.

They believed that entrepreneurs, investors and producers were the prime movers on which the economy depended. It was the increase in the supplies of capital and labor and increase in their productivities that determined growth. Of course, free trade and capital movements internationally were instrumental in a faster growth rate of the economy.

Main Features of Supply-side Economics

Modern supply-side economics lays emphasis on providing all types of economic incentives to raise aggregate supply in the economy. According to Bethell, "The essential argument of supply-side theory is that adding to supply unlike adding to demand is not a zero-sum task. In order to make something, a producer does not need to be given any money. Instead, he has to be given an incentive." Incentives to producers are essential to invest, produce and employ. Similar incentives are to be given to individuals to work and save more.

The government plays a limited role in liberalising markets, reducing taxes and freeing the labor market. The main objectives of supply-side policies are to keep inflation at a low level, achieve and maintain full employment and attain faster economic growth. Supply-side economists suggest the following policy measures in order to achieve these objectives.

Tax-induced Change in Aggregate Supply

Supply-siders regard tax cuts as an effective means of raising the growth rate of the economy. To assess the likely effects of tax reductions, they distinguish between income and substitution effects of a cut in the marginal rate of income tax.

The substitution effect of a wage cut induces people to work more and have less leisure, and the income effect causes people to work less and enjoy more leisure. It is only when the substitution effect of a tax cut is larger than the income effect that there will be an incentive to work more, thereby leading to reduction in unemployment.

A reduction in personal tax rates increases the incentive of people to work and save more. High savings reduce short-term interest rates and lead to increased investment and thus to an increase in the economy's capital stock. Reduction in marginal tax rates by improving the work effort of the people also increases their productive capacity and the level of output and employment in the economy.

Thus supply-side tax cuts by raising work, effort, saving and investment, increase the supplies of labor and capital and shift the aggregate supply curve to the right. The effect of a supply-side tax cut is illustrated in figure where AS is the aggregate supply curve and AD is the given demand curve.

Real output or GDP is measured along the horizontal axis and the price level on the vertical axis. AS and AD curves intersect at point T and determine OP price and OQ real output of the economy. Suppose there is a tax cut both on persons and firms. This increases work effort and saving on the part of workers and investment by firms.

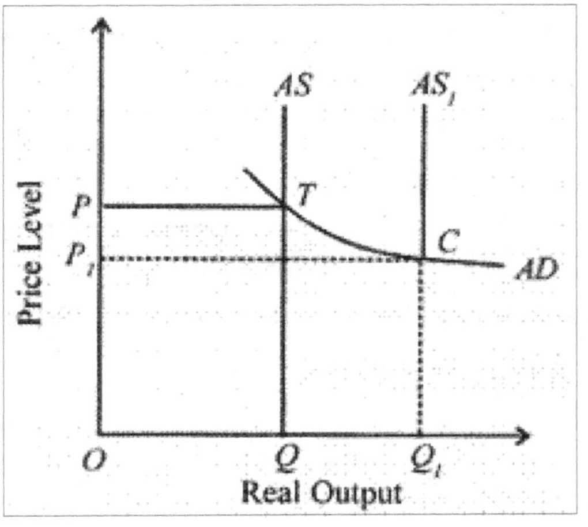

As a result, supplies of labor and capital increase which shift the aggregate supply curve AS to the right as AS_1. Now the AS_1 curve cuts the AD curve at point C. As a result, the price level falls to OP_1 and the real output increases to QQ_1 as a result of a tax cut.

Similarly, reduction in corporate tax rates, by giving incentives to the corporate sector in the form of increasing tax credit for larger investment and providing higher depreciation allowance, encourage investment. Higher investment leads to the production of more goods and services per unit of labor and capital.

Supply-siders also advocate an additional tax relief for firms employing researchers because R&D help in increasing productivity. They also favour reduced estate taxes for small farmers which will induce them to spend more on inputs so as to increase production.

Further, tax cuts reduce diversions to "shelter" (protected) industries and minimise or eliminate the need for accountants, investment consultants and tax-lawyers. Moreover, tax reductions reduce 'underground' (black market) activity where exchange is not recorded in the books and no taxes are paid.

Increasing Growth Rate

According to supply-side economists, tax cuts increase the disposable income of the people who raise additional demand for goods and services. On the other hand, the faster growth in productivity leads to the production of additional goods and services to match the additional demand.

This leads to balanced growth in the economy without shortages. When the economy is moving towards balanced growth, the rate of inflation is low. This, in turn, leads to an increase in the real disposable income of the people which raises consumption, output and employment.

Low inflation leads to increase in net exports which strengthen the value of national currency in relation to foreign currencies. The increase in productivity increases the production of more goods for export, thereby further strengthening the country's currency.

Thus supply-side economists advocate reduction -in tax rates in order to increase the incentives to work, save and invest and to get more tax revenue by the government. Increase in investment leads to an increase in the economy's capital stock, to increase in productivity, to larger output, low inflation, high level of employment and high growth rate of the economy.

These policy prescriptions shift the aggregate supply curve of the economy to the right. This is illustrated in the figure below, where AS is the aggregate supply curve and AD is the given aggregate demand curve. They intersect at point E which is the initial equilibrium point of the economy with OP price level and OQ real output.

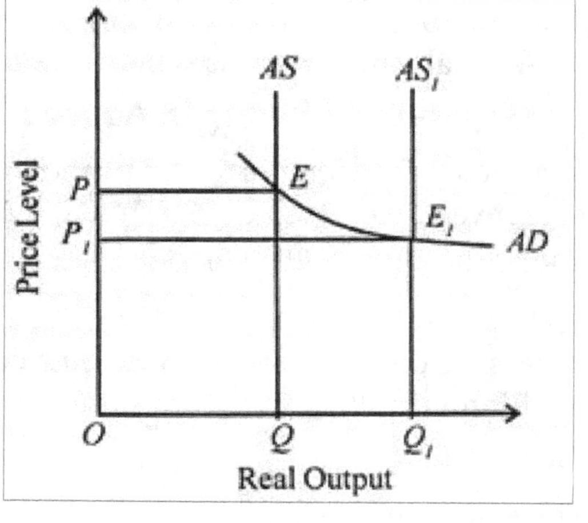

Suppose the supply-side policies increase the total supply of factors like labor and capital due to tax policies, incentives, etc. They increase real output and shift the AS curve to the right as AS_1. The new equilibrium is at where the AS_1 curve cuts the AD curve. Now real output increases to OQ_1 and the price level falls to OP_1 thereby increasing the growth rate of the economy.

Policy Prescriptions of Supply-side Economics

The Laffer Curve: Tax Rate vs. Tax Revenue

The most popular aspect of supply-side economics is the Laffer curve named after its originator Prof. Arthur Laffer. The Laffer curve depicts the relation between tax rate and tax revenue. It is based on the assumption that a cut in the marginal rate of tax will increase the incentives to work, save and invest. This tax cut, in turn, will increase the tax revenue. The Laffer curve shows two extremes of tax rates: A 0% tax rate and a 100% tax rate.

Both yield no tax revenue. If the tax rate is 0%, no revenue will be raised. If the tax rate is 100%, people will have no incentive to work, save and invest at all because the whole income will go to the government. Thus the tax revenue will again be zero. As the tax rate increases from 0% to 100%, tax revenue correspondingly rises from zero to some maximum level and then starts declining to zero. Thus the optimum tax rate is somewhere between the two extremes.

Figure below shows the Laffer curve where the tax rate (0%) is taken on the horizontal axis and the tax revenue on the vertical axis. As the tax rate is raised above zero, the tax revenue starts increasing. The Laffer curve is upward sloping. At the relatively low tax rate, it is upward sloping. At the relatively low tax rate T_1, the tax revenue is R_1.

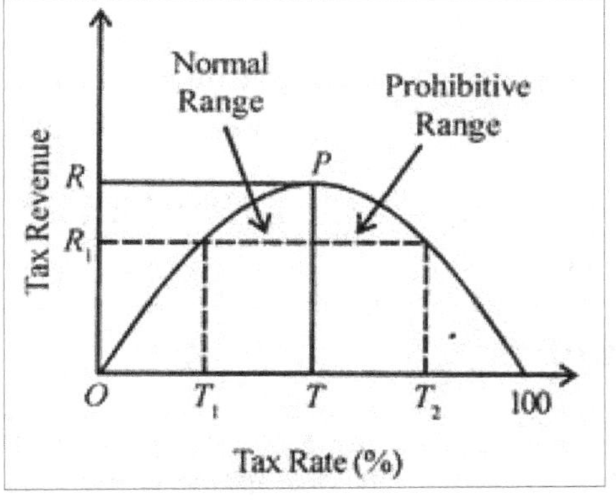

As the tax rate rises to T, the tax revenue continues to increase and the curve reaches the peak, P where the tax revenue R is the maximum. Thereafter, further rise in the tax rate will reduce revenue to the government. Thus T is the optimum rate of tax.

According to Laffer, “Except for the optimum rate, there are always two tax rates that yield the same revenue.” In the figure, the revenue R_1 at the high tax rate T_2 is the same as the revenue collected at the low tax rate T_1. If the government wishes to maximise tax revenue, it will choose the optimum tax rate T.

An important feature of the Laffer curve is that it has a normal range and a prohibitive range. The normal range is to the left of the optimum tax rate T and the prohibitive range is to its right. In the normal range, increases in the tax rate bring more revenue to the government.

But in the prohibitive range, when the tax rate becomes high, it reduces the incentives to work, save and invest. Consequently, the fall in output more than offsets the rise in tax rate. When the tax rate reaches 100%, the revenue falls to zero because no one will bother to work.

Thus high tax rate stifles economic growth and results in high unemployment. Therefore, a reduction in the tax rate will actually increase revenue by encouraging the incentives to work, save and invest. People not only produce and earn more but also switch money out of low-yielding "tax shelters" and untaxed "underground" economy into more productive and socially desirable investment. The result would be higher employment and economic growth leading to high tax revenue.

Reduction in Government Spending

To achieve full employment, low inflation and high growth rate of the economy, the supply-side economists emphasise reduction in government expenditure accompanied by tax cuts. They are against monetization of budget deficit which the Keynesians advocate.

But the reduction in government expenditure should be more than or equal to tax cuts so that savings increase to finance larger investments. This will increase employment, income and growth rate of the economy.

Monetary Policy

Another plank of supply-side policy is to have restrained monetary expansion in order to keep the inflation rate low.

Increased Depreciation

To encourage more investment, supply-siders suggest increased investment allowance and/or higher depreciation on buildings, machines vehicles, and other capital goods.

Reduction in Welfare Benefits

To reduce unemployment, supply-side economists emphasise reduction in welfare benefits, especially unemployment allowance. This will encourage workers to accept jobs at lower wages, thereby reducing unemployment in the economy.

Reducing Trade Union Power

Supply-siders also advocate reduction in the power of trade unions through legislation which will make the labor market more competitive. Trade unions raise wages above the competitive level which the employers cannot afford. Thus they destroy jobs and increase unemployment. When the government restricts union power, unemployment and cost-inflation are reduced.

Deregulation and Privatisation

Deregulation and privatisation are important supply-side policies. They are used to encourage more competition within the economy. Removal of public sector monopolies and sale of public sector enterprises and transfer of public utilities in private hands lead to increase in productive efficiency, wider consumer choice and lower prices.

Free Trade and Capital Movements

Free trade and free capital movements among countries are another policy measure of supply-siders. The removal of exchange controls and free inflow and outflow of both short- term and long-term capital lead to the maximisation of output and growth by widening markets and checking monopolies.

Criticisms of Supply-side Economics

The prescriptions of supply-side economics have been criticised by economists on the following grounds.

Laffer Curve Controversial

The Laffer curve is an interesting but a controversial concept. No one knows with certainty either the location of the optimum point or the exact shape of this curve. The curve may peak at 40% or 90% tax rate, or it may peak in-between these rates.

For instance, if we take the curve which peaks at point A in figure below, the present tax rate-T should be cut to T_1 to maximise revenue. On the other hand, if another curve peaks at point B, the tax rate T should be increased to T_2. Without the knowledge of either the peak or the shape of the curve, it is not possible to know the effect of reducing (or increasing) the tax rate or tax revenue and economic activity. In fact, nobody knows the exact shape of the Laffer curve or the relationship between tax rate and tax revenue.

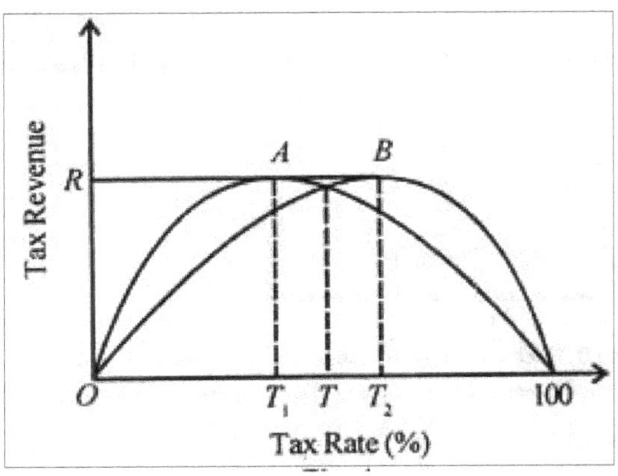

Tax Cuts do not bring High Growth Rate

Economists do not agree that cutting tax rates will lead to high growth rate and more tax revenue. They point out that high growth rate generates higher incomes which, in turn, generate higher tax revenue. Therefore, it is not reduction in tax rates that leads to the high growth rate of the economy.

Tax Cuts do not Measure Work Effort

It is not possible to measure work effort specifically as a result of tax cut. No doubt, increased work effort leads to higher incomes and to increase in tax revenue. But the increased tax revenue may not be sufficient to compensate the government for the decrease in revenue due to the lower tax rate. Moreover, it is possible that people may work less when their disposable income increases with the lower tax rate.

Tax Cuts do not Affect Target Incomes

Critics argue that some persons have 'target' real income. When taxes are reduced, they will work less and have more leisure to maintain their target income.

State Intervention Necessary

Supply-siders have been criticised for their policy of non-intervention by the state. But there are many contradictions in the working of the capitalist system which cannot sustain balanced growth of the economy. When the economy reaches full employment, a number of distortions and imbalances develop which fail to maintain full employment. Therefore, state intervention is necessary to remove them.

Supply-side Policies Fail to bring Social Justice

Supply-side economists emphasise reduction in social spending, subsidies, grants and budget deficit with reduction in taxes. But such a policy has actually led to huge budget deficits in the United States. Further, the policy of reducing social spending, subsidies and grants adversely affects the poor and unemployed and fails to bring social justice.

Demand-side Economics

In Macroeconomics, Demand Side Policies are attempts to increase or decrease aggregate demand in order to affect output, employment and inflation.Demand Side Policies can be classified into fiscal policy and monetary policy.

In general, demand-side policies aim to change the aggregate demand in the economy. Aggregate Demand is made up of Consumer Spending + Government Spending + Investment + Net Exports (exports-imports). So anything that affects these factors will affect demand. We tend to use demand-side policies for short-term changes – if inflation is getting too high, we can increase interest rates to cool the economy down.

Demand-side policies may be expansionary or contractionary. Expansionary policies are intended to stimulate spending in a recessionary economy; contractionary policies designed to reduce expenditures in an inflationary economy.

Fiscal Policy

Fiscal Policy refers to policies affect government spending or tax policy. In Keynesian economics, the level of Aggregate Demand determines the output. To increase production, we would need to increase aggregate demand. Thus, fiscal policy can be used to increase Aggregate Demand. These policies can be used to help close the deflationary gap.

Fiscal expansions tend to be politically popular (i.e., more spending and/or less taxes) and thus easier to execute. However, fiscal expansions can make existing deficits worse and add to the national debt, which may not be sustainable. Contractionary policies (spending cuts or higher taxes) tend to be politically unpopular and less likely to be used even if required by economic conditions.

Monetary Policy

Monetary Policy refers policies that affect the interest rate or money supply. Monetary policy involves the country's central bank controlling the interest rate and money supply. Monetary policy affects Aggregate Demand (AD). An expansionary monetary policy increases Aggregate Demand, while a contractionary monetary policy decreases AD.

Monetary expansions are often less efficient and less predictable as compared to monetary contractions. For example, if the Central Bank is concerned about weak economic growth or relatively high rates of unemployment. The policy reaction would be to increase bank reserves (excess reserves) through open market purchases. Banks would then be expected to convert these excess reserves into loans with their customers. However, if banks are pessimistic about their future reserve position (expecting higher than usual withdrawal activity or fewer new deposits), they might just sit on these reserves with no change in lending rates.

Open market operations that remove reserves from the banking system will require that these banks reduce lending activity and allowing competition for fewer available loans to push interest rates upward. Higher interest rates will always make certain investment projects unprofitable thus leading to the abandonment of these projects.

Middle-out Economics

Middle-out economics is a principle that Henry Ford understood when he decided to pay his workers enough so they could afford to buy his cars. Entrepreneurs start companies not because of tax breaks, but because there are consumers out there who want and can afford what the entrepreneurs make. And most entrepreneurs don't start rich; most start in the middle class or below. Steve Jobs's father, Paul, was high-school educated and his mother was a payroll clerk they struggled to send Steve to college. Sam Walton's father was a farmer, and Walton started his business with $5,000 saved from his Army pay and a loan from his in-laws. Neither of these entrepreneurs would have benefited from tax breaks for the rich. Think of all the potential Steve Jobses and Sam Waltons who didn't make it because their parents couldn't afford to send them to college or because they couldn't get a small-business loan. Government doesn't make entrepreneurs, but it can help them help themselves.

Trickle-down economics may work in textbook economic theory with ivory-tower assumptions about perfectly rational people and perfectly efficient markets. But in the real world of politics and interests, it simply provides a cover story for rentier economics. It dresses up anti-market behavior in free-market rhetoric.

Other have presented Middle-out economics as a progressive argument but it can just as easily be presented as a conservative argument. It is a call for a return to a truer form of American capitalism. It is an argument for going back to the values that have described American capitalism since de Tocqueville competition, meritocracy, equality of opportunity, innovation, risk taking, and reward for hard work, self-improvement, and fair play. Both Randians and modern conservatives such as Koch claim to disdain rentier capitalism and celebrate these values. But what Rand's acolytes, Koch, and the Tea Party fail to see is the constructive role government must play if these conservative values are to be made real. This is not the heavy-handed interventionism or disdain for markets by socialists or the far left. This is the enabling and investing role of government supported by generations of both centrist Republicans and Democrats.

Modern Monetary Theory

There is a school of thought among economists who aren't worried about the so called "budget black hole", where tough choices have been called for to reduce government spending. Proponents of modern monetary theory, like Bernie Sanders' chief economic adviser Professor Stephanie Kelton, claim the Australian government need not balance its budget and are instead calling for the government to balance the economy, which they argue is a different thing entirely.

Modern monetary theory is an approach to economic management developed since the 1990s by Professor Bill Mitchell, alongside American academics like Professor Randall Wray, Stephanie Kelton, and investment bankers and fund managers like Warren Mosler. It builds on the ideas of a previous generation of economists, such as Hyman Minsky, Wynne Godley and Abba Lerner, whose interpretation of the work of the famous economist J. M.Keynes was very different from that which became dominant by the 1980s.

By the 1980s, most people saw Keynes as an advocate of budget deficits only during periods of high unemployment. Lerner, as early as 1943, in a paper entitled Functional Finance and the Federal Debt, had argued that Keynesian economics involved running whatever government deficit was necessary to maintain full employment, and that deficits should be seen as the norm. Keynes, in a letter to fellow economist James Meade written in April 1943, said of Lerner, "His argument is impeccable. But heaven help anyone who tries to put it across".

While the theory has attracted its own interpretations and criticism it's also gaining traction in a global economic environment that continues to defy the efforts of policymakers to restore sustained economic growth.

There are three core statements at the heart of modern monetary theory. The first two are:

1) Monetary sovereign governments face no purely financial budget constraints.

2) All economies, and all governments, face real and ecological limits relating to what can be produced and consumed.

The first statement is the one which is widely misunderstood. A monetary sovereign government is one with its own currency and central bank, a floating exchange rate, and no significant foreign currency debt. Australia has a monetary sovereign government. So does the UK, the US and Japan. The Eurozone countries are not monetary sovereigns, as they do not have their own currencies.

The second of these statements confirms the obvious fact that governments can cause inflation, if they choose, by spending too much themselves, or not taxing enough. When this happens, the total level of spending in the economy exceeds what can be produced by all the labor, skills, physical capital, technology and natural resources which are available. We can also destroy our natural ecosystem if produce too many of the wrong things, or use the wrong processes to produce what we want to consume.

The Australian government is a currency-issuing central government. It cannot run out of Australian dollars. It's never forced to borrow Australian dollars, although it can and does choose to do so, and its debt securities play a useful role in our financial system.

It doesn't exactly need to tax us to pay for its spending either. Taxes exist to limit inflation. It's necessary for us to pay taxes to keep total spending government and private at a level which will not be inflationary.

This doesn't mean government spending and taxation have to equal each other, and in countries like Australia this rarely happens in practice. This leads to the third principle of modern monetary theory:

3) The government's financial deficit is everybody else's financial surplus.

For every lender, there must be a borrower. That means that across our financial system, surpluses and deficits always add up to zero.

This is clear in the following chart, which shows the financial balances of the Australian private sector, the rest of the world, and the Australian government sector, since 1994.

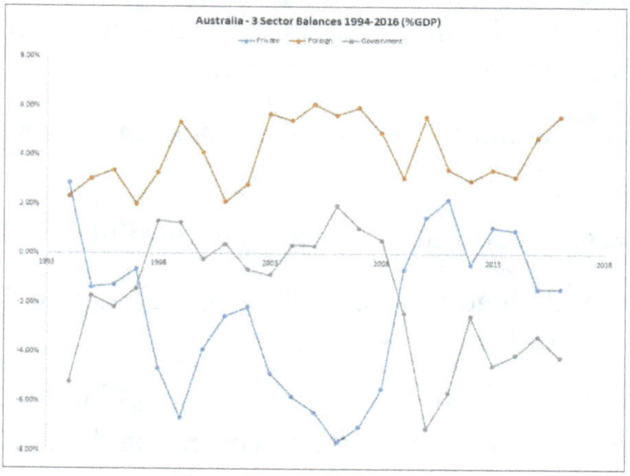

For every saver who earns more than they spend, there must somebody or some institution which spends more than it takes in. If we want the private sector as a whole to save rather than go further into debt, the government will probably have to spend more than it taxes (depending on what the rest of the world is doing).

It works the other way around too. The Howard government was only able to run fiscal surpluses because the private sector went heavily into deficit.

Household debt trebled during the Howard years. Since then, we have been in a tie with a couple of other countries for the highest household debt to income ratios in the world.

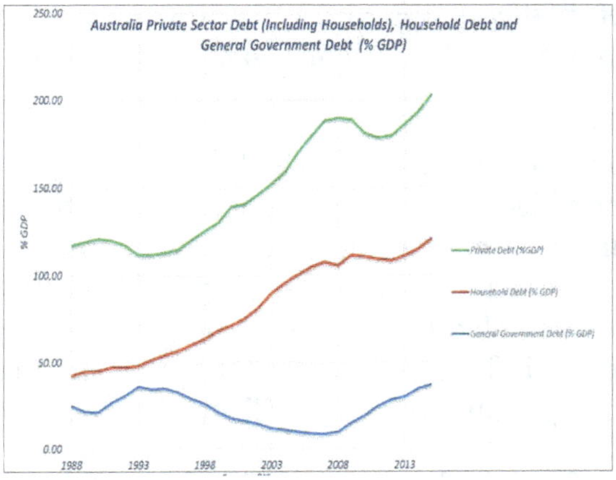

So, the government cannot run out of dollars; that doesn't mean the government should "spend like a drunken sailor" or that we don't have to pay taxes; it does mean balanced budgets are unnecessary. It also means government deficits can play a supportive role, allowing the private sector to build up its saving.

Australian governments have nearly always run deficits anyway. None of the above ought to be shocking. On average, governments of both left and right have run deficits, ever since federation. It just might be that you have been misled by that metaphor of the government as a household.

In a country with nearly 15% underutilisation of labor, over 30% youth underutilisation, fragile private balance sheets, and a growing need for green and other infrastructural investments, it does imply that budget repair is a red herring. This means the government could and should be using its role as the currency issuer to promote full employment, social inclusion, ecological repair, and healthy private sector balance sheets.

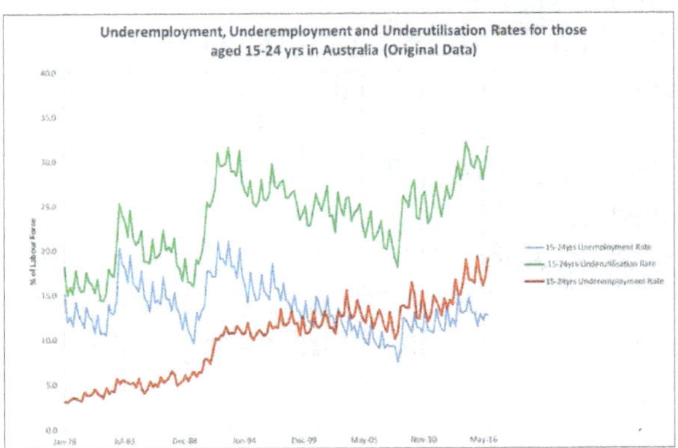

Politicians are, according to modern monetary theorists, currently obsessed with something which doesn't matter (balancing their budget), and are ignoring many things which do matter a great deal for the future of the country.

This is the perspective you get when you start to see Australia and the world through the prism of modern monetary theory. It's based on nothing more than a comprehension of how modern financial systems actually work, and in that sense, perhaps it should not be controversial at all.

Modern monetary theory proponent, Professor Bill Mitchell, advocates for governments to use the policy space provided for them by monetary sovereignty to introduce a job guarantee and pursue a return to unemployment rates of 2% or less. These rates were achieved in Australian across the 1960s and early 1970s. He proposes a return to full employment through a federally funded and locally managed program of public employment. He does not believe that this need be inflationary - indeed the job guarantee is an essential part of the modern monetary theory framework for stabilising the economy and avoiding inflation.

In Australia, the three major political parties have as yet paid little attention to his ideas. But his fellow modern monetary theorists got close to government in the USA (with Senator Bernie Sanders) and two micro-parties have been set up in the last year with the express intention of promoting modern monetary theory as a frame for understanding economic issues. So you can expect to hear a lot more from both the proponents and the critics of modern monetary theory.

Vertical Transactions

MMT labels any transactions between the government, or public, sector and the non-government, or private, sector as a "vertical transaction". The government sector is considered to include the treasury and the central bank. The non-government sector includes domestic and foreign private individuals and firms (including the private banking system) and foreign buyers and sellers of the currency.

At any given point, the government's budget can be either in deficit or in surplus. A deficit occurs when the government spends more than it taxes. A surplus occurs when a government taxes more than it spends. MMT states that as a matter of accounting, it follows that government budget deficits add net financial assets to the private sector. This is because a budget deficit means that a government has deposited more money into private bank accounts than it has removed in taxes. A budget surplus means the opposite: the government has overall removed more money from private bank accounts via taxes than it has put back in via spending. Therefore, budget deficits add net financial assets to the private sector; whereas budget surpluses remove financial assets from the private sector. This concept is widely represented in macroeconomic theory by the national income identity,

$$G - T = S - I - NX$$

where G is government spending, T is taxes, S is savings, I is investment and NX is net exports.

Based on the national income identity, MMT states that it is possible for the non-government sector to accumulate a surplus only if the government runs budget deficits. As most private sectors want to accumulate a surplus, MMT economists usually advocate for government budget deficits.

Horizontal Transactions

MMT economists describe any transactions within the private sector as "horizontal" transactions, including the expansion of the broad money supply through the extension of credit by banks.

MMT economists regard the concept of the money multiplier, where a bank is completely constrained in lending through the deposits it holds and its capital requirement, as misleading. Rather than being a practical limitation on lending, the cost of borrowing funds from the interbank market (or the central bank) represents a *profitability consideration* when the private bank lends in excess of its reserve and/or capital requirements.

According to MMT, bank credit should be regarded as a "leverage" of the monetary base and should not be regarded as increasing the net financial assets held by an economy: only the government or central bank is able to issue high-powered money with no corresponding liability. Stephanie Kelton argues that bank money is generally accepted in settlement of debt and taxes because of state guarantees, but that state-issued high-powered money sits atop a "hierarchy of money".

Policy Implications

MMT claims that the word "borrowing" is a misnomer when it comes to a sovereign government's fiscal operations, because what the government is doing is accepting back its own IOUs, and nobody can borrow back their own debt instruments. Sovereign government goes into debt by issuing its own liabilities that are financial wealth to the private sector. "Private debt is debt, but government debt is *financial wealth* to the private sector."

In this theory, sovereign government is not *financially* constrained in its ability to spend; it is argued that the government can afford to buy anything that is for sale in currency that it issues (there may be political constraints, like a debt ceiling law). The only constraint is that excessive spending by any sector of the economy (whether households, firms or public) has the potential to cause inflationary pressures.

Some MMT economists advocate a government-funded job guarantee scheme to eliminate involuntary unemployment. Proponents argue that this can be consistent with price stability as it targets unemployment directly rather than attempting to increase private sector job creation indirectly through a much larger economic stimulus, and maintains a "buffer stock" of labor that can readily switch to the private sector when jobs become available. A job guarantee program could also be considered a powerful automatic stabilizer to the economy, expanding when private sector activity cools down and shrinking in size when private sector activity heats up.

Recursive Competitive Equilibrium

An equilibrium concept associated with dynamic programs. Recursive competitive equilibrium (RCE) is characterized by time-invariant equilibrium decision rules that specify actions as a function of a limited number of state variables, which summarize the effects of past decisions and current information. Economic agents with knowledge of these state variables assess the current state of the economy. As their actions determine in part the values of the state variables in the next sequential time period, this structure is termed 'recursive'.

The RCE concept is used in exploring various economic issues, including monetary and fiscal policy and business-cycle fluctuations. RCE decision rules include a number of functions, such as pricing and value.

The beauty of the recursive representation lies in the fact that, in a stationary environment, the nature of the problem do not change with passage of time. Unlike the sequential formulation, in which the solution to the problem depends on at what point in time you solve it, the solution to the recursive problem do not depend on time and we do not have to keep track of time.

So what do we keep track of? Everything that matters to the structure of our problem. These are the variables that our agents respond to either directly or indirectly and we call them the STATE VARIABLES. State variables need to satisfy the following criteria:

1. Predetermined: when decisions are made, the state variables are taken as given and cannot be effected by the agent.
2. It must matter for decisions of agents: there is no sense of adding irrelevant variables as state variable.
3. It must vary across time and state: otherwise, we can just take it as a parameter.

One important thing is to be able to distinguish the aggregate and individual state variables. Aggregate state is not affected by individual choice. But aggregate state should be consistent with the individual choice (we will consider the meaning of "consistency" more formally later), because aggregate state represents the aggregated state of individuals. In particular, in our RANGM aggregate state turns out to be the same as individual state in equilibrium, but this does not mean that the agent decide the aggregate state or the agent is forced to follow the average behavior, but rather the behavior of the agent turns out to be the aggregate behavior, in equilibrium.

Also note that prices (wages, and rental rates of capital) is determined by aggregate capital, rather than individual capital, and since individual takes aggregate state as given, she also takes prices as given (because they are determined by aggregate state).

Again, the aggregate capital turns out to coincide with the individual choice, but it is not because of the agent's choice, rather it is the result of consistency.

Example: Victor is going to use a for individual capital and K for aggregate capital, in order to avoid the confusion between K and k. But the problem with aggregate and individual capital is often called as "big-K, small-k" problem, because the diff of aggregate capital and individual capital is crucial. So for our case, the counterpart is "big-K, small- a" problem.

What does the agent has to know in order to solve her problem? Our agent has to know how wealthy she is. She also needs to know the prices but we do not need $\{R, w\}$ directly. Why? Because they are redundant: K is a sufficient statistic to calculate $\{R, w\}$ as they must be equal to marginal products in the firm problem at equilibrium.If we put K as a state variable instead of these prices, we do not need $\{R, w\}$ So are we done? Not yet. As the problem of the HH is formulated below, our agent not only needs to know $\{R, w\}$ but $\{R', w'\}$ as well thus Ko. But this is a variable that our agent has no control over and the best she can do is to have a belief about it. These beliefs in our model are parameterized by the GF function which vmaps today's state to a unique belief about next period's value. As it is formulated, it is an exogenous parameter, i.e. we can solve this problem for any sort of beliefs under which the problem is well defined. But from the beginning of this course we want to be able to 'predict' the outcome, once we setup our environment as precise as possible. To continue to be able to do so, as we will see later, we will impose an additional constraint on the beliefs and make them an equilibrium object as well, i.e. endogenize them.

The recursive form of the problem of the agent (that does not value leisure) is:

$$V(K,a;G^F) = \max_{c,a'}\left[u(c) + \beta V(K',a';G^F)\right]$$

$$s.t \quad c + a' = Ra + w$$

$$R = R(K) = F_K(K,1)$$

$$w = w(K) = F_N(K,1)$$

$$K' = G^F(K)$$

Note that F is indexing the beliefs. This means that for different beliefs F, different equilibria will arise. Of course, in this course we will only focus on rational expectations equilibria.

How do we deal with the problem written above? The first step is to assume that the solution (for the decision rule) is of the form, $a' = g\left(a,\ K;\ G^F\right)$. So use this fact to write:

$$\begin{aligned} &V(K,a;G^F) \\ &= u\left(R(K)a - g(a,K;G^F)\right) + \beta V\left(G^F(K), g(a,K;G^F); G^F\right) \end{aligned}$$

Note that the FOC implies that:

$$-u_c(c)+\beta\frac{\partial V}{\partial a'}=0$$

and in order to obtain a more useful expression for the derivative we use the Envelope condition. This is where equation above the last one is useful. From, take the derivative with respect to a:

$$\frac{\partial V}{\partial a}=u_c(c)\left[R(K)-\frac{\partial g}{\partial a}\right]+\beta\frac{\partial V}{\partial a'}\frac{\partial g}{\partial a}=u_c(c)R(K)+\frac{\partial g}{\partial a}\left[-u_c(c)+\beta\frac{\partial V}{\partial a'}\right],$$

so by the above equation: $\frac{\partial V}{\partial a}=u_c(c)\,R(K)$.

We will assume that there exist a $\overline{K}$ such that $\overline{K}\geq F(\overline{K},1)+(1-\delta)\overline{K}$. In words $\overline{K}$ is the amount of capital stock which is impossible to reproduce. The assumption is that such a value of K exists.

A Recursive Competitive Equilibrium with arbitrary beliefs G^F is a list of functions $\{V^*(.),g^*(.),G^*(.),R(.),w(.)\}$ such that:

1) Given $\{G^F(.),R(.),w(.)\},\{V^*(.),g^*(.)\}$ solves the household problem above,
2) $\{R(.),\ w(.)\}$ are characterized by the optimal decisions of firms, and
3) $G^*(K;\ G^F)=g^*(K,\ K;\ G^F)$ (agent is representative).

Some comments on the third condition. This condition is called 'Representative agent condition' and is a specific case of the compatibility condition that any equilibrium must satisfy. It basically means that if a consumer turns out to be average this period (her individual capital stock is K, which is aggregate capital stock), the consumer will choose to be average in the next period (she chooses $G^*(K)$, which is a belief on the aggregate capital stock in the next period if today's aggregate capital stock is K). This condition guarantees that in an equilibrium, individual choice turns out to be consistent with the aggregate law of motion. This is true not because our agent is constrained to do so but because the prices are such that she choses to do so.

Twin Deficits Hypothesis

Twin deficit identity is used to refer to a nation's current account deficits and a simultaneous fiscal deficit. The term became widely used in the 1980s until the 1990s because the United States experienced the "twin" deficits during this time frame. However, there is no reason why current account deficits and government budget deficits occurs at the same time. The term "twin deficit" is now mostly used to refer to the relationship between the country's current account deficit and fiscal deficit. It's one of the reasons due to which the precious metals market is likely take off in the coming years.

In the twin deficit hypothesis, economists relate a large fiscal deficit to a large current account deficit. The logic behind it is that tax cuts which increase the deficit and reduce revenues result in increased consumption. This spending lowers the national savings rate which increases the amount of money a nation has to borrow from other countries. However, the fiscal deficit and current account deficit are just two parts of the puzzle. There are many other inputs that determine a nation's fiscal situation.

Simply put the twin deficit hypothesis is the view that an economy running a fiscal budget deficit will also run a current account deficit. It stems from a national accounting equation which says that NX = S-I. We arrive at this point because Classical economists take S = Y-C-G, so we can arrange our national accounting equation of Y = C + I + G + NX to get the above NX = S – I. Where Y is national output (i.e. GDP), S is savings, C is consumption, I is investment, G is government spending and NX is net exports (exports minus imports).

Since 2004, the United States found itself back into the "twin deficit" scenario. To get a deeper understanding of this, it may be helpful to study how fiscal deficits and current account deficits occur independently.

Fiscal Deficit

Fiscal deficit is also called government budget deficit. It occurs when a nation's expense exceeds its revenues. Running a deficit doesn't seem like a positive development for an economy. However, some would argue that it is necessary to boost a sluggish economy. A nation in recession would find that deficit spending can finance infrastructure projects (which hires workers, boost corporate profits, and builds important networks for commerce).

Government can fund these projects by issuing bonds to investors. In effect, the buyers of these bonds are loaning money to the government. When the government repays the debt, investors will get their principal plus an interest on the loan. These bonds are considered safe if it is issued by a stable government because of its ability to print money or raise taxes to generate revenue.

The problem is that history shows that ultimately governments don't act responsibly: they spend to much and ultimately print too much currency causing hyperinflation.

Current Account Deficit

Current account deficit occurs when a nation imports more than it exports. Intuitively, many would argue that running a current account deficit is not good for the economy. But there are two sides to the story. Views on a country's "trade balance" are relative to the economy and business cycle.

For example, a country in recession will find that exports can create jobs. During economic expansion, imports cause price competition which keeps inflation manageable. Trade deficit is essentially bad news during recession but it may help when an economy is expanding. It is also worth noting that countries may run short-term current account deficits if it imports unfinished products. Once these products are exported, the deficits can turn into surplus.

Twin Deficit and Gold

The twin deficits may reduce confidence in the economy and thus spur safe-haven demand for gold. This was exactly what happened in 2000s. President Bush has become the biggest spender in decades and created the twin deficits in the USA. The deteriorated fiscal position of the USA erased investors' confidence in the American economy. As investing in the USA became riskier (or the country risk premium decreased, since the USA is a benchmark country) and the greenback plunged, gold started its huge rally. Therefore, gold may be an excellent safe-haven against fiscal irresponsibility, increase in country risk and twin deficits in the USA.

References

- Trickle-down-vs-middle-out-economics-the-real-history-of-economic-growth: mostlyeconomics.wordpress.com, Retrieved 21, June 2020
- Explainer-what-is-modern-monetary-theory-72095: theconversation.com, Retrieved 25, July 2020
- Recursive-competitive-equilibrium: investopedia.com, Retrieved 15, July 2020
- Kelton, Stephanie (Bell) (2001), "The Role of the State and the Hierarchy of Money"(PDF), Cambridge Journal of Economics, Cambridge (25): 149–163
- Macroeconomics, the-supply-side-economics-features-and-policy-prescription-31217: yourarticlelibrary.com, Retrieved 31,March 2020
- Tcherneva Pavlina R. "Chartalism and the tax-driven approach to money", in A Handbook of Alternative Monetary Economics, edited by Philip Arestis & Malcolm C. Sawyer, Elgar Publishing (2007), ISBN 978-1-84376-915-6
- Murphy, Robert P. (9 May 2011). "The Upside-Down World of MMT". Ludwig von Mises Institute Retrieved 17, July 2020
- Demand-side-policies: intelligenteconomist com Retrieved 11, April 2020

7

Microeconomic Theories

The branch of economics which is concerned with the decision making behavior of individuals to allocate scarce resources is known as microeconomics. This chapter covers economic decision making, general equilibrium theory, search theory, theory of the second best, information economics, etc. The aim of this chapter is to explore these concepts and theories related to microeconomics.

Economic Decision Making

Let us consider an example. After several weeks of interviewing, you have received job offers from three firms. The offers differ greatly, which leaves you quite confused. You have made this list of the offers:

1. Large national firm, $12 per hour starting wage, life insurance and dental benefits paid by the company, a two-week paid vacation each year, and potential for rapid advancement.
2. Small local firm, $20 per hour starting wage, life insurance and dental benefits available but you must pay the premiums, a two week paid vacation each year, share options and pension plan benefits, and potential for advancement.
3. Regional firm, $15 per hour starting wage, full life insurance and dental benefits, one-week paid vacation, good pension plan, and moderate advancement potential.

Will you consider the short run or the long run for this decision? Which offer provides you with the most today and which one the most over the next five years? What is the real economic value of the benefits? Aside from the monetary considerations, do you like the work you will perform in each position and the people with whom you will work.

Regardless of the form of organization or the business activity, success in the world of business sometimes even survival depends on making wise economic decisions. A key ingredient is an understanding of the decision-making process itself. Because economic decision making relies heavily on accounting information, it is crucial for that information to be useful to economic decision makers.

Life is a never-ending sequence of decisions, some very complex and others relatively simple. Because we cannot know the future, we strive to reduce uncertainty in any decision by collecting as much information as possible.

Decision making is the process of identifying alternative courses of action and selecting an appropriate alternative in a given decision situation. This definition presents two important parts:

1. Identifying alternative courses of action means that an ideal solution may not exist or might not be identifiable.

2. Selecting an appropriate alternative implies that there may be a number of appropriate alternatives and that inappropriate alternatives are to be evaluated and rejected. Thus, judgment is fundamental to decision making.

Choice is implicit in our definition of decision making. We may not like the alternatives available to us, but we are seldom left without choices.

Rewards and Sacrifices: The Trade-off

In general, the aim of all decisions is to obtain some type of reward, either economic or personal. Reward requires sacrifice. When you made the decision to attend college or university, for example, you certainly desired a reward.

Think of some things you cannot do because you are attending college. Some sacrifices cannot be measured in dollars (such as loss of sleep, lack of home-cooked meals, and loss of leisure time). Some, however, can be measured. Suppose that instead of attending college you could work full time and earn $15,000 a year. Attending college, therefore, costs you that $15,000, in addition to what you pay for tuition and books. We call the $15,000 an opportunity cost of making the decision to attend college. An opportunity cost is the reward we forego because we choose a particular alternative instead of another. Most decisions include opportunity costs.

Decision makers want the reward or benefit from a decision to be greater than the sacrifice or cost required to attain it. Examining the relationship between rewards and sacrifices is known as cost/benefit analysis. In a condition of absolute certainty, in which the outcome of a decision is known without doubt, cost/benefit analysis provides a certain outcome. Unfortunately, absolute certainty rarely, if ever, exists.

Economic decision making, in this book, refers to the process of making business decisions involving money. All economic decisions of any consequence require the use of some sort of accounting information, often in the form of financial reports. Anyone using accounting information to make economic decisions must understand the business and economic environment in which accounting information is generated, and they must also be willing to devote the necessary time and energy to make sense of the accounting reports. Economic decision makers are either internal or external. Internal decision makers are individuals within a company who make decisions on behalf of the company, while external decision makers are individuals or organizations outside a company who make decisions that affect the company. Table illustrates some decisions made by internal and external decision makers.

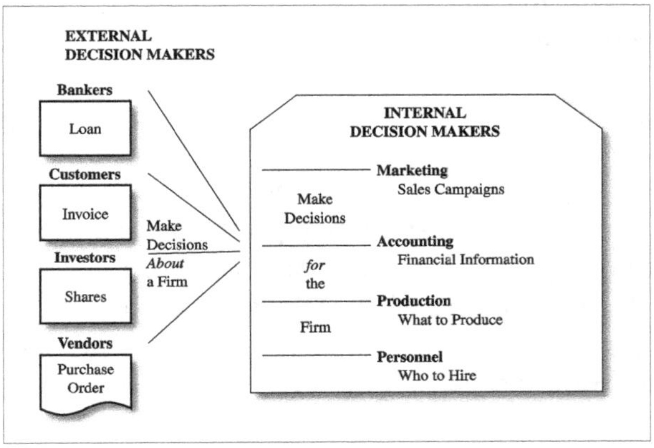

Internal Decision Makers

Internal decision makers decide whether the company should sell a particular product, whether it should enter a certain market, and whether it should hire or fire employees. Note that in all these matters, the responsible internal decision maker makes the decision not for himself or herself, but rather for the company.

Depending on their position within the company, internal decision makers may have access to much, or even all, of the company's financial information. They do not have complete information, however, because all decisions relate to the future and always involve unknowns.

External Decision Makers

External decision makers make decisions about a company. External decision makers decide whether to invest in the company, whether to sell to or buy from the company, and whether to lend money to the company.

Unlike internal decision makers, external decision makers have limited financial information on which to base their decisions about the company. In fact, they have only the information the company gives them—which in most cases is not all the information the company possesses.

The decisions made by internal and external decision makers are similar in some ways, but so different in other ways that the accounting profession developed two separate branches of accounting to meet the needs of the two categories of users. Management accounting is not constrained by GAAP and generates information for use by internal decision makers, whereas financial accounting is constrained by GAAP and generates information for use by external parties.

All Economic Decision Makers want to Know

Although internal and external parties face different decision situations, both attempt to predict the future, as do all decision makers. Specifically, all economic decision makers attempt to predict future cash flow—the movement of cash in and out of a company. So one of the major objectives of financial reporting is to provide helpful information to those trying to predict cash flows.

The difference between cash inflows and cash outflows is net cash flow. Positive net cash flow indicates that the amount of cash flowing into the company exceeds the amount flowing out of the company during a particular period. For example, a company that collects $1,000,000 during a period when it pays out $950,000 has a positive cash flow of $50,000. Negative net cash flow indicates that the amount of cash flowing out of the company exceeds the amount flowing into the company during a particular period.

Cash inflow	-	Cash outflow	=	Cash outflow
$1,000,000	-	$950,000	=	$50,000
Cash inflow	-	Cash outflow	=	Negative net cash flow
$ 500,000	-	$575,000	=	-$75,000

All economic decisions involve attempts to predict the future of cash flows by searching for the answers to the following three questions:

1. Will you be paid?

This question refers to the uncertainty of cash flows:

2. When will you be paid?

This question refers to the timing of cash flows:

3. How much will you be paid?

This question refers to the amounts of cash flows.

The answer to each question contains two parts: return on investment and return of investment. Return on investment consists of the earnings and profits an investment returns to the investor. Return of investment is the ultimate return of the principal invested.

Table shows the conceptual link between the three major questions posed by economic decision makers and the resulting cash flows using the following example. Assume you wish to invest in a $1,000 term deposit at your bank, which will earn 10 percent interest per year, payable every three months, over the course of two years. If you invest in this term deposit, you must hold it for two years, after which the bank will return your $1,000.

Three Big Questions for Economic Decision Makers:

Table

		Cash Outcome	
Questions	Concepts	Return on Investment	Return of investment
1. Will I be paid?	Uncertainty	Interest	Term deposit maturity
2. When will I be paid?	Timing	Quarterly	2 years
3. How much will I be paid?	Amount	$25 per quarter	$1,000
		Total of $200	

Before you make this economic decision, you must attempt to answer the three questions:

1. Will you be paid? Because it is impossible to know the future, making an economic decision always involves risk. However, assuming the economy does not collapse and the bank stays in business, you will be paid both your return on investment and your return of investment.

2. When will you be paid? You will receive an interest payment every three months for two years (return on investment), and then you will receive your initial $1,000 investment back (return of investment).

3. How much will you be paid? The return on your investment is the interest you receive quarterly of $\$25\ (\$1{,}000 \times 10\ \textit{percent} \times 3/12)\$$, and the return of your investment is the $1,000 the bank gives you back. The total received in interest in two years is $\$\ 200\ (8 \times \$25)$.

Initial Investment		$1,000
Return on Investment	200	
Return of Investment	1,000	
Total Return		1,200
Profit on Investment		$ 200

We can answer these questions easily for the insured term deposit. In the vast majority of economic decision situations, the answers to the three questions we asked are much less certain. We will show you how to use accounting information to answer them in various economic decision situations throughout this text.

Cash is the "Ball" of Business

If business were any game such as baseball, football, or soccer, then cash would be the ball. To be successful, the players must keep their eye on the ball. Because the business game is so complex, businesspeople easily become distracted and lose sight of (the ball) cash. Various measures of performance such as gross profit, net income, net worth, and equity help those in business to make economic decisions. These are important measures of financial performance, but they are not cash! Never allow yourself to become so focused on any of them that you lose sight of cash, because when a company runs out of cash, it dies. Only cash pays the bills that keeps the company in business. The secret to becoming a street-smart user of accounting information is learning to balance the complexity of business with the simple rule of keeping your eye on cash flow.

General Equilibrium Theory

General equilibrium analysis is an extensive study of a number of economic variables, their interrelations and interdependences for understanding the working of the economic system as a whole. It brings together the cause and effect sequences of changes in prices and quantities of commodities and services in relation to the entire economy.

An economy can be in general equilibrium only if all consumers, all firms, all industries and all factor-services are in equilibrium simultaneously and they are interlinked through commodity and factor prices. As Stigler has said: "The theory of General Equilibrium is the theory of interrelationship among all parts of the economy."

General equilibrium exists when all prices are in equilibrium; each consumer spends his given income in a manner that yields him the maximum satisfaction; all firms in each industry are in equilibrium at all prices and output; and the supply and demand for productive resources (factors of production) are equal at equilibrium prices.

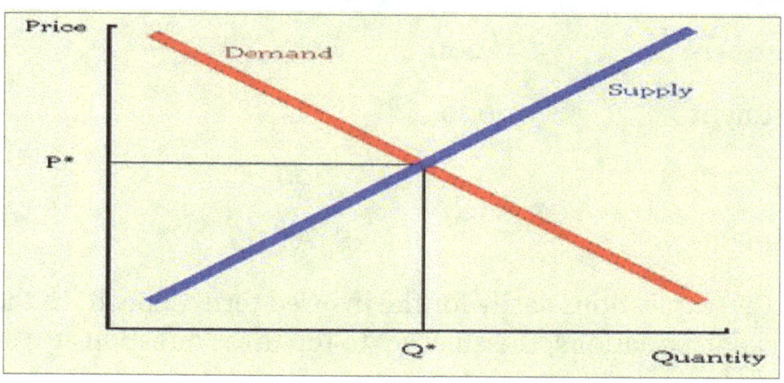

Assumptions

The general equilibrium analysis is based on the following assumptions:

- There is perfect competition both in the commodity and factor markets.
- Tastes and habits of consumers are given and constant.
- Incomes of consumers are given and constant.
- Factors of production are perfectly mobile between different occupations and places.
- There are constant returns to scale.
- All firms operate under identical cost conditions.
- All units of a productive service are homogeneous.
- There are no changes in the techniques of production.
- There is full employment of labour and other resources.

Working of the General Equilibrium System

Given these assumptions, the economy is in a state of general equilibrium when the demand for every commodity and service is equal to the supply for it. It implies perfect harmony of the decisions made by all the market participants. The decisions of consumers for the purchase of each commodity must be in perfect accord with the decisions of producers for the production and sale of each commodity.

Similarly, the decisions of owners for selling each factor service must be in perfect harmony with the decisions of their employers. It is only when the decisions of buyers of goods and services fit in perfectly with the decisions of sellers that the market is in general equilibrium.

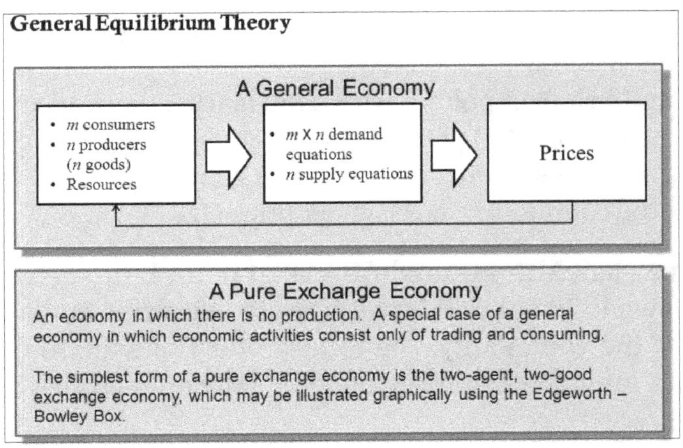

Product Market

Given the tastes, preferences and aims of the consumers in the economy, the quantity of each commodity demanded depends not only on its own price but also on the price of each other commodity available in the market. Thus, each consumer maximizes his satisfaction relative to the prices ruling the market. For him, the marginal utility of each commodity equals its price.

Each consumer is assumed to spend his entire income on consumption, so his expenditure equals his income. His income, in turn, depends on the prices at which he is selling his productive services. In other words, a consumer earns by selling the productive services he owns. Thus, the demand of consumers for the various commodities depends upon their prices and the prices of services.

Let us take the supply side. Given the market structure, the state of technology and the aims of firms, the price at which a commodity sells depends on its costs of production. The costs of production, in turn, depend on the quantities of the various productive services employed and the prices paid for them.

Assuming constant returns to scale and identical cost conditions for all firms, each producer will produce and sell that quantity of output at which the demand price for the commodity equals both the minimum average cost and the marginal cost. The equilibrium of the commodity market is illustrated in Figure below.

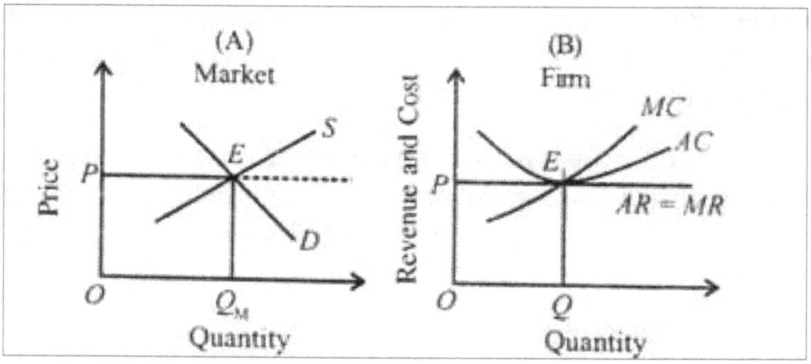

The market is in equilibrium at point E where the market demand and supply curves D and S intersect. It determines OP price at which OQ_M quantity of the product is bought and sold in the market. There being identical cost conditions, each firm in the market produces and sells the commodity at the given price OP.

It is in equilibrium when MC=MR and AC=AR at point E_1producing OQ units of the commodity, as shown in Panel B. If, say, there are 100 firms in the market each producing 60 units of the commodity, the total production will be 6000 (=100 x 60) units. This analysis inter alia can be extended to all commodities being produced in the economy.

Factor Market

Like the equality of demand and supply of commodities, the equality of demand and supply of factor services is also essential for the general equilibrium system. The demand for productive services comes from the producers and supply from the consumers. Given the state of technology and the profit maximization objective of the producers, the quantity of a factor used in producing a commodity depends on the relationship between the prices of that factor and of all other factors and on the prices of commodities.

Each producer maximises his profits relative to the ruling factor prices by employing the various factors in such proportions and quantities that their marginal revenue productivities are equal to their prices. Since there is full employment in the economy, the markets for factors are in equilibrium when the total quantities of factors offered and the total quantities employed are equal.

The equilibrium of the factor market is illustrated in Figure below, where in Panel (A), the price of a factor OP and its quantity ON are determined in the market by the interaction of its demand and supply curves D and 5 respectively at point E. Panel (B) shows that the supply curve of this factor to an individual firm is perfectly elastic and is the same as the marginal cost of that factor, MFC.

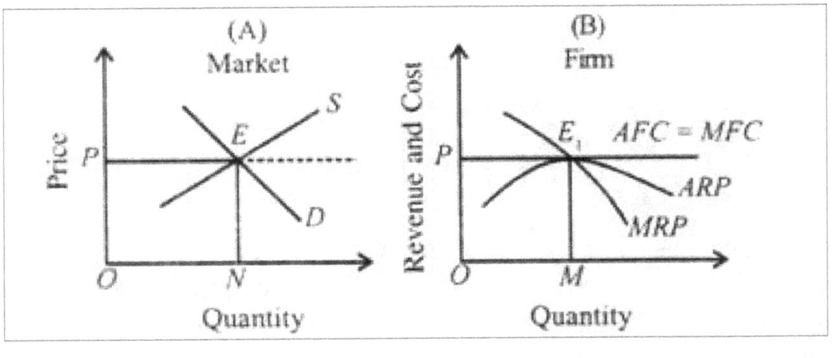

The firm will employ units of the factor at the given factor price OP where MFC=MRP and average factor cost, AFC=ARP (average revenue product) to the firm. Such an equilibrium point is E_1 at which it employs OM units of the factor. If there are 10 identical cost firms and each employs 100 units of the factor, the total market demand and supply of this factor will be 1000 units in the market. This analysis can be extended to the economy as a whole.

General Equilibrium

Thus the economy is in general equilibrium when commodity prices make each demand equal to its supply and factor prices make the demand for each factor equal to its supply so that all product markets and factor markets are simultaneously in equilibrium.

Such a general equilibrium is characterised by two conditions in which the set of prices in all product and factor markets is such that:

(1) All consumers maximise their satisfactions and all producers maximise their profits;

(2) All markets are cleared which means that the total amount demanded equals the total amount supplied at a positive price in both the product and factor markets.

To explain it, we begin with a simple hypothetical economy where there are only two sectors, the household and the business. The economic activity takes the form of flow of goods and services between these two sectors and monetary flow between them.

These two flows which are called real and monetary are shown in figure where the product market is shown in the lower portion and the factor market in the upper portion. In the product market, consumers purchase goods and services from producers while in the factor market, consumers receive income from the former for providing services.

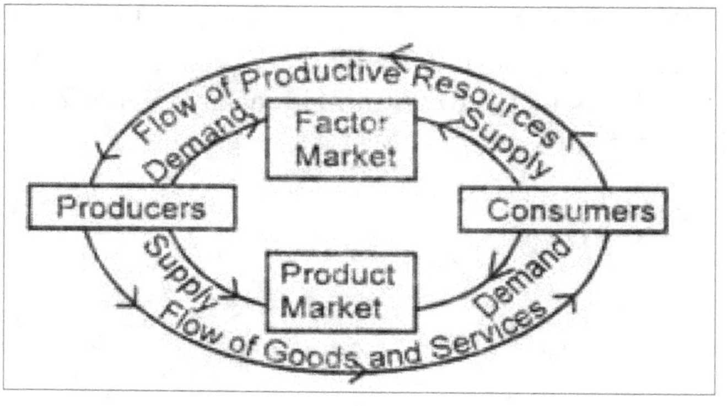

Thus consumers purchase all goods and services provided by producers and make payments to the latter in lieu of these. The producers, in turn, make payments to consumers for the services rendered by the latter to the business, wage payments for labour services, interest for capital supplied, etc. Thus payments go around in a circular manner from producers to consumers and from consumers to producers, as shown by arrows in the outer portion of the figure.

There are also flows of goods and services in the opposite direction to the money payments flows. Goods flow from the business sector to the household sector in the product market, and services flow from the household sector to the business sector in the factor market, as shown in dies inner portion of the figure.

These two flows are linked by product prices and factor prices. The economy is in general equilibrium when a set of prices is allowed at which the magnitude of income flow from producers to consumers is equal to the magnitude of the money expenditure from consumers to producers.

Limitations

The general equilibrium analysis of the economy has several limitations:

1. It is based on a number of unrealistic: Assumptions which are contrary to the actual conditions prevailing in the world. Perfect competition, the very basis of this analysis, is a myth.

2. It is a static analysis: All consumers and producers in this analysis consume and produce the same products day in and day out without any time-lag. Their tastes, preferences, and aims are the same, and their economic decisions are in perfect harmony with each other.

In reality, nothing of this sort happens. Producers and consumers never act and think alike. Changes are taking place continuously in tastes and preferences. There are no constant returns to scale and no two factor services are homogeneous. Thus cost conditions differ from producer to producer. Since the given conditions are continuously changing, the movement towards general equilibrium is ever thwarted and its attainment has ever remained a wishful ideal.

3. Prof. Stigler regards general equilibrium as a misnomer: According to him, "No economic analysis has ever been general in the sense that it considered equilibrium studies as more inclusive than partial equilibrium studies, never that they are complete. Moreover, the more general the analysis, the less specific its content must necessarily be."

Search Theory

Search theory is a study about transactional frictions between two parties that prevent them from a match in an efficient time frame. Search theory has mainly been used to explain inefficiencies in the market for employment, but it also has broad applicability to any form of "buyer" and "seller" whether for a product, house or even a spouse/partner. Under classical competitive equilibrium models, buyers and seller can transact in a frictionless world with complete and open information; clearing prices are immediately met because supply and demand forces react freely. However, in the real world, this does not happen.

Two parties that wish to transact in business - an employer and job seeker, a seller of a good and a buyer - encounter frictions in their search for each other. These frictions can take the form of mismatched geographies, price expectations and specification requirements, as well as slow response and negotiation times by one of the parties involved. Government or corporate policy may even interfere with an efficient search process. For example, overly generous unemployment benefits may induce a qualified worker to sit at home and collect unemployment checks instead of seeking a job.

Economists Peter Diamond, Dale Mortensen and Christopher Pissarides won the 2010 Nobel Prize in Economics for their "analysis of markets with search frictions." Their search theory puzzled over a basic empirical observation that there can be many unemployed job seekers (as opposed to unemployed who are not looking for a job) at a time when there are many job openings that are suitable for them. Diamond initiated search theory research into retail markets and Mortensen and Pissarides spearheaded focus on labor markets. Their discoveries of frictions that lead to less- than-optimal outcomes have helped to explain chronic unemployment issues, price and wage differences, and inefficient uses of search resources. In turn, findings of their search theory offer guidance to policy makers to adjust unemployment programs to minimize benefit payments and promote more matching activity between buyers and sellers of work.

Theory of the Second Best

The theory of the second-best was formalized by Richard Lipsey and Kelvin Lancaster in 1956.

The primary focus of the theory is on what happens when the optimum conditions are not satisfied in an economic model. Lipsey and Lancaster's results have important implications for the understanding of, not only, trade policies but many other government policies as well.

First of all, one must note that economic models consist of exercises in which a set of assumptions are used to deduce a series of logical conclusions. The solution of a model is referred to as an equilibrium. An equilibrium is typically described by explaining the conditions or relationships that must be satisfied in order for the equilibrium to be realized. These are called the equilibrium conditions. In economic models these conditions arise out of the maximizing behavior of producers and consumers. Thus the solution is also called an optimum.

For example, in a standard perfectly competitive model, the equilibrium conditions include:

- Output price equal to marginal cost for each firm in an industry,
- The ratio of prices between any two goods is equal to each consumer's marginal rate of substitution between the two goods,
- The long-run profit of each firm is equal to zero,
- Supply of all goods is equal to demand for all goods. In a general equilibrium model, with many consumers, firms, industries and markets there will be numerous equilibrium conditions that must be satisfied simultaneously.

Lipsey and Lancaster's analysis asks the following simple question: What happens to the other optimal equilibrium conditions when one of the conditions cannot be satisfied for some reason? For example, what happens if one of the markets does not clear, i.e. supply does not equal demand in that one market? Would it still be appropriate for the firms to set price equal to marginal cost? Should consumers continue to set each price ratio equal to their marginal rate of substitution? Or, would it be better if firms and consumers deviate from these conditions? Lipsey and Lancaster show that, generally, when one optimal equilibrium condition is not satisfied, for whatever reason, all of the other equilibrium conditions will change. Thus if one market does not clear, it would no longer be optimal for firms to set price equal to marginal cost or for consumers to set the price ratio equal to the marginal rate of substitution.

First-Best vs. Second-Best Equilibria

Consider a small perfectly competitive open economy that has no market imperfections or distortions, no externalities in production or consumption, no public goods. An economy in which all resources are privately owned, where the participants maximize their own well-being, firms maximize profit and consumers maximize utility always in the presence of perfect information. An economy in which markets always clear, in which there are no adjustment costs or unemployment of resources.

The optimal government policy in this case is laissez-faire. With respect to trade policy the optimal policy is free trade. Any type of tax or subsidy implemented by the government under these circumstances can only reduce economic efficiency and national welfare. Thus with a laissez-faire policy the resulting equilibrium would be called first-best. It is useful to think of this market condition as economic nirvana since there is no conceivable way of increasing economic efficiency at a first-best equilibrium.

Of course, the real world is unlikely to be so perfectly characterized. Instead markets will likely have numerous distortions and imperfections. Some production and consumption activities have externality effects. Some goods have public good characteristics. Some markets have a small number of firms, each of which has some control over the price that prevails and makes positive economic profit. Governments invariably set taxes on consumption, profit, property and assets, etc. Finally, information is rarely perfectly and costlessly available.

Now imagine again a small open perfectly competitive economy with no market imperfections or distortions. Suppose we introduce one distortion or imperfection into such an economy. The resulting equilibrium will now be less efficient from a national perspective than when the distortion was not present. In other words the introduction of one distortion would reduce the optimal level of national welfare.

In terms of Lipsey and Lancaster's analysis, the introduction of the distortion into the system would severe one or more of the equilibrium conditions that must be satisfied to obtain economic nirvana. For example, suppose the imperfection that is introduced is the presence of a monopolistic firm in an industry. In this case the firm's profit maximizing equilibrium condition would be to set its price greater than marginal cost rather than equal to marginal cost as would be done by a profit maximizing perfectly competitive firm. Since the economic optimum obtained in these circumstances would be less efficient than in economic nirvana, we would call this equilibrium a second-best equilibrium. Second-best equilibria arise whenever all of the equilibrium conditions satisfying economic nirvana cannot occur simultaneously. In general, second-best equilibria arise whenever there are market imperfections or distortions present.

Welfare Improving Policies in a Second-Best World

An economic rationale for government intervention in the private market arises whenever there are uncorrected market imperfections or distortions. In these circumstances the economy is characterized by a second-best rather than a first-best equilibrium. In the best of cases the government policy can correct the distortions completely and the economy would revert back to the state under economic nirvana. If the distortion is not corrected completely then at least the new equilibrium conditions, altered by the presence of the distortion, can all be satisfied. In either case an appropriate government policy can act to correct, or reduce the detrimental effects of the market imperfection or distortion, raise economic efficiency and improve national welfare.

It is for this reason that many types of trade policies can be shown to improve national welfare. Trade policies, chosen appropriate to the market circumstances, act to correct the imperfections or distortions. This remains true even though the trade policies themselves would act to reduce economic efficiency if applied starting from a state of economic nirvana. What happens is that the policy corrects the distortion or imperfection and thus raises national welfare by more than the loss in welfare arising from the application of the policy.

Many different types of policies can be applied even for the same distortion or imperfection. Governments can apply taxes, subsidies or quantitative restrictions. It can apply these to production, to consumption, or to factor usage. Sometimes it even applies two or more of these policies simultaneously in the same market. Some policies, like tariffs or export taxes, are designed to directly affect the flow of goods and services between countries. These are called trade policies. Other policies, like production subsidies or consumption taxes, are directed at a particular activity that occurs within the country but is not targeted directly at trade flows. These can be referred to as domestic policies.

One prominent area of trade policy research focuses on identifying the optimal policy to be used in a particular second-best equilibrium situation. Invariably this research has considered multiple policy options in any one situation and has attempted to rank order the potential policies in terms of their efficiency enhancing capabilities. As with the ranking of equilibria described above, the ranking of policy options is also typically characterized using the first-best and second-best labels.

Thus, the ideal or optimal policy choice in the presence of a particular market distortion or imperfection is referred to as a first-best policy. The first-best policy will raise national welfare, or enhance aggregate economic efficiency, to the greatest extent possible in a particular situation.

Many other policies can often be applied, some of which would be welfare-improving. If any such policy raises welfare to a lesser degree than a first-best policy, then it would be called a second-best policy. If there are many policy options which are inferior to the first-best policy, then it is common to refer to them all as second-best policies. Only if one can definitively rank three or more policy options would one ever refer to a third-best or fourth-best policy. Since these rankings are often difficult, third-best policies are not commonly denoted.

Trade Policies in a Second-Best World

In a 1971 paper a framework for understanding the welfare implications of trade policies in the presence of market distortions was provided. This framework applied the theory of the second-best to much of the welfare analysis that had been done in international trade theory up until that point. The paper demonstrated the result that trade policies can improve national welfare if they occur in the presence of a market distortion and if they act to correct the detrimental effects caused by the distortion. However, the paper also showed that in almost all circumstances a trade policy will be a second-best rather than a first-best policy choice. The first-best policy would likely be a purely domestic policy that is targeted directly at the distortion in the market. One exception to this rule occurs when a country is "large" in international markets and thus can affect international prices with its domestic policies. In this case, as was shown with optimal tariffs, quotas, VERs and export taxes, trade policy is the first-best policy.

Since the paper, international trade policy analysis has advanced to include market imperfections such as monopolies, duopolies and oligopolies. In many of these cases it has been shown that appropriately chosen trade policies can improve national welfare. The reason trade policies can improve welfare, of course, is that the presence of the market imperfection means that the economy begins at a second-best equilibrium. The trade policy, if properly targeted, can reduce the negative aggregate effects caused by the imperfection and thus raise national welfare.

Theory of the Second-Best

Theory of the second-best provides the theoretical underpinning to explain many of the reasons that trade policy can be shown to be welfare enhancing for an economy.

In most (if not all) of the cases in which trade policy is shown to improve national welfare, the economy begins at an equilibrium that can be characterized as second best. Second best equilibria arise whenever the market has distortions or imperfections present. In these cases it is relatively straightforward to conceive of a trade policy which corrects the distortion or imperfection sufficiently to outweigh the detrimental effects of the policy itself. In other words, whenever there are market imperfections or distortions present it is always theoretically or conceptually possible to design a trade policy that would improve national welfare. As such the theory of the second best provides a rationale for many different types of protection in an economy.

The main criticism suggested by the theory is that rarely is trade policy the first best policy choice to correct a market imperfection or distortion. Instead trade policy is second best. The first best policy, generally, would be a purely domestic policy targeted directly at the market imperfection or distortion.

Information Economics

Though economists often talk in terms that seem impenetrable, what they study is very simple and basic. The "economy" is how resources are distributed throughout society. Since the 1960s, the world has been described as an information economy, rather than an industrial or agricultural economy. Buying, selling, and using information are at the heart of economic activity for businesses and consumers, as well as for the governments that regulate them.

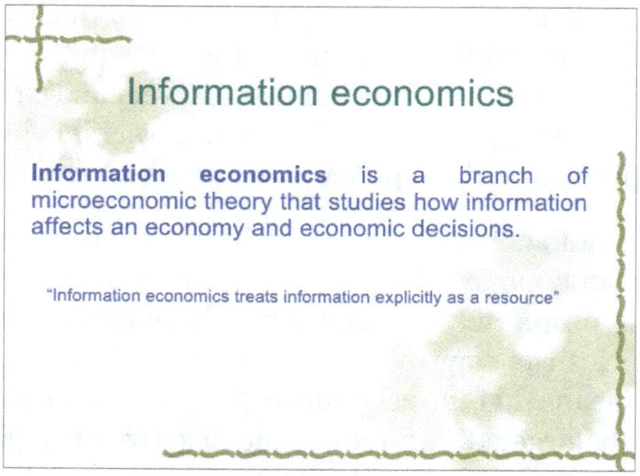

The earliest way of understanding the information economy was set forth in the 1960s. According to this product-based theory, an information economy operates just like any other economy except for the simple difference that there is a larger proportion of informational goods and services being bought and sold. This approach continues to underlie most governmental decision making, and it is the approach that is used to generate statistics to describe the growth of the information economy. This approach is useful as far as it goes, and it has the advantage of permitting decision makers to continue to work with the kinds of analytical tools that they have always used. However, people in the business world increasingly began to feel that this approach did not adequately capture what was going on in the contemporary economy where value was being created and money was being made.

By the 1970s, some people began to look for an alternate understanding of the information economy because of the problems that were associated with treating information as a commodity and with the social inequities that resulted from differential access to information. This led to a domain-based theory that said the information economy resulted from the expansion of the boundaries of the economy itself through commodification of forms of information that had never before been treated as a commodity. Some of the forms of information newly commodified could be public, as when governmental databases such as those generated by the U.S. satellite surveillance system are turned over to the private sector. Some of it is private, as in the example of the details of one's personal life that are now bought and sold. Again, there is some truth in the insights offered by this approach. However, it has been limited in its influence upon policymaking because it has not offered alternative analytical tools that can help policymakers solve problems.

In the early 1990s, a third way of defining the information economy appeared, focused not on products or on the domain but on how the economy functions. Led by Cristiano Antonelli, proponents of this approach argue that the contemporary economy is an information economy because it operates in qualitatively different ways from how the economy operated in earlier stages. Antonelli and others argue that in the information economy, cooperation and coordination are as important as competition for long-term economic success. Because different types of economic, political, and social entities are so intertwined in all of their activities, these economists argue that there is little that actually still takes place in the market as idealized by the neoclassical economists of the late nineteenth century. Rather, most economic activity takes place via the "harmonization" of different types of information systems with each other.

While all three of these perspectives are used to support decision making by various groups, both public and private sector decision makers are gradually shifting from the most traditional approach to an appreciation of the unique informational features of what many now call the "net-work economy." Corporations are changing because they are finding that traditional ways of thinking do not account for what they are experiencing. Governments are changing in order to remain competitive with other types of organizations such as transnational corporations in contemporary struggles for power.

Economic Analysis of Information

- Focuses on the application of IT in areas where its intangible benefits contribute to performance on key aspects of organizational strategies and activities.
- It incorporates the technique of scoring methodologies, which are used in many evaluation situations.
- Scoring methodology is used by analysts to first identify all the key perfomance issues and assign a weight to each one.
- Organizational objectives are used to determine which factors to inculde, and what weights to assign in the scoring methodology (tangible and intangible benefits).

Information is important economically both as a good (i.e., an object that can be bought and sold, such as a book) and as a service (i.e., a process that can be bought and sold, such as data processing). One of the reasons it has been so difficult to deal with information in economic terms has been that it is more difficult to deal with the economic features of commodities that are intangible than with those that are material, or tangible.

Consumers tend to think most of primary or final information goods and services, those that are bought by users in the form in which they are produced. Movies, television programs, databases, books, and magazines are all examples of information as a final good. In the contemporary economy, however, informational goods and services are also important in secondary or intermediate form, meaning that they are not products bought and sold in the retail market. Rather, they are inputs into the production of other types of goods and services. For example, data about marketing and sales trends is an important input into the production of goods for sale. Data about the functioning of the global information infrastructure through which the communications of the Internet flow is another example of information as a critically important secondary good. Information as a secondary good may be in the form of raw data, as in these examples. It is also said to be embedded in advanced technologies that embody information because they are the outcome of lengthy research processes that produce information. It is also embedded in the people who use those technologies as a form of what is called "human capital."

One of the first problems economists faced in thinking about information was defining the information sector of the economy (i.e., those industries involved in working with information) so they could be analyzed separately from other types of economic activities. This is not a problem with a precise and fixed solution because many companies are involved in both information-based and materials-based businesses and new information businesses are being created all the time. Generally, the information sector is defined as those industries that have a primary focus of producing, distributing, processing, or storing information. Important examples of industries that belong to the information sector include education, media (e.g., television, radio, book and magazine publishing, and film), Internet companies, telephone companies, libraries, database providers, and data processors.

It is precisely because so many new businesses are being created all the time that it is difficult to draw clear lines between different information industries. For example, a film archive may become a content producer, a law firm may launch a data processing venture, and a radio station may make money transferring data files as a side business. Furthermore, many of the new types of businesses that are emerging, such as Internet service providers and cable television, do not quite fit into the previously standard ways of categorizing industries.

Historically, an economic analysis of an industry would have focused on the activities of individual corporations, what economists call the "firm." Accounting systems and the governmental regulation for which they provide the frame-work have long been in place, and they support the continued reliance on such an approach. However, economists are developing analytical techniques that look at the long-term project rather than the firm as the unit of analysis because so much activity in the network economy takes place not within single firms but within a network of interdependent organizations of different types that interact in a multitude of ways.

The Information Production Chain

The fundamental principle of the economics of information is that value is added every time information is processed. Donald Lamberton, a key figure in the development of the subfield, points out that the division of labor involved in information processing the way in which processes are broken up into small pieces for handling may be the most fundamental form of the division of labor. Awareness of this has led to the use of models of an "information production chain" as a way of identifying the different points at which value is added and as a means by which information commodities can be distinguished from each other.

While different industries and governments break up the steps of the information production chain in different ways, work by Machlup and Boulding suggests a basic model that includes the following stages: information creation (de novo, or through generation or collection), processing (algorithmic [computerized] or cognitive [human]), storage, transportation, distribution, destruction, and seeking. Those who think about the informational value of production chains for other types of goods and services often think of each stage of manufacturing and distribution as spinning off an informational "value chain."

This emphasis on distinctions among types of information processing as a source of economic value has another consequence, exacerbated by the fact that ongoing technological innovation processes continue to offer new opportunities to entrepreneurs. Though, historically, analysis of functions within the firm were organized around the product, the task, or the job description, economists, led by Roberto Scazzieri, are learning to analyze activities within individual and networked firms in terms of their processes. Thinking in terms of an information production chain also heightens awareness of the value of information as a resource.

Creating Information Goods and Services

In the agricultural and industrial economies, fundamental resources were material. In order to have more (whether it was, for example, land, oil, or iron ore), more had to be found physically, or new ways of getting at known resources had to be invented. In the information economy, however, the discovery of new resources is conceptual. Distinctions among types of information processing and the informational states they produce must be understood in a new way so that a new type of product or service niche becomes available. It is this emphasis on thinking as a way of creating new products that has made it possible for so many young people to have succeeded so well in information businesses. In the past it might have taken years for an entrepreneur with a good idea to accumulate the needed capital and capacities, but today, even someone who is very young can come up with a new way of thinking about ways to create, process, distribute, and use information and turn that into a business.

Creativity is needed in order to form a successful information-based business, but economists are able to offer a number of basic generalizations regarding how best to think about information from a business perspective. These approaches begin by segmenting the market into different niches, each of which can be served with a different product. Marketing equipment and software for web access to the elderly population that would use it primarily for family correspondence, for example, might stress features that would be very different from the ones emphasized in marketing the same equipment and software to teens who might be more interested in games, music, and other web-based activities. Through product differentiation, different products are developed for each niche. Versioning, or developing several different versions of the same product, is a popular approach to product differentiation for information goods and services. A different version can be developed for each market segment. If such a breakdown is not evident, information economists Carl Shapiro and Hal R. Varian suggest that a business should create three versions because psychologically, the market will at the least break down into those segments that are attracted to each of the extremes and to the central choice. Versions can be distinguished from each other along a number of dimensions, depending on which are most important to the specific good or service involved. Shapiro and Varian identify the following as possibilities: delay, interface (e.g., nature of and ease of use), convenience (e.g., how long does it take to learn to use it, how troublesome is it), image resolution, speed of operation, flexibility of use, capability, features and functions, comprehensiveness, annoyance, and support.

The cost of producing information is independent of the scale on which it is produced; that is, the cost of producing information is the same whether it results in one commodity for sale or a million. The difference between the "first unit cost" and subsequent reproduction means that there can be enormous "economies of scale" in the information industries. This is the reason for the economic appeal of mass market products such as television programs, films, and books to those who produce and sell them.

The features of information technologies are critical to understanding the economics of information. Two features worth mentioning here are those of "lock-in" and "network externalities." Lock-in reflects the fact that the "sunk costs" involved in building any specific communications network are so high that it is hard to change technologies once the network is built. (This is also called "path dependence.") Lock-in makes decision making even more difficult during a period in which innovation is constant and experience with existing and new technologies is so thin that it is difficult to know how to evaluate various technologies relative to each other. One way to reduce the risks associated with lock-in is to respond to network externalities (i.e., the characteristic that the greater the number of individuals and organizations using a network good or service, the greater will be the value of that service). The greater the market for an informational product, the more likely it will be that users will develop an experiential base that facilitates use, that maintenance systems will be in place, and that complementary goods and services will be available.

Lock-in also facilitates what antitrust law refers to as "tying" and those in the information industries refer to as "bundling" linking together different informational goods and services for joint purchase and use. One of the discoveries of experimentation within the newly emergent information economy has been that many types of informational goods previously thought of as discrete and unique entities can themselves be "unbundled," or broken down into their parts, for separate sale and use. Vendors of magazines, for example, have realized that in the digital environment they can sell article titles, summaries, texts, references, and tables of contents separately. A very famous example of unbundling was the result of the 1983 insistence by the antitrust division of the U.S. Department of Commerce that AT&T divest itself separate off and sell local telephone services, which had always historically been bundled with long-distance telephony in one service package.

While ownership of material goods, land, capital, and resources remains important in the information economy, many would say that property rights in information and ideas have become the most important form of property. Intellectual property rights law determines the nature of property rights in information. In the United States, there are several different types of intellectual property. The most important are copyright (i.e., ownership of the expression of ideas), patent (i.e., ownership of the expression of ideas in an invention), trademark (i.e., the right to control the use of symbols), and working papers (i.e., privacy for and control over the results of information processing conducted in the course of completing a work process).

Policymakers struggle with adapting the intellectual property rights system to the contemporary technological environment. It has been difficult, for example, to figure out just how to deal with computer software from an intellectual property rights perspective. Should it be covered by copyright or by patent? Which kinds of software programs should be available to everyone and which kinds should have to be purchased? These problems are made even more difficult by the need to reach international agreement on these matters, since the global nature of the information infrastructure means that property rights issues that arise anywhere are global in nature.

The Limits to Information as a Commodity

While both governments and corporations make policy based on economic analyses of information and the processes by which it is created, stored, distributed, and used, the same matters can be analyzed from political, social, cultural, or ecological perspectives. The greatest value can be derived from economic analyses when they are placed within the wider context. From this point of view, the weaknesses as well as the strengths of the economic approach can be identified.

One of the most striking features of the last half of the twentieth century was the way in which forms of information never before treated as economic goods and services were commodified, or turned into something that could be bought and sold. Examples of such newly commodified forms of information include those that are most private, such as what thoughts are in one's mind, or what chemicals are in one's urine. They also include those that had historically been most public, such as databases put together by governments in order to serve the public interest or the traditional stories that ensure survival of ancient cultures. The fact that such forms of information can be com-modified, however, does not mean that they should be. Growing numbers of economists, policymakers, and communities have begun to realize that the pursuit of the economic value of information must be balanced with the pursuit of other types of important value. Even when information is treated as a commodity, it remains important in other ways as knowledge structures and as a constitutive force in society. Information is critical to the social construction of reality to the ways in which people together build the social world. Information policy for a thriving political culture and creative expressive environment may have to temper economic profit with other social values.

Even within the economically defined world, the unique characteristics of the network economy make clear that competition is not the only important way of relating to others for long-term economic survival. Cooperation and coordination are important as well. Incorporation of this knowledge into planning is to some degree just a shift in the way planners are thinking. For example, while in the short term it may be economically inefficient to let the children of illegal immigrants attend public school in the United States, the U.S. Supreme Court has realized that, considering the long-term costs to the community as a whole should those children not receive an education, it makes more sense economically to permit those children into the schools.

The problem of differences in access to information, including the ability to use it once it is acquired, is as important to economists as it is to society as a whole because research consistently shows that those differences are often due to differences in economic class. In the Internet environment, this is known as the problem of the "digital divide." With this in mind, policymakers struggle to ensure that access to the Internet is equal within and across communities. The problem is, of course, not unique to the Internet environment. Before there was any such thing as a digital divide, sociologists were studying the effects of the "knowledge gap" as it played out between the poor and the rich, the rural and the urban, the uneducated and the educated, the female and the male, and the black and the white.

Permissions

All chapters in this book are published with permission under the Creative Commons Attribution Share Alike License or equivalent. Every chapter published in this book has been scrutinized by our experts. Their significance has been extensively debated. The topics covered herein carry significant information for a comprehensive understanding. They may even be implemented as practical applications or may be referred to as a beginning point for further studies.

We would like to thank the editorial team for lending their expertise to make the book truly unique. They have played a crucial role in the development of this book. Without their invaluable contributions this book wouldn't have been possible. They have made vital efforts to compile up to date information on the varied aspects of this subject to make this book a valuable addition to the collection of many professionals and students.

This book was conceptualized with the vision of imparting up-to-date and integrated information in this field. To ensure the same, a matchless editorial board was set up. Every individual on the board went through rigorous rounds of assessment to prove their worth. After which they invested a large part of their time researching and compiling the most relevant data for our readers.

The editorial board has been involved in producing this book since its inception. They have spent rigorous hours researching and exploring the diverse topics which have resulted in the successful publishing of this book. They have passed on their knowledge of decades through this book. To expedite this challenging task, the publisher supported the team at every step. A small team of assistant editors was also appointed to further simplify the editing procedure and attain best results for the readers.

Apart from the editorial board, the designing team has also invested a significant amount of their time in understanding the subject and creating the most relevant covers. They scrutinized every image to scout for the most suitable representation of the subject and create an appropriate cover for the book.

The publishing team has been an ardent support to the editorial, designing and production team. Their endless efforts to recruit the best for this project, has resulted in the accomplishment of this book. They are a veteran in the field of academics and their pool of knowledge is as vast as their experience in printing. Their expertise and guidance has proved useful at every step. Their uncompromising quality standards have made this book an exceptional effort. Their encouragement from time to time has been an inspiration for everyone.

The publisher and the editorial board hope that this book will prove to be a valuable piece of knowledge for students, practitioners and scholars across the globe.

Index

A

Administrative Activities, 172

C

Cash Flow, 212, 214

Commodity Markets, 134

Complementary Goods, 111, 121, 229

Composition, 19, 21, 48, 69, 99, 102, 122

Conceptualization, 83

Consumer Goods, 23

Consumer Income, 122, 133

Convergence, 46

Cookies, 127

Cost Curves, 111

D

Data Mining, 2, 160

Datum, 55

Demand Curve, 9-11, 104, 107, 110-113, 116, 118-123, 128-129, 133, 140-141, 144, 146, 190

Demand Model, 113

Denominator, 182, 188

Digital Divide, 231

Domestic Policy, 223-224

Duopoly, 129-130, 164

E

Economic Activity, 5, 117, 195, 224-225

Economic Development, 18-20, 24, 46, 48, 51, 72-77, 79, 169, 174

Economic Growth, 2, 17-24, 30, 36, 44, 47, 50-51, 61, 65-66, 70, 72, 75-78, 189-190, 194, 197, 199

Economic Planning, 75

Economic Policy, 21, 49, 148, 163

Eigenvalues, 154

Equitable Distribution, 72

Error Correction, 149

Exogenous, 44, 66, 90, 114, 129, 133, 159, 176-178, 181, 187, 205

F

Factorisation, 156

Financial Markets, 2, 124, 133, 146

Fiscal Policy, 3, 148, 163, 183, 196-197, 204

Foreign Direct Investment, 47

Free Markets, 3

G

General Equilibrium, 48, 91-92, 113, 116, 162-163, 209, 214-215, 219-220

Globalization, 17-18

Great Depression, 7

Gross Domestic Product, 2, 19, 72

I

Identity Matrix, 150-151

Income Tax, 190

Inflation, 2, 5, 13-14, 36, 52, 133, 162, 177, 183, 190, 194, 196, 199-200, 202, 208

Information Systems, 225

Integer, 155, 159

Intellectual Property, 229-230

Intellectual Property Rights, 229-230

Inventory, 8, 12

K

Keynesian Economics, 3, 114, 197, 199

L

Labor Markets, 134, 220

Labour Force, 24, 42, 55, 57, 69, 71

Laissez-faire Policy, 221

Linear Equations, 53

M

Managerial Economics, 14

Marginal Cost, 11, 110-111, 126-128, 220-222

Marginal Product, 103, 126, 169

Market Economy, 114, 173

Market Equilibrium, 111-112, 128, 133

Market Intervention, 12

Market Position, 15

Market Price, 110-111, 128-130, 132, 135, 166

Mercantilism, 17
Meritocracy, 198
Metaphor, 201
Microeconomics, 1-2, 6-8, 13, 111, 146, 209
Mixed Economy, 174
Monetary Policy, 2-3, 52, 94, 114, 175, 183, 194, 196-197
Money Markets, 95, 182
Money Supply, 6, 82, 85-87, 89, 91-92, 94-101, 104-105, 114, 124, 133, 176, 178-181, 197, 203
Monopoly, 57, 75, 127, 131, 166-167
Monopsony, 168

O

Organizational Theory, 73

P

Perfect Competition, 68, 110, 116, 127-128, 173, 215, 219
Physical Capital, 30-31, 67, 72, 110, 133, 199
Policy Analysis, 223
Polynomial, 156
Product Development, 164-165
Product Differentiation, 228
Product Market, 216
Production Function, 16, 28, 31, 44-45, 49, 66-67, 69-71, 136, 170-172
Production System, 103
Public Agencies, 76
Public Sector, 18, 75, 91-92
Purchasing Power, 79-81, 170
Python, 154, 159

Q

Quantity Demanded, 9-13, 104, 111-113, 116, 118-119, 121-123, 128-129, 131-133, 136, 139-140, 143, 145-146
Quantity Supplied, 10-13, 110-111, 113, 116-117, 124-133, 135-138

R

Radio Station, 227
Real Numbers, 155
Realism, 163
Resolution, 228
Resource Allocation, 4, 69
Retail Markets, 220

S

Staffing, 15
Stock Market, 14
Supply Curve, 10-11, 104, 107, 110, 112-114, 116-117, 124-127, 129, 136, 138, 190
Supply Function, 89, 125, 127-128

T

Tax System, 163
Top Management, 16

V

Value Chain, 227
Variable Costs, 11
Variable Factors, 8, 127, 138
Variables, 2, 5-6, 9-10, 13, 51-52, 69, 89-90, 112, 114, 122, 124-125, 128, 135, 148-149, 151-152, 155, 159, 161, 163, 165, 176, 178, 186-188, 204, 214

www.ingramcontent.com/pod-product-compliance
Lightning Source LLC
LaVergne TN
LVHW080617210926
848485LV00003B/176